워치 & 칠

장기화되는 팬데믹은 사회적 거리두기로 우리 삶을 점점 더 어렵게 하고 있습니다. 이에 동시대 지구는 문화의 활력을 잃어가는 것처럼 보이기도 합니다. 이를 극복하기 위한 초연결 소통과 네트워크 창출이 그 어느 때보다 간절해졌습니다. 국립현대미술관은 이러한 위기를 극복하기 위한 방편으로 미술관의 자원들을 디지털 콘텐츠로 전환하는 프로젝트를 추진했습니다. 미술관 콘텐츠의 디지털 전환은 온라인에서도 미술관의 역할을 확장할 수 있는 다양한 시도의 발판이 되었습니다.

«우리 집에서, 워치 앤 칠»은 미술관이 관객과 만나는 또 다른 가능성을 제시하고자 합니다. 본 프로젝트를 통해 국립현대미술관은 마닐라 현대미술디자인미술관, 치앙마이 마이암현대미술관, 홍콩 서구룡문화지구 M+와 협력하여 온라인 스트리밍 플랫폼 '워치 앤 칠'(https://watchandchill.kr)을 구축하고, 각 미술관의 미디어 소장품과 지역 작가들의 작품을 공유합니다. 이번 프로젝트는 미술관이 변화하는 관객의 매체 소비 습관에 어떻게 대응하는지, 동시에 기관 소장품에 새로운 가치를 어떻게 부여할 것인지, 발상의 전환을 촉구하고 있습니다. 또한 네 개의 아시아 미술관이 다자간 교류의 장으로서 디지털 플랫폼을 활용하며 기술적 목적보다는 긴밀한 대화로 서로의 지식, 경험과 자원을 공유하는 기회를 열며, 나아가 미술 한류를 시도하는 독특한 모델이라 하겠습니다.

작품의 온라인 스트리밍과 함께 개최되는 오프라인 순회전 또한 «우리 집에서, 워치 앤 칠»의 중요한 요소로서 서울, 마닐라, 치앙마이, 홍콩 네 개의 도시에서 각기 다른 모습으로 전시가 구현되었습니다. 물리적 장소와 디지털 세계의 결합을 적극 유도하여 상호 보완하는 전시 유형을 구축한 것입니다. 본 프로젝트는 온·오프라인 공간의 하이브리드라는 전시 공간의 불가역적 변화를 제시합니다. 3개년으로 계획된 '워치 앤 칠' 플랫폼이 앞으로도 더 다양한 협력자들과 교류를 넓혀가기를 기대합니다. 이번 «우리 집에서, 워치 앤 칠»에 참여한 작가들과 이 기획이 실현될 수 있도록 애써준 우리 미술관 내외의 여러분, 해외 협력 기관 관계자분들께 감사의 말씀을 드립니다.

윤범모
국립현대미술관장

As the Covid-19 pandemic has continued, social distancing has been creating more and more difficulties for our lives. It also seems as though the world today is losing cultural vitality. More than ever before, we are in need of hyper-connected communication and networks to overcome this. As a way to triumphing over the crisis, the National Museum of Modern and Contemporary Art, Korea (MMCA) has been carrying out a project to convert its resources into digital content. The digital transformation of museum content has laid the groundwork for different experiments for broadening the museum's role.

The ambition of *Watch and Chill: Streaming Art to Your Homes* is to propose a different possibility for museums to connect with viewers. For this project, MMCA collaborated with the Museum of Contemporary Art and Design (MCAD) in Manila, the MAIIAM Contemporary Art Museum in Chiang Mai, and M+ in Hong Kong's West Kowloon Cultural District to create the online streaming platform *Watch and Chill* (https://watchandchill.kr/en) and shared the works from each museum's media collection and the local artists. The project calls for a shift in attitude on how museums should respond to viewers' changing behaviors of media consumption, and how they can add new value to their existing collections. Through the use of a digital platform as a setting for multilateral exchange, these four Asian museums gained an opportunity to share knowledge, experience, and resources based on dialogue that was closer than it would be for any technical objective. It can also be seen as a unique model for attempting to make visible the dynamics of Korean art and its potentials.

In conjunction with streaming of artworks, the offline traveling exhibition are another key part of *Watch and Chill: Streaming Art to Your Homes*, taking on varying forms in the four Asian cities of Seoul, Manila, Chiang Mai, and Hong Kong. It has created a complementary form of exhibition that actively encourages the blending of physical venues and the digital world. The project proposes an irreversible change to the condition of exhibition making: the hybridization of online and offline spaces. The *Watch and Chill* platform has been designed to continue for a three-year period, and I look forward to seeing the interchange broadening with a wider range of partners. I would like to give thanks to all of the artists who took part in *Watch and Chill: Streaming Art to Your Homes*, and to all the staff members of MMCA and our overseas partner institutions who worked with enthusiasm to bring this project to fruition.

Youn Bummo
Director, National Museum of Modern and Contemporary Art, Korea

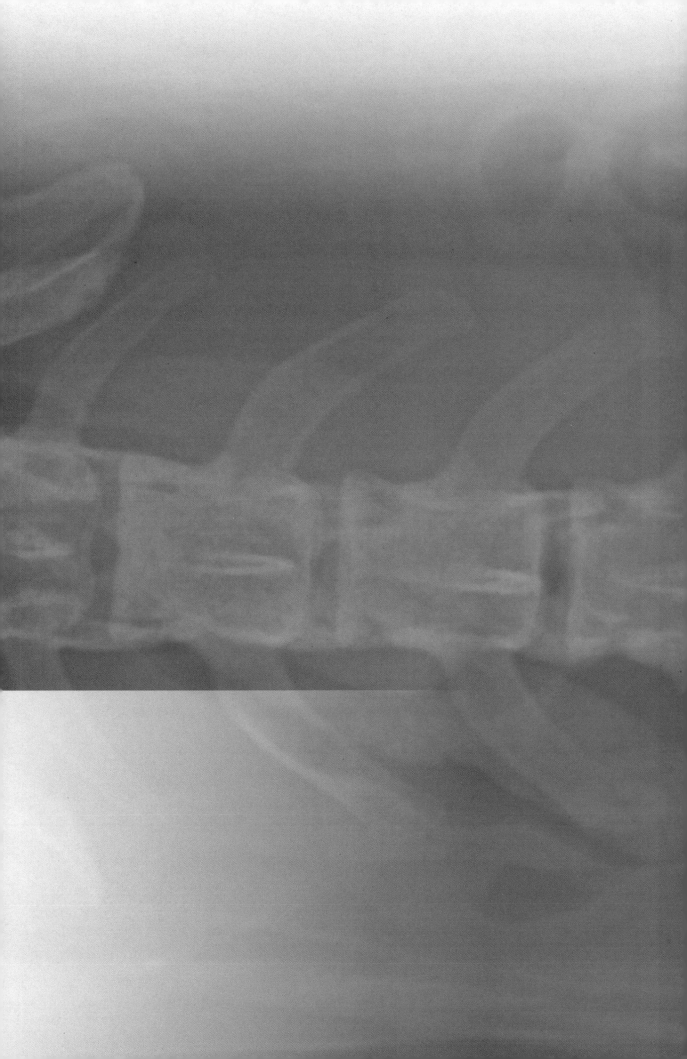

칠*chill* 할 것이냐 말 것이냐?
우리 집에서 당신의 집으로, 스트리밍하는 미술

팬데믹은 전통적인 집의 개념을 파괴했다.
위안 광밍, ‹주거›(2014) 영상 스틸 이미지

'워치 앤 칠'의 그래픽 아이덴티티. 한국의 디자인 스튜디오 워크스가 작업했다.

전 세계를 휩쓴 팬데믹으로, 인터넷 사용자에게 집은 유례 없는 데이터 전송의 집합지로 변모했다. 넷플릭스, 튜토리얼, 뮤직비디오, 업무 회의부터 친목 모임까지, 무엇이든 우리 집 거실 안으로 또 거실 밖으로 송출된다.

하지만 미술관의 상황은 다르다. 상업용 영상 스트리밍 업계가 속도를 붙여 새로운 영역으로 들어서는 동안, 많은 미술관의 영상 소장품은 놀라우리만치 제자리에 정체해 있다. 온라인에 단순 시놉시스와 영상 스틸 정도가 제공되는 수준이다. 어떻게 하면 미술관의 영상 소장품을 집에서 감상할 수 있을까?

이런 질문을 바탕으로 국립현대미술관의 이지회 학예연구사는 2021년 초, 홍콩의 M+, 마닐라의 현대미술디자인미술관(MCAD), 치앙마이의 마이암현대미술관(MAIIAM) 등 아시아 곳곳의 큐레이터들에게 연락을 취했다. 영상 작품을 위한 온라인 스트리밍 플랫폼을 개발하기 위함이었다. 이렇게 만들어진 스트리밍 기반 서비스 '워치 앤 칠'은 2021년 8월 출범하여 2022년 2월까지 온라인 상에서 운영되었다. 아래는 이지회 학예연구사, 키티마 차리프라싯(MAIIAM 큐레이터), 호셀리나 크루즈(MCAD 관장), 실케 슈미클(M+ 무빙이미지 선임 큐레이터)이 나눈 대화이다. 네 사람은 이번 협력을 가능하게 한 온·오프라인 큐레토리얼 전략에 관해 이야기를 나누었다.

실케 슈미클(이하 실케)   안녕하세요, 이지회 님! 몇 달 전 저희 M+에 연락해 '워치 앤 칠'에 대한 아이디어를 공유해 주셨죠. 마음이 바로 들뜨더라고요. '워치 앤 칠'은 미술 기관이 당면하고 있는 시급한 문제를 다루며 혁신적인 해답을 제공하는 것이었습니다.

먼저, 미술관은 물리적 공간을 넘어 관객 참여의 새로운 방식을 상상할 필요가 있습니다. 팬데믹으로 분명히 드러났듯, 여행이 불가능한 시대에 디지털을 통한 관객의 참여를 유도하는 것은 미술관과 관객의 관계를 이어가는 중요한 요소가 되었습니다. 팬데믹으로 이러한 요구가 가속화되었지만, 이미 2000년대부터 미술관에 있어 핵심 사명을 유지하면서 디지털화하는 세계에 적응하는 것, 즉 창의적으로 소장품을 활용하여 관객에게 다가가는 것은 시급하지만 대체로 해결되지 못한 과제로 남아있었습니다.

두 번째로 이 프로젝트는 기관 간 협력의 새로운 형식을 제시합니다. 아시아의 주요 미술관 네 곳이 보유한 영상 작품들을 온라인 스트리밍 플랫폼과 각 기관의 물리적 공간 양쪽에서 주고받는 것이죠. 작품 본연의

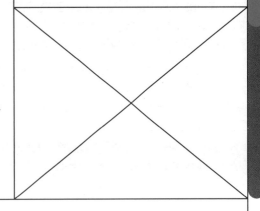

디지털적 특성과 복제가능성에 기대어, '워치 앤 칠'은 자연스러운 유동적 순환을 재가동합니다. 작품을 수집 가능한 유일무이한 오브제로 다루는 미술관 소장품의 맥락에서는 종종 가로막히던 순환을요.

에이미 미디어, 〈어머니와 미디어〉(2016)에서 작가는 일상의 오브제를 물건을 역동적 시각적 패턴으로 엮는다.

이지회(이하 지회) 무수히 많은 미디어 콘텐츠가 쉴 새 없이 정신을 흩뜨리는 가운데, 공공성의 측면에서 미술관의 역할이 실로 시험대에 오른 시대입니다. 팬데믹으로 분명 이런 추세에 탄력이 붙었죠. 대중의 접근을 확대하는 디지털 플랫폼은 관객의 변화한 습성에 부응하는 방법으로, 말 그대로 미술을 사람들의 '집'으로 가져다줍니다. '워치 앤 칠'은 미술관, 작가, 관객의 경로가 교차하는 플랫폼으로서, 그러한 교류를 가능케 하는 매개물이 되도록 기획되었습니다.

본 프로젝트는 한국 정부의 재정 지원을 받았습니다. 문화체육관광부 산하의 국립 미술관으로서, 국립현대미술관의 과업 중 하나는 '미술 한류' 등 국제 교류 사업으로 한국 문화를 해외에 소개하는 것입니다. 사업의 틀을 감안해, 먼저 떠오른 생각은 단순히 우리 소장품을 알리는 데 머무르지 않고, 이를 여러 나라 간의 교류로 삼을 방법을 찾아보자는 것이었습니다. 교류의 중심에는 자원의 공유가 있었습니다. 여기에는 소장품만이 아니라 인력, 행정, 미술관의 물리적 기반시설도 포함되었죠.

미술관 소장은 영원이라는 가치를 위해 오브제를 좀 더 전통적인 방식으로 다루는 쪽에 자연스레 기울기 마련이고, 저도 이 점을 무척 중요하게 생각합니다. 하지만 사실상 디지털 파일을 담은 채 수장고에 놓인 하드 드라이브가 미디어 소장품 대부분이 처한 물리적 현실입니다. 미술관 웹사이트에 올라온 작품 정보는 단순 설명과 영상 스틸에 국한되는 경우가 많고, 작품을 이해하는 데 결코 충분하지 못해요. 더 많은 관객에게 다가가면서 작품들을 활성화하고 동원할 방법은 무엇일까요? 공유 경제의 측면을 차용할 수 있을까요?

'워치 앤 칠'은 참여 작가와 협력 미술관의 너그러운 협조 아래, 영상 소장품의 유동 가능성을 끌어올리는 시공간의 실험이자 일종의 포털로 작동하기를 바랐습니다.

호셀리나 님, 제가 협력 제안을 위해 가장 먼저 접촉한 미술관이 MCAD였고, 보여주신 긍정적인 반응이 큰 힘이 되었다는 이야기를 꼭 하고 싶어요. 어느 정도는, 코로나19가 처음 전 세계를 강타했던 2020년 당시 각자 같은 작가의 전시를 기획하면서, 우리 사이에 이미 연대가 이뤄졌기 때문이었다고 생각합니다.

호셀리나 크루즈(이하 호셀리나) 처음 지회 님이 아이디어를 제안했을 때, 놀랍고 또 근사한 아이디어로 다가왔습니다. 지회 님도 마찬가지셨을 듯한데, 처음 생각에는 그렇게 크지 않은 규모의 기획이 되겠구나 싶었어요. 미술관들이 미래 모습을 그리려 애쓰는 가운데, 코로나19가 야기한 과제들을 다루는 작업이 되리라는 생각이었죠. 지역의 다른 공간들을 초청하는 방안에 대해서도 이야기를 나눴습니다. 미술관뿐만이 아니라 팬데믹에도 불구하고 적극적이고 열심인 큐레이터까지요.

필리핀도 다른 나라들처럼 현 상황과 씨름 중이었지만, 관람객의 상실로 대부분의 미술관과 갤러리는 대규모의 타격을 입었습니다. 필리핀에서 영향력 있는 미술 기관들은 대체로 대학에 부속해 있어요.

차오 페이의 〈아지랑이와 안개〉(2013). 좀비들이 출몰하는 이 작품은 일상적인 가정 공간 속에 초현실적인 순간을 연출한다.

바르가스 미술관은 필리핀대학에, 아테네오 미술관은 아테네오대학에 속해 있습니다. MCAD는 성베닐데대학 디자인미술학교 안에 자리 잡고 있고요. 학교가 문을 닫고 온라인으로 전환되면서, 저희는 큰 타격을 입었습니다. 다른 미술관들이 일반 대중을 잃었다면, 저희는 주된 관객층을 잃었어요. 할 수 있는 일은 온라인으로 접근 가능한 프로그램들을 통해, 또 교육 프로그램 측면 대부분을 줌 강의와 온라인 워크숍으로 옮겨 학생 집단의 관객 참여를 강화하는 방법뿐이었습니다.

저희가 아티스트 필름 인터내셔널(AFI) 측과 영상 작품 전시를 준비하던 와중에 '워치 앤 칠'과 관련해 대화를 나누었고, 저는 지회 님의 초청을 팬데믹을 헤치며 작업하는 지역의 작가들을 최대한 지원할 행운의 순간으로 봤어요. 소장품 없는 전시 공간인 MCAD에 있어 언제나 전시는 저희가 전시 작품의 창작 과정에 참여하는 기회였습니다. 저희는 종종 작가들의 신작 작업에 함께 하거나 아니면 다른 다양한 방식으로 프로젝트 제작을 지원해왔는데요. 여기에는 작가들에게 본인의 실천과 관계 맺고 맥락을 부여하고 확장하며 심지어 도전하는 환경 안에서 작품을 보여줄 수 있는 공간과 기회를 제공하는 것도 포함됩니다. 비록 작품이 소장되지는 못하더라도, 단체전에 참여하면 자신의 작품을 동료들과 나란히 또는 역사와 세대를 가로질러 보여주게 되죠. 우리는 MCAD의 전시가 지역이나 국가를 넘어서면서도 여전히 지역의 논의에 깊이 융합된 더 큰 담론의 일부가 되도록 최대한 노력합니다.

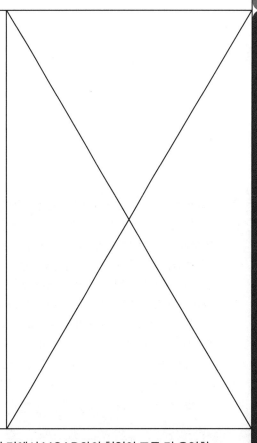

차이 시리손이 〈엉샵만 닌〉(2016). 태국 람팡 지역을 달리는 이동식 야외 영화 항해 트럭은 1990년대 이 지역에서 발견된 호주 에렉투스 화석의 흔적 바지는 공룡이 이미로 영화를 상영한다.

실케 ▬▬▬▬▬ 그런 면에서 MCAD와의 협업이 조금 더 유연한 행위자로서 기관의 역할을 《우리 집에서, 워치 앤 칠》이 강조하는 중요한 내용 중 하나로 다룰 수 있게 되었다고 봐요. 그리고 지회 님이 언급한 미디어 소장의 물리적 현실에 관해서도, 다른 미술 작품에 적용하는 것과 마찬가지의 전문적인 기준으로 영상 작품을 수집하고 보존하는 미술관의 접근 방식이 지극히 중요하다는 데 저 역시 동의합니다. 보존이라는 목적뿐만 아니라, 영상 작품이 20세기 및 21세기의 시각 문화에 불가결한 부분이라는 점을 인정하기 위해서죠.

소장품의 유의미한 활성화는 어떤 기관에든 핵심입니다. '워치 앤 칠'은 제약 없이 자의적으로 자유롭게 접근 가능한 인터넷상의 스트리밍 콘텐츠와 면밀하게 연구된 미술관 소장품의 서사 사이에 개입할 흥미로운 기회를 제공합니다. 우리는 종종 이 양극단의 접근 사이에 놓이는데요. 각각 나름의 타당성과 기능을 지니고 있죠.

지난 10년에 걸쳐, 넷플릭스 같은 온라인 영화 제공 서비스 업체들이 기획된 콘텐츠는 물론이고 접근성 높은 엔터테인먼트를 제공하며, DVD 대여 업체에서 디지털 영역으로 활동 무대를 넓혀 시장의 틈새를 성공적으로 공략했습니다. 우리 프로젝트도 강렬한 예술 콘텐츠를 관객의 집으로 전달함으로써 이 사이의 공간을 탐색합니다. 관객이 작품을 새로운 환경에서 자신만의 속도로 발견할 수 있게요.

또한 전시 제목은 넷플릭스와 관련해 집에서 영상 콘텐츠를 단순 소비는 아니더라도 시청하는 습관을 가리키는 '넷플릭스 앤 칠'이라는 표현에 도전합니다. '워치 앤 칠'과 다른 스트리밍 플랫폼의 차이는 어떻게 설명될까요? 특히, 저는 미술관에서 수행해 온 진지한 연구와 해석을 새로운 시청 습관과 연관시킨 큐레토리얼 태도에 관심이 갑니다.

지회 통상적인 오버더톱(OTT) 서비스와 달리, '워치 앤 칠' 플랫폼은 휴면에 들어가기 전까지 일정 기간만 일반 관객에게 열립니다. 2021년의 야심 찬 출범을 시작으로, '워치 앤 칠'은 앞으로 다른 미술관들과 협력하며 2.0, 3.0 버전으로 이어질 예정입니다. 이처럼 일정 기간을 두고 잠시 정기적으로 열린다는 특성은 미술관 전시의 주기적 특성과 유사합니다. 더 나은 시스템을 만들고 큐레토리얼 노력을 심화하기 위해 영원히 베타 버전으로 운영하는 셈이죠.

스트리밍 플랫폼 '워치 앤 칠'의 주 소비 장소로 '집'을 상정하면서, '가정'이라는 개념에 대한 인식이 어떻게 변해왔는가를 고찰하는 데서 큐레토리얼 연구가 시작됐습니다. 유례없는 대량의 데이터 전송과 연결된 집은 '주거'라는 단순 사적 기능을 넘어 공공 영역으로 진입한 지 오래입니다. 선정된 22편의 작품은 집의 확장된 성격을 성찰하며, 구체적으로 짜인 서사들에 따라 나뉘어 묶었습니다.

플랫폼의 콘텐츠는 협력 미술관에 물리적으로도 구현되었습니다. 서울에서는 전시로, 마닐라에서는 자동차 극장의 형태로, 치앙마이에서는 이번 전시를 위해 특별히 설계한 건축 공간에서, 홍콩에서는 일련의 상영, 토크, 미디어테크 전시의 형식으로요. 현실과 가상의 전시라는 이원성이 각 감상 경험의 특유함을 재확인하는 동시에, 유의미한 수준의 유연성을 제공한다고 생각합니다.

실케 이 혼성적 형식은 서로에 대한 신뢰와 호기심을 증명하는 진정 선구적인 큐레토리얼 실험이기도 합니다. 미술관마다 각자의 소장품과 미술 공동체를 대상으로 자유롭게 작품을 선정했는데요. 이런 혼성의 형식에 또 '집'과 관련된 네 가지 주제에 적합하다 싶은 작품들을 골랐습니다.

《우리 집에서, 워치 앤 칠》은 '거실의 사물들'로 시작합니다. 집 안의 물건들과 그것들이 배치되고 나열되고 순환하는 장면에 초점을 맞추죠. 두 번째 챕터 '내 곁에 누군가'는 물건을 넘어 동물, 식물, 로봇, 침입자를 포함해 가정의 다양한 반려자로 범위가 확대됩니다. '집의 공동체'는 실제의 이웃을 넘어, 전 지구화된 세계에서 물리적으로 또 가상으로 이어진 복잡한 네트워크 안에서 일어나는 새로운 버전의 공동체 생활을 제안합니다. 마지막으로 '메타-홈'은 집의 물리적, 정신적 개념들을 시적으로 일깨워주죠.

이런 주제적 접근이 서로 다른 큐레이터들의 취향과 작가들의 스타일을 프로젝트의 강점으로 전환하는 데 도움이 되었다고 보시나요? 지리적인 관점도 기관마다 맥락도 그토록 다양한 가운데 하나의 전시를 공동 기획하면서 어려운 점은 무엇이었고 어떤 점이 가장 흥미로웠을까요?

지회 우선, 협력 큐레이터들 사이에 곧바로 기대감이 돌았어요. 그 바탕에는 코로나19의 영향으로 모든 미술관이 직면한 불확실성의 문제가, 또 이 프로젝트가 모두가 안은 어려움 속에 일종의 돌파구 역할을 한다는 사실이 있겠죠.

네 가지 소주제들은 각각 익숙한 일상 환경이 불안정해져 가는 현실에 대한 각기 다른 응답이라 할 수 있습니다. 맨 처음 MMCA의 미디어 소장품을 들여다보는 과정에서 주제의 윤곽이 대략 그려졌어요. 오민은 〈에이 비 에이 비디오〉(2016)에서 여러 사물을 재배열하고, 차재민은

‹안개와 연기›(2013)에서 변해가는 지역 공동체의 모습을 담아냅니다. 구동희는 사적임과 공적임의 서먹한 결합을 ‹타가수분›(2016)에서 탐구합니다. 이런 작품들이 가정이라는 공간의 확장된 개념들과 관련해 가능한 주제들을 타진해보는 출발점이 되었습니다.

느슨한 큐레토리얼 구조로 협력 미술관의 파트너 큐레이터가 협의를 통해 작품 목록을 더하거나 빼고, 또 수정하는 것이 가능했습니다. 작품 목록 초안을 작성하는데 M+의 소장품을 살펴본 것도 도움이 많이 되었어요. 온라인 상영이 가능한 작품들의 광범위한 목록을 보유한 덕분에요. 협력한 큐레이터 모두 프로젝트에 적합하다 생각한 후보작을 제안하면서, 이 작품들이 어떤 이유로 또 어떤 방식으로 특정 분류에 어울리는 흥미로운 서사를 표현하는지 서로의 생각을 나누었습니다.

키티마 님과는 세부적인 촬영 기법, 작가의 주관성, 응시 등과 관련해 기나긴 이메일을 주고받았습니다. 이미 세계적으로 알려진 작가들 대신에 젊은 세대의 작가들을 소개해주신 점이 무척 좋았어요.

‘내 곁에 누군가’ 챕터에 전시된 시린 세노의 ‹꽃을 따는 것›(2021). 한 조각의 나무가 나무에서 탁자가 되기까지 지나온 여정을 담는다.

‘집의 공동체’ 섹션에 전시되던 템포의 ‹만에서 만을 거쳐 만으로›(2013). 작품은 인도의 삼선에서 생활하는 선원들이 손에 카메라를 들려주었다.

키티마 차리프라싯(이하 키티마) MAIIAM은 작은 사립 미술관으로 동남아시아 전역의 현대미술 작품을 소장하고 있습니다. 태국을 비롯해 동남아시아 지역의 신진 미술가들을 소개하고 지원하는 것이 저희의 기본 과업입니다. 지회 님과 전시 기획을 위해 관련 주제를 논의한 후, 소장품들을 살펴보기 시작했어요. 현대 태국 사회의 맥락에서 (집 또는 가정이라는 뜻의) ‘반’(บ้าน, Baan)이라는 개념을 반영하면서, 더 중요하게는 ‘워치 앤 칠’의 네 가지 하위주제에 해당되는 영상 작품들을요. ‘반’이라는 단어를 번역하려고 보니, 그에 상응하는 영어 단어를 찾을 수가 없었습니다. 왜냐면 ‘반’은 대체로 ‘가족’이라는 말과 불가분하거든요. 예를 들어 “집에서 저녁을 먹다”라는 표현은 말 그대로 자기 집에서 저녁을 먹는다는 뜻이라기보다, 자기 가족과 저녁을 먹는다는 뜻입니다. 그래서 저희는 소장품을 넘어 더 넓은 정의의 ‘반’을 전달할 수 있도록 프로그램을 채워줄 젊은 작가들의 영상 작품을 더 찾아보았습니다.

카와타 바타나즈얀쿠르의 ‹어머니와 나(진공청소기 III)›(2021)는 제목이 암시하듯 어머니와 함께 만든 작품으로, 집 안 가족 구성원의 신체적 안전을 논의합니다. 한편 완타니 시리파타나눈타쿨의 ‹모든 이는…›(2017)은 반려동물과 보호자 간의 가족 같은 관계를 묘사하고요. 타다 행삽쿨의 ‹당신은 나를 대양으로 내려가게 한다›(2018)는 집의 이슈들을 민족주의의 영향 아래 있는 민족국가의 국경에서 벌어지는 동요 사태와 연결 짓는다면, 반면에 차이 시리즈의 ‹포시즌스›(2010)는 현대 민족국가 체제에서 벗어난 집을 그립니다. 더 나아가, 태국 사람들이 생각하는 ‘집’ 개념은 심지어 보이지 않는 존재로까지 확장되는데요, 지역 신앙에 따르면 집을 지켜준다고 믿는 존재들이죠. 사룻 수파수티벡의 ‹보안원의 CCTV›(2019)는 무릇 건물이 사람뿐 아니라 유령과 신비로운 존재의 집일 가능성을 다룹니다. 언급한 작품들은 다양한 배경과 이데올로기를 지닌 관객들에게 최대한 어필할 수 있게 신중하게 선별했습니다.

이번 프로젝트에 참여한 작가들 중에는 앞서 우리와 협업한 경험이 있는 사람들도 있고 그렇지 않은 사람들도 있습니다. 그럼에도 그들의 작품을 보면 작품 제작 과정과 그 윤곽을 잡는데 있어 흥미로운 연결점들을 발견할 수 있었어요. 그런 이유 때문에 이번 프로젝트로 선보인 작품 중

일부를 우리 미술관이 소장하기로 하기도 했습니다. 이 작가들을 지원하고 작품의 향후 전시를 추진하기 위해서요.

실케   'M+ 컬렉션 온라인'은 저희 미술관의 디지털 환경과 오픈소스 정책을 보여주는 중요한 특징입니다. 이 컬렉션이 지회 님에게 영감이 되고 초반의 작가 명단 논의에 기여했다는 점이 무척 기뻤어요. 제안했던 차오 페이, 위안 광밍, 캠프 모두 참여 작가가 되었는데요. 차오 페이의 경우 인간 관계, 장소와의 상호작용, 현대화가 초래한 여러 형태의 소외를 계속해서 살펴온 부분이 자연스럽게 맞아 들었고, 공동체를 중심으로 뛰어난 작업과 더불어 여러 분야를 교차하는 협력의 실천을 보여준 캠프도 마찬가지였지요.

왕 공신과 지앙 지의 작품으로는 저희 M+ 개막전 주제와의 연관성을 진전시키고 싶었습니다. 왕 공신의 〈브루클린의 하늘 – 베이징에서 구멍 파기〉(1995)는 《개인, 네트워크, 표현》 전의 주제였던 디아스포라, 전 지구적 연결과 공명합니다. 지앙 지의 〈날아, 날아〉(1997)는 《M+ 지그 컬렉션: 혁명에서 세계화로》 전반에 걸쳐 제기된 변화의 개인적 경험과 일상의 근본적 변모를 그리죠. 이런 연결 지점을 통해 영상 전시를 둘러싼 논의를 확장하고 매체의 본질적이고 끊임없이 진화하는 현대성과의 관계를 조명할 수 있다고 봤습니다.

위안 광밍의 경우, 저희 소장품이 아닌 〈주거〉(2014)를 '워치 앤 칠' 출품작으로 선정했습니다. 씨씨 우와 차오 페이와는 실제 공간과 온라인의 전시 방식을 달리하기로 했고요. 참여 작가와 나눈 대화가 MMCA 작품 선정의 윤곽을 잡는 데 어떤 영향을 주었나요?

왕 공신의 중요한 영상 설치작 〈브루클린의 하늘 – 베이징에서 구멍 파기〉(1995). 작품에서 그는 본가의 거실 바닥에 구멍을 팠다. 이는 미국에서 관음적으로 사용되는 '중국까지 땅을 파다'라는 표현을 야유한 것이다.

지회   순회 전시와 연동된 온라인 플랫폼이라는 형식에 대해서 작가들과 이야기를 나누던 중, 몇 작가분들이 미술관 소장품이 아닌 다른 최근 작업, 혹은 신작을 포함하면 어떻겠냐고 말씀해 주었어요. 김희천은 게임 엔진에 임베드된 단채널 영상 작품인 〈나 홀로 '멈블' 보기〉(2020)를 넣자고 제안했고, 차지량은 전시를 위해 새로운 작업을 진행하고 싶어 했죠. 십 년 전 퍼포먼스를 기록한 MMCA 소장작 〈뉴 홈〉(2012)은 오늘의 시점에서 다시 제작한 작업으로 구현되었습니다. 이러한 유기적인 과정을 통해서 작품을 선정하는 범위, 소위 게임의 규칙은 협력 미술관 소장품에 국한하지 않고, 소장 작가의 관련 작품까지 두루 살펴보도록 확장되었습니다. 그렇게 이 프로젝트를 함께 상상함에 있어 제한을 두기보다는 어느 정도의 자유도를 가질 수 있게 한 것이죠. 물론 작품을 소장하지 않는 MCAD와의 협력 또한 그러한 확장성의 맥락 안에 있고요.

이제 《우리 집에서, 워치 앤 칠》의 물리적 구현에 대해서 좀 더 이야기 해 볼까요? 순회전이라는 형식을 취하긴 했지만 각 기관의 상황에 따라 보여지는 방식이 정말 다를 것이라 기대했고, 또 여러 이야기를 나누고 구체화 하는 과정 속에서 흥미로운 지점들이 있었습니다. 먼저 MMCA에서는 건축농장(최장원)을 참여 작가로 초청해 전시의 네 챕터를 연출할 공간 설계를 부탁했습니다. 순회전의 시작점으로 인상적인 미디어스케이프를 선보이고 싶었죠. 전시장은 '워치 앤 칠' 플랫폼을 경험하는 견본주택, 즉 미디어 환경으로 변모한 가상의 집 형태를 취하는데요. 건축가는 챕터 별로 서로 구분되는 네 가지 개념의 공간을

현대 사회의 도시 재개발로 거처를 잃은 사람들을 기록한 차지량의 〈인계획 연기〉(2013)가 MMCA 전시장 내 원형 감상 공간 후벽에 영사되고 있다.

구상했습니다. 긴 의자와 스크린 등으로 구현된 집의 일부, 감상실 기능을 하는 부유하는 방, 모든 장소를 연결하는 인상적인 원형 의자 가구, 마지막으로 미래의 홈시어터를 위한 기울어진 벽과 같은 방식으로요.

호셀리나 MCAD는 자동차 극장에서 영감을 받아 야외에서 물리적 전시를 구현하기로 했습니다. 야외를 활용해 영화를 상영하는 방식은 아시아 일부 지역에서 인기 있는 대중오락의 수단이 되었는데요. 특히 태국에서는 예전에도 지금도 대단히 인기가 높죠. 한편, 1950년대 미국에서도 자동차 극장이 유행했는데, 온 가족이 야외에서 먹고 마시며 거실을 자동차 안으로 옮겼던 사례입니다. 역사적으로 필리핀은 어느 쪽에도 해당하진 않지만, 팬데믹 시기 영상 매체를 중심으로 기획한 전시에 적합한 실현 가능한 구현으로서 이러한 자동차 극장을 생각하게 했습니다. 자동차 극장 공간에서 열린 '워치 앤 칠' 전시는 팬데믹의 영향 속에서 영상 작품을 선보이는 가능성과 한계를 충분히 생각하며 이뤄졌습니다. 팬데믹이 미술 기관에 안긴 어려움으로 인해, 저희는 또 다른 관점에서 전시를 바라보게 되었던 것이죠. 공중 보건을 위협하지 않고, 이 시기 시행되는 정부 방침을 준수하며 미술관 공간 너머와 바깥에서 실행할 수 있는 새로운 수평적 가능성들을 제안하게 된 것입니다. '워치 앤 칠'의 자동차 극장은 관객에게 본인의 차량 안에서 감상하는 사적 경험 뿐만 아니라 세심하게 조율된 환경에서 야외에서도 감상할 수 있도록 공간을 제공했습니다. 교내의 야외 주차장에서 자동차 극장 본래의 방식을 따라 FM 라디오 신호로 음향을 각자의 자동차로 전송하여 영상을 감상할 수 있었어요. 주 관객은 바이러스 감염 노출의 위험이 덜한 자동차 극장까지 기꺼이 운전해 온 차량 안 관객들이었습니다. 또 대학 주변 도보로 접근 가능한 지역에 사는 주민들도 있었는데, 이 분들 역시 야외에서 안전하게 작품을 감상할 수 있도록 했습니다.

키티마 저희는 MAIIAM에 '워치 앤 칠' 프로그램을 위한 야외 상영 플랫폼으로 '원형 감상 공간'을 만들었습니다. 2021년 12월부터 2022년 1월까지 한 달간 금요일부터 토요일까지 열려, 한 번에 30명을 수용할 수 있는 공간이죠. 현장 상영 플랫폼의 설계는 마치 자기 집 거실처럼 안락한 관람 환경을 조성하는데 중점을 두었습니다. 치앙마이의 젊은 건축가 집단인 폼볼스튜디오가 설계한 '원형 감상 공간'은 건축농장이 설계한 MMCA 서울관의 《우리 집에서, 워치 앤 칠》 전시 구조물과 스타일에서 영감을 얻었습니다. '워치 앤 칠' 프로젝트가 끝난 이후에도 이 공간을 활용해 신진 작가와 감독들이 작품을 대중에게 선보일 수 있도록 지원할 계획입니다.

실케 M+에서는 두 가지 전시 형식을 택했습니다. 2022년 1월과 2월에는, 저희가 소장한 단채널 작품을 위한 M+의 온디맨드 미디어 도서관인 미디어테크의 아늑한 감상 부스에서 '워치 앤 칠'을 볼 수 있고요. '대형 계단'에서 열리는 주말 상영도 있습니다.[1] 우리 미술관에서의 '워치앤 칠' 프로젝트는 2022년 3월에 열릴 연계 심포지엄으로 마무리될 텐데요. 공동의 경험과 풍부한 자료를 여러 국가의 다양한 관객들과 논의하는 자리가 될 예정입니다.

이 토크 행사들은 당연히 '워치 앤 칠'의 정신에 충실하게 온라인과 우리의 집, 즉 물리적 미술관 양쪽에서 열립니다.[2]

1.
2022년 1월부터 전 세계적으로 급상한 코로나19의 오미크론 변이의 여파로 인해 다수의 관객을 초대하고자 계획했던 '대형 계단'에서의 LED 스크린 상영 행사는 취소되었다.
2.
장기화된 M+의 휴관으로 '워치 앤 칠' 연계 행사들은 모두 온라인으로 대체되었다.

이 글은 Jihoi Lee, Silke Schmikl, "To Chill or Not to Chill? Streaming Art from Our Home to Yours," *M+ Magazine*, https://www.mplus.org.hk/en/magazine/to-chill-or-not-to-chill/, 2021년 10월 29일. 에서 발췌되었으며 저자 및 M+의 허락 하에 다시 쓰였다.

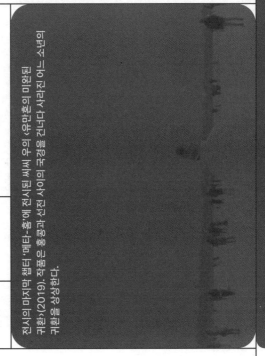

전시의 마지막 챕터 '메타-홈'에 전시된 씨씨 우이 〈양민훙이 미얀마 국경을 건너다 사라진 어느 소년이 귀환〉(2019). 작품은 홍콩과 선전 사이의 국경을 건너다 사라진 어느 소년의 귀환을 상상한다.

To Chill or Not to Chill?
Streaming Art from Our Home to Yours

The pandemic has exploded traditional notions of home for many. Still image from Yuan Goang-ming's *Dwelling* (2014).

The graphic identity for *Watch and Chill*, created by Korean design studio WORKS.

For those with an internet connection, the global pandemic has turned the home into a nexus of unprecedented data transmissions. We stream anything and everything into and out of our living rooms-news flashes and Netflix, tutorials and music videos, business meetings, and happy hours.

But museums? We've got a bit of a problem. Even as the commercial video streaming industry has accelerated into new territories, many museums' moving image collections have remained remarkably stagnant, with online information limited to simple synopses and video stills. How can we share video art from our home to yours?

Enter curator Lee Jihoi of the National Museum of Modern and Contemporary Art, Korea (MMCA). Earlier this year, Lee reached out to curators across Asia-at M+ in Hong Kong, the Museum of Contemporary Art and Design (MCAD) in Manila, and MAIIAM Contemporary Art Museum in Chiang Mai-to develop an online streaming platform for video art. *Watch and Chill*, a subscription-based service, launched in August 2021 and will stay online until February 2022. Below is a conversation between Lee Jihoi, Kittima Chareeprasit (Curator, MAIIAM) Joselina Cruz (Director/Curator, MCAD), and Silke Schmickl (Lead Curator, Moving Image, M+) about the online/offline curatorial strategies behind this collaboration.

Silke Schmickl   Hi Jihoi! When you reached out to us at M+ a few months ago to share your idea of *Watch and Chill: Streaming Art to Your Homes*, we felt immediately excited. The project addresses several urgent questions that art institutions are facing and offers some innovative answers.

Firstly, the need to imagine new ways of audience engagement beyond the physical space of museums. The pandemic made it clear that engaging audiences through the digital in times when we can't travel is key to staying close and connected. While the pandemic accelerated this need, it has been an urgent and to a large extent unresolved challenge for museums since the 2000s to adapt their activity to an increasingly digital world without losing focus on their core mission, which is to creatively work with the collection and make it accessible to audiences.

Secondly, the project invents a new form of inter-institutional collaboration: the exchange of moving image works from four significant Asian museums on both an online streaming platform and in the physical spaces of these institutions. Drawing on the digital nature and reproducibility of these works, *Watch and Chill* reactivates their natural, fluid circulation—a circulation often interrupted in the context of museum collections, where they are treated as unique, collectable objects.

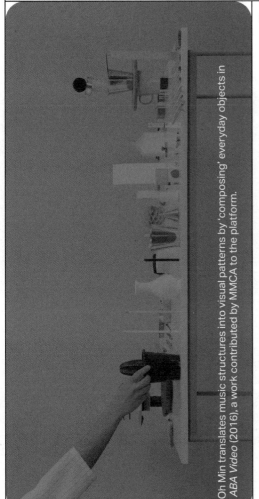

Oh Min translates music structures into visual patterns by 'composing' everyday objects in *ABA Video* (2016), a work contributed by MMCA to the platform.

Jihoi Lee Indeed, it is an era where the role of art museums is put to the test in terms of public engagement when myriads of media content constantly distract us. This tendency has certainly gained momentum, particularly so with the pandemic. Creating a digital platform that aims to broaden public access is a way to respond to the changing habits of audiences, quite literally bringing art into their 'homes'. *Watch and Chill* is intended as a platform where museums, artists, and audiences cross paths, becoming a mediator that enables such an exchange.

This project is funded by the Korean Government. As a national museum under the Ministry of Culture, Sports, and Tourism, one of our missions at the MMCA is to execute a global outreach program, Art Hallyu, in an attempt to introduce Korean culture abroad. Given the program's framework, the first thought that came to my mind was to find ways to make this opportunity a multilateral exchange, rather than simply informing others of the content of our collections. At the core of this exchange, there was a question of sharing resources, which included not only collections, but also manpower, administration, and the physical infrastructures of each museum.

I do value how the museum collection gravitates towards more conservative ways of treating objects for the sake of eternity. However, a digital file in a hard drive that sits in storage is, in effect, the material reality of most video collections. Information about these works on a museum website is often limited to a simple description and a still image, which is never enough to comprehend the works. How do we find ways to activate and mobilize these collections while seeking further audiences? Can we adopt aspects of the sharing economy?

Watch and Chill is that experimental portal of time and space which enhances the fluid possibilities of moving image collections, thanks to the kind permissions of the artists and each collaborating museum.

Joselina, I must say that MCAD was the first museum that I contacted to pitch the collaboration and was very much encouraged by your congenial reaction. Because, in part, there was already solidarity built among us for curating shows of the same artist in 2020 when the Covid-19 hit the entire globe for the first time.

Joselina Cruz It came as a surprise, and a wonderful one when Jihoi first pitched the idea. I thought initially that it was, and I think so did Jihoi, that it would be a modest undertaking, with us addressing the challenges of Covid-19 as institutions struggled to figure out what the future would look like. We spoke about inviting other spaces around the region, but not only institutions but curators engaged and active despite the pandemic.

The Philippines was struggling with the situation as with other countries, but the loss of an audience hit most of the museums and galleries in a large way. Here in the Philippines, the most active art institutions were attached to the universities: Vargas Museum was part of the University of the Philippines, Ateneo Art Gallery was part of Ateneo University, and MCAD was ensconced within the School of Design and Arts of the College of Saint Benilde. It was a huge blow for us when the schools closed themselves and migrated

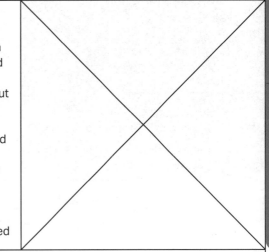

online. While other museums lost their general public, we lost our primary audience. We could only do so much to shore up audience engagement from the student population through projects made accessible online and transferring most aspects of our learning programs to zoom lectures and online workshops.

The talks regarding *Watch and Chill* came at a time when MCAD was working on the presentation of moving image works with Artists' Film International (AFI), and I looked at Jihoi's invitation as a fortuitous moment, to go full-on with support for local artists who were working through the pandemic. MCAD, as an exhibition space without a collection, has always been an opportunity for us to be part of the production of artworks for presentation. Often we have worked with artists to make new work or support the production of a project in various ways, and this includes giving them the space and the opportunity to show their work within a setting that engages, contextualizes, expands, and even challenges their practices. When shown within group shows their works are shown together with their peers, or across history and generations, despite not being part of a collection.

We try as much as possible to ensure that exhibitions at MCAD are part of larger conversations that go beyond the local or national but are still deeply integrated with local discussions.

Cao Fei's zombie-infested *Haze and Fog* (2013), an M+ work on the platform, stages surreal moments in everyday domestic scenes.

In Chai Siris's *500,000 Years* (2016), an outdoor cinema truck screens a film in Lampang, Thailand as an offering to the ghost of a homo erectus fossil found there in the 1990s.

Silke It is precisely that integrating attribute of MCAD colored an important aspect of *Watch and Chill: Streaming Art to Your Homes*, which pictures a possibility that an art institution can be an accommodating actor to this extend. And I agree, Jihoi, that museums' approaches to collecting and preserving moving-image work with the same professional care and standards that are applied to other art objects are extremely important. Not only for the purpose of conservation but also to acknowledge that artists' moving images are an integral part of twentieth- and twenty-first-century visual culture.

The meaningful activation of a collection is also key for any institution, and *Watch and Chill* offers an exciting opportunity to intervene in the intermediate space between unlimited, arbitrary, and freely accessible streaming content on the internet and the extremely well-researched narrative of a museum collection. We are often caught between these two extreme approaches, which both have their own relevance and function.

Over the last decade, online film services such as Netflix have successfully addressed this market niche by expanding their activity as a former DVD rental company into the digital realm, offering a wide range of accessible entertainment as well as curated content. Our project also explores this interstitial space by bringing compelling artistic content to viewers' homes, allowing them to discover these artworks in a new setting and at their own pace.

The title obviously also critically challenges Netflix's associated habit of watching, if not simply consuming, moving image content from home: 'Netflix and chill'. How would you describe the difference between *Watch and Chill* and other streaming platforms? I'm especially interested in the curatorial gestures we've taken to relate it back to the serious research and interpretation we practice in our institutions.

Jihoi Unlike the general over-the-top (OTT) services, the *Watch and Chill* platform will only be open to the public for a certain period of time before turning dormant. Starting from this year's grand launch, the *Watch and Chill* platform will re-launch with versions 2.0 and 3.0 in the coming years with different collaborating art institutions. The ephemeral character of this periodic opening is similar to the cyclical nature of exhibitions at art museums, a forever beta run to better our systems and deepen our curatorial endeavors.

Staging the "home" as a primary site for consuming the *Watch and Chill* streaming platform, our curatorial research began by speculating how the perception of the very notion of "domesticity" has changed. Linked via an unprecedented amount of data transmissions, our homes have gone beyond the mere private function of "dwelling" and have long entered the public realm. The twenty-two selected video works reflect on this expanded ethos of the home and have been grouped together with specifically constructed narratives.

The content of the platform is also physically embodied at each collaborating museum, in the form of exhibitions in Seoul, a drive-in cinema in Manila, a special architectural space built specifically for the occasion at Chiang Mai, and a series of screenings, talks, and a Mediatheque display in Hong Kong. I think this duality of actual and virtual presentation offers a meaningful level of flexibility, while re-affirming each watching experience to be a unique one.

Videos are presented both online and onsite at each institution. Shown here is MMCA's presentation of Wantanee Siripattananuntakul's *Everyone is···* (2017), a video contributed by MAIIAM.

A hand soars through a cramped domestic space against a classical score in Jiang Zhi's *Fly, Fly* (1997), a video presented under the theme 'Meta-Home'.

Silke This hybrid format is a truly pioneering curatorial experiment that also speaks of mutual trust and curiosity. Each institution had the freedom to select works from their own collection and arts communities, which they felt were relevant for this format and the four themes relating to this notion of "home."

The project opens with "Things in My Living Room," which focuses on objects in the house and scenes of their replacement, arrangement, and circulation. The second program, "By the Other Being," expands beyond material objects to a wider range of domestic companions, including animals, plants, robots, and intruders. "Community of Houses" proposes an updated vision of community living that occurs outside actual neighborhoods in a complex network of physical and virtual connections in our globalized world. And finally, there is "Meta-Home," in which physical and spiritual notions of home are poetically evoked.

From your point of view, did the thematic approach help to transform the diversity in curatorial tastes and artistic styles into a strength of the project? What were some of the challenges and highlights in co-curating an exhibition from such diverse geographical perspectives and institutional contexts?

Jihoi To begin with, there was instant excitement from all parties. It had to do with the uncertainty that all museums faced under the influence of Covid-19, and the fact that the project is a breakthrough in the hardship that we all share.

The four sub-themes equally respond to the destabilizing reality of our everyday environment as we know it. In the beginning, these categories were roughly structured as I looked into the MMCA's media collection. Oh Min rearranges an array of objects in *ABA Video* (2016), Cha Jeamin portrays a changing regional community in *Fog and Smoke* (2013), Koo Donghee examines the estranged linkage between privacy and publicity in *Cross×Pollination* (2016). These videos were the starting point of potential themes related to expanded notions of domesticity.

Shireen Seno's *To Pick a Flower* (2021), presented under the theme 'By the Other Being', narrates a piece of wood's journey from a tree into a household table.

The loose curatorial structure allowed other stakeholders to add to, subtract, and modify the selections. Going through your collection at M+, Silke, helped a lot because you have an extensive list available online. I proposed some candidates to all of you that I thought fit with this project, as did you, and we exchanged ideas as to why and how these works could render interesting narratives for specific categories.

Kittima and I had exchanged lengthy emails in regards to detailed camera works, the artist's subjectivity, and its gaze. And I love the fact that she introduced the younger generation of artists instead of those who were already well-known internationally.

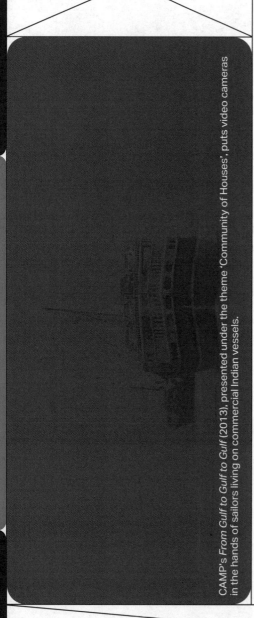

CAMP's *From Gulf to Gulf to Gulf* (2013), presented under the theme 'Community of Houses', puts video cameras in the hands of sailors living on commercial Indian vessels.

Kittima Chareeprasit MAIIAM is a small private museum that houses a collection of contemporary artworks from all over Southeast Asia. Our primary mission is to present and support emerging artists both in Thailand and throughout the region. After discussing the curation topic with Jihoi, we began to search the collection for moving images that can reflect the concept of "Baan"(บ้าน, meaning house or home) in the context of contemporary Thai society and, more importantly, fall under the four sub-themes of *Watch and Chill*. When we first started translating the word "Baan," we couldn't find its English equivalent, partly because the word "Baan" is in most cases inseparable from the word "Family." "Having dinner at home," for example, doesn't literally mean having dinner in one's own house, but rather means having dinner with one's own family. As a result, we looked for additional young artists' moving images beyond the collection to round out this program so that it delivers a broader definition of "Baan."

Kawita Vatanajyankur's *My Mother and I (Vacuum III)* (2021), which—as the name suggests—she created with her mother, discusses the physical safety of family members in the home, while *Everyone is···* (2017) by Wantanee Siripattananuntakul describes the family-like relationship between owners and their pets. Tada Hengsapkul's *You Lead Me Down, to the Ocean* (2018), on the one hand, likens home issues to the turbulence at the borders of a nation-state under the influence of nationalism, yet *Four Seasons* (2010) by Chai Siris, on the other hand, depicts a home that has broken away from the framework of a modern nation-state. Furthermore, the Thai people's concept of "Home" extends even to the invisible presences that, according to local belief, protect the home; *CCTV of Security Guard* (2019) by Saroot Supasuthivech addresses the possibility that buildings, in general, are home to not only humans, but also ghosts and mysteries. The above-mentioned artworks were handpicked with the intention of appealing to as many audiences as possible from a variety of backgrounds and ideologies.

Some of the artists in this project have previously collaborated with us, while others have not. Nonetheless, when viewing these artworks, one will find an intriguing connection between the creation process and framing choice. It is partly because of this aspect that we decided to acquire some of the moving images presented in this project into the collection of our museum in order to support the artists and promote the future presentation of these works.

We were so thrilled that the M+ Collection Online, an important feature of our digital presence and open-source policy, inspired you and sparked the discussion around the initial artist list. Cao Fei, Yuan Goang-ming, and CAMP all made it into the final selection. Cao Fei's ongoing interest in human relationships, interactions with places, and various forms of alienation that come from modernization was a natural fit, as were CAMP with their extraordinary work around communities and cross-disciplinary, collaborative practice.

We were also keen to develop a relationship with the themes in our opening exhibitions with the works by Wang Gongxin and Jiang Zhi. Wang Gongxin's *The Sky of Brooklyn – digging a hole in Beijing* (1995) resonates with the themes of diaspora and global connections in the exhibition Individuals, Networks, Expressions. *Fly, Fly* (1997) by Jiang Zhi illustrates a personal experience of change and the profound transformation of everyday life that is evoked throughout *M+ Sigg Collection: From Revolution to Globalisation*. These connections allow us to further expand the discussion around exhibiting moving images and highlight the medium's intrinsic and ever-evolving relationship with modernity.

With Yuan Goang-ming, we chose *Dwelling* (2014), a non-collection work, as a pertinent contribution, and agreed with Cici Wu and Cao Fei on distinct presentations for the physical and online exhibitions. Jihoi, how did your conversations with the artists shape your selection?

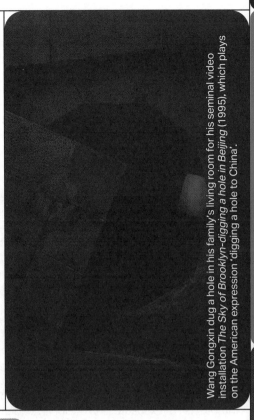

Wang Gongxin dug a hole in his family's living room for his seminal video installation *The Sky of Brooklyn-digging a hole in Beijing* (1995), which plays on the American expression 'digging a hole to China'.

Cha Jeamin's *Fog and Smoke* (2013), which documents people displaced by a modern housing development, is projected on the back wall of this circular viewing area at the MMCA exhibition.

While talking to individual artists about the format of an online platform combined with exhibitions, some of them proposed including other recent works that were not part of the museum collection. Kim Heecheon suggested we include *Watching 'Mumbling in Hell, Tumbling down the Well' Alone* (2020)— a single-channel video piece embedded in a game engine—and Cha Jiryang was eager to make new work specifically for this presentation—a re-enactment of *New Home* (2012), a performance he had done a decade ago and whose documentation was acquired by the MMCA.

So, by this time already, the rule of the game was not only to present the museum collection but also to work around it so that it doesn't limit our imagination. Not to mention building a partnership with MCAD, without a museum collection, meant the intended expansive quality of the project at large.

Shall we now talk a little bit more about how *Watch and Chill: Streaming Art to Your Homes* has been embodied in each museum? We expected varied forms of stagings depending on the situations we find ourselves in. And, in effect, we had incredibly fruitful conversations as we narrowed down each of our plans in the making. For the physical For the physical exhibition at MMCA, we invited Farming Architecture (Choi Jangwon) as a participating artist to design the spaces of four chapters of the exhibition. It takes the form of a model house for experiencing the *Watch and Chill* platform, a simulated home that has transformed into media environments. At each chapter, the architect had envisioned a spatial embodiment of four distinctive concepts: as fragments of home materialized into benches and screens; as floating pods functioning as viewing chambers; as an impactful, circular sitting furniture that connects all places; and, finally, as slanted walls for future home cinema.

Joselina MCAD decided to have its physical presentation in an outdoor space and took inspiration from the drive-in theatre. The use of the outdoor for cinema has been a popular means for mass entertainment in some parts of Asia, I think this was, is, very popular in Thailand especially, while drive-in theatres on the other hand rose to popularity in the US during the 50s where entire families brought their living room to their vehicles with drinks and food in the open air. The Philippines did not have either historically, but these two elements fed into thinking about the drive-in as a feasible project during the pandemic for an exhibition that centered on the moving image. The presentation of *Watch and Chill* within the space of a drive-in theatre came as we thought through the possibilities and limitations of showing the moving image during a pandemic. The difficulties brought on by the pandemic for art institutions led us to examine exhibition presentation through different lenses and propose lateral possibilities that could be undertaken beyond and outside the institution's space without endangering public health, and keep within government rules that were in play during that period. MCAD's *Watch and Chill* drive-in theatre gave our audience the possibility of privacy in their own cars, but also the opportunity for carefully orchestrated open-air engagement. Presented within the open-air car park of the college, and using FM radio signal for audio in keeping with original drive-in technology, *Watch and Chill* attracted those who lived further out willing to make the drive, without risk of exposure; and the local residents who lived around the college, who could simply walk into the car park, and safely see the works, in the open air.

Kittima At MAIIAM, we made The Circular Viewing Zone an outdoor screening platform for the *Watch and Chill* program, which happens from Friday to Sunday for one month from December 2021 to January 2022 and can accommodate 30 viewers at a time. The design of the on-site screening platform stresses viewing comfort, like being in one's own living room. Designed by pommballstudio, a Chiang Mai-based group of young architects, the Circular Viewing Zone is inspired by the structure and style of Farming Architecture's *Watch and Chill* exhibition at the National Museum of Modern and Contemporary Art, Seoul (MMCA). Following the *Watch and Chill* project, the museum will continue to use this area in supporting emerging artists and directors by allowing them to screen their work to the public.

1.
The screenings at the Grand Stairs, which intended to invite a large number of audiences, were cancelled due to M+'s temporary closure under Covid-19 restrictions.
2.
Due to the prolonged closure of M+, all the events relation to *Watch and Chill* were replaced by online formats.

Silke At M+, we chose two different forms of presentation. In January and February 2022, *Watch and Chill* will be available in the cozy viewing booths of our Mediatheque, the museum's on-demand library for single-channel works from the collection, and at weekend screenings in our Grand Stair.[1] We will end the project with our next M+ International in February 2022, in which we'll discuss our collective experiences and rich documentation with international audiences. These talks will take place online and from our homes, of course, to stay true to the spirit of *Watch and Chill*.[2]

Extracted from: Jihoi Lee, Silke Schmikl, "To Chill or Not to Chill? Streaming Art from Our Home to Yours" in *M+ Magazine*, October 29, 2021, https://www.mplus.org.hk/en/magazine/to-chill-or-not-to-chill/. Reproduced with the permission of the authors and the M+.

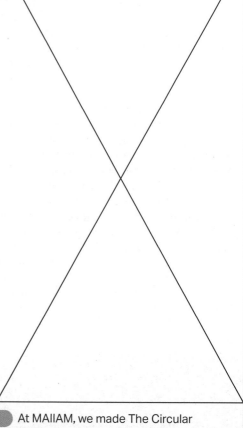
Cici Wu's *The Unfinished Return of Yu Man Hon* (2019), under 'Meta-Home', imagines the return of a boy who disappeared over the Shenzhen–Hong Kong border.

나는 계속 내가 된 누군가를 만나요

...peatedly come across people who turned into myself?

사자　8살이야
Saza is 8 years old.

나만
The Tales
아는
I Tell
이야기

⟨나만 아는 이야기⟩는 '워치 앤 칠'을 개인의 취향대로 유영하면서 경험한 것을 풀어낸 이야기나 비평적 관점을 담은 텍스트를 생산하고, 온라인 플랫폼을 통해 공유하는 전시 연계 위성 프로젝트이다. 이 프로젝트는 다양한 미디어 플랫폼의 등장으로 영상 콘텐츠의 감상 방식이 급변함에 따라 예술 작품이 온라인 미디어 플랫폼에서 어떻게 감상되는지 보다 개인적이고, 내밀한 시각에서 바라보고자 기획되었다. ⟨나만 아는 이야기⟩는 전시와 동일하게 3개년 프로젝트로 진행되면서 후속 전시 주제의 확장 가능성을 고려하여 담론 생산을 지속할 예정이다.

⟨나만 아는 이야기⟩는 총 3부로 구성된다.

오늘날 우리는 미디어 플랫폼 덕분에 언제 어디서든 간편하게 영상 콘텐츠를 소비할 수 있게 되었다. 이제 관람객이 콘텐츠가 있는 곳으로 찾아가는 것이 아니라, 관람객의 현재 위치가 콘텐츠를 감상하는 장소가 된 것이다. 이 글을 통해 문화예술 콘텐츠를 온라인 미디어 플랫폼에서 감상하는 방식에 대해 비평적 관점에서 바라보고자 한다.

코로나19 시대의 집은 거주뿐 아니라 사무, 육아, 친목 등 다양한 용도로 사용되는 공간이 되었다. 「내밀함에 관하여」에서는 집을 다양한 층위가 중첩된 공간으로 사용하는 동시대 문화계 인사들이 '워치 앤 칠' 플랫폼을 경험하고 작성한 일기를 공유하고자 한다. 이들의 일기를 소개함으로써 개인의 취향, 주변 환경 등에 따라 달라질 수 있는 경험과 감상의 방식을 엿볼 수 있다.

'워치 앤 칠'은 개인의 취향에 따라 웹페이지를 떠돈다는 점에서 여행의 경험 방식과 유사하다고 할 수 있다. 물리적인 여행이 제한된 이 시기에 소설가가 여행하듯이 온라인 플랫폼을 경험하고, 그 경험을 단편 에세이를 통해 공유하여 새로운 예술작품 감상 경험을 긴 호흡으로 공유해보고자 한다.

The Tales I Tell is an exhibition-related satellite project in which texts containing everyday stories or critical perspectives on experiencing online platform *Watch and Chill* according to writers' own tastes are produced and shared on the platform. The project was planned to examine from a personal and private perspective how artworks can be viewed on online media platforms in accordance with the rapid changes in video content viewing methods brought by the appearance of diverse media platforms. Like the exhibition itself, the project will last for three years, continuously producing discourses in consideration of the direction and expansive potential of the themes of later iterations of *Watch and Chill*.

The project consists of three parts.

Today, thanks to media platforms, we are able to watch video content with ease, any time and anywhere. The viewer no longer goes to find content in its location; rather, the viewer's location becomes the venue for viewing. In this text, Professor Yoo Hyunjoo attempts to examine ways of viewing cultural and artistic content on online media platforms from a critical perspective.

In the age of Covid-19, the home has become not just a place of dwelling but a multipurpose space of work, childcare, friendship and more. In *On Privacy*, contemporary cultural figures using their homes for a variety of purposes share the diaries they kept while experiencing the *Watch and Chill* online platform. Their diary entries offer a glimpse of how experiences and viewing methods differ according to factors such as personal taste and environment.

Watch and Chill allows users to wander around the website in accordance with personal taste. In this sense, it can be seen as similar to the modes of experience found in travel. At a time of restricted physical travel, a novelist experiences an online platform as if on a journey of his own, then conveys the outcome in a short essay, sharing his new art viewing experiences in long breaths.

체험하는 미술관,
사적 공간 안으로 구겨져 들어오다

유현주(연세대학교 교수)

아마도 아주 새로운 풍경은 아닐 것이다. 이미 지난 세기말에 시작된 디지털화는 우리의 사회 전반의 모습을 빠르게 바꾸어 놓았고, 이때부터 우리가 만질 수 있었던 모든 물질적인 것들은 대부분 전자적 추상화의 길로 들어섰던 것을 기억한다. 그렇게 우선 도서관이 (저항이 전혀 없던 것은 아니었지만) 전자화가 되었다. 한때는 직접 책을 대출하여 카피를 해야 했던 많은 자료들을 이제 간단히 네트워크에서 파일 형태로 다운로드하는 것이 가능해졌다. 마치 장밋빛 비전을 우리에게 약속했던 1990년대의 '캘리포니아 이데올로기'가 이야기했던 '당신 손 끝 위의 정보'가 실현된 듯이 말이다. 돌이켜 생각하면, 동시에 그것은 플랫폼의 변화이기도 했다. 처음에는 PC를 통해, 그리고 그 다음에는 모바일 기기를 통해 온라인에서만 존재하는 통로가 열리기 시작하였고, 점점 그 범위를 넓혀 갔다. 다시 도서관의 예를 들자면, 현실의 도서관을 실제로 방문하는 사람들보다, 가상의 도서관에서 자료를 열람하는 사람들의 숫자가 훨씬 더 늘어나기 시작했다는 말이다. 그렇지만 모두를 위한 장밋빛 미래가 정말 펼쳐진 것은 아니었다. 새로운 소통의 네트워크는 누구에게나 활짝 열려 있는 것처럼 보였지만, 실제로는 ─ 원래 현실 사회가 그러하듯이 ─ 경제적 기술적 지역적 그리고 정보 부족의 이유로 네트워크에서 탈락하는 사람들은 계속해서 발생했다.

지난 30년간 휘몰아쳤던 이 파도 속에서 그럼에도 이 전자화를 조금이나마 비껴갔던 분야가 있다면, 아마도 공연예술 영역과 함께 바로 전시문화를 언급할 수 있을 것이다. 여기에서의 키워드는 구체적인 장소와 시간이 결합된 '현장성'이다. 고전적인 매체학자라면 벤야민의 '아우라'를 언급했을지도 모르겠다. 공연예술과 예술작품의 전시에 한해서만큼은 (그리고 물론 점점 증가하는 그 혼합의 형태도) 오프라인이 그 중심이 되는 것이 일반적이며 당연한 것이었다. 적어도 이곳에서는 광섬유로 이루어진 새로운 통로보다 기존의 방식이 계속해서 사용되었던 것이다. 일회성, 체험성, 그리고 바로 그 대체불가한 현장성이 이유가 되었다.

그러나 이제 또다시 새로운 전환의 물결이 밀려온다. 이번 파도는 좀 더 가파르고, 시급하며, 이전보다 더 즉각적으로 작용한다. 사회적 거리가 필수적인 요청이 된 코비드-19의 상황이 그것이다. 우리는 근미래를 다루는 영화에서나 나올 것 같은 풍경 속에서 이제는 밖으로 나가지 않고 되도록 집에 머무르게 되었다. 아침에 일어나면 서재 안으로 수업을 하러 들어가고 거실 책상으로 출근을 한다. 그리고 이번에는 공연예술과 예술작품의 전시까지도 빠르게 비대면 원거리 소통으로 대체되고 있다. 갈 수 없는 오프라인 공연 대신 연일 실시간 온택트 콘서트와 VOD가 제공되고 있으며 (가상의 아티스트가 아닌 가상의 관객들과 함께!) 미술전시관은 구글 아트 앤 컬쳐와 같은 대규모 플랫폼을 필두로 자신의 소장품들을 가상의 미술관에서 기획하여

Part. 1

The Experienced Museum: Arriving Folded into Private Spaces

Yoo Hyunjoo (Professor, Yonsei University)

The landscape may not be an entirely new one. The digital transformation that began late last century has swiftly transformed all aspects of our society, and I can recall how most of those material things we once could touch began traveling a path of electronic abstraction. First, libraries were made electronic (a process not entirely without resistance). Many materials that we once had to borrow and copy ourselves can now be downloaded easily as files from a network. It is like the realization of the "information at your fingertips" described by the "California ideology" of the 1990s, with all the rosy visions it promised us. In retrospect, it was also a change in platforms. First with PCs and later with mobile devices, channels began to open that solely existed online; over time, their scope has broadened. To go back to the library example, far more people began accessing material at virtual libraries than people actually visiting physical libraries. But this optimistic future was not truly for everyone. The new communication networks seemed wide open to all, but in practice—as it always is with real-world societies—people kept being shut out of these networks for economic reasons, technological reasons, regional reasons, or a lack of information.

Yet if there are any areas that managed to somewhat avoid this electronic shift amid the surging of this wave for the past 30 years, they may be the fields of performing arts and exhibition culture. The key concept here is "immediacy," a mixture of concrete place and time. A classical media scholar might mention Walter Benjamin's "aura." At least when it came to the performing arts and art exhibitions (along with the growing number of hybrid forms, of course), it seemed ordinary and natural for them to be offline-centered. They continued to use the same methods rather than introducing new channels made of optical fibers. The reasons had to do with their one-time nature, their experiential element—that irreplaceable immediacy.

Yet we now see another new wave of transformation arriving. It's steeper than before, more urgent, and more immediate. It's the Covid-19 pandemic, which commands social distancing as an essential practice. Living in landscapes we might find in a film set in the not-too-distant future, we try to stay home as much as possible without going outside. We wake up in the morning and go to classes in our study; we clock in for work at our living room desk. Now even the performing arts and art exhibitions are quickly being replaced by long-distance, non-face-to-face communication. Day after day, real-time "online face-to-face" concerts and VOD are offered in place of the offline performances we can no longer visit (with virtual audiences rather than virtual artists!), while art institutions organize "virtual museums" to show their collections through vast platforms like Arts & Culture. Performance venues and museums are now transported into the laptop on my desk and the mobile device in my hand.

선보이고 있다. 내 방 데스크 위 랩톱 속으로, 내 손 안의 모바일 디바이스 속으로 이제 공연장과 미술관이 들어온다.

　　　　단순한 이미지의 제시 그 이상을 목표로 하는 전자 미술관에 있어 관객체험의 문제는 새로운 매체기술이 구현하는 '체험'의 가능성과 밀접한 관련을 가진다. 이러한 체험은 구체적이어야 하며, 현실의 미술 전시장에서 느낄 수 있듯이 어느 정도는 동일한 전시에 참여하는 집단과의 의식적이며 무의식적인 유대관계가 필요하다. 새로이 제기되는 질문은, 기술이 구현하는 관객체험이란 무엇을 제공할 수 있는지에 대한 논의이며, 또한 앞서도 언급했듯이 여기에서 처음부터 배제되거나 탈락되는 존재에 대한 인지이다. 만약 대면과 비대면이 혼합된다면, 즉 이질적인 것들의 네트워크화가 다시 한번 하이퍼-연결로 실현된다면, 이러한 전시는 또 이전과는 다른 어떠한 특징을 가지게 될 것인가? 우리는 이러한 질문과 함께 이제 진화된 미디어 조건과 생태 환경에서의 예술적 체험에 대한 융합적 구상을 펼쳐볼 수 있을 것이다.

인간의 몸, 체험, 수행성과 상호작용성

이 이야기를 시작하기 위해서는 짧은 미디어문화사를 통해 디지털 미디어와 인간의 몸, 체험의 관계에 대해 먼저 살펴봐야 할 것 같다. 비대면으로 이루어지는 소통에서 몸으로 겪는 체험이란 언뜻 멀어 보이기도 하지만, 디지털 매체에서의 체험 문제를 다루는 '상호작용성'은 실상 디지털 미학의 중추 개념이며, 전자적 네트워크의 시작과 함께 크게 주목받았던 개념이기도 했다. 물론 처음부터 몸과 체험이 전면에 등장한 것은 아니었다. 초기 상호작용성 논의에서는 무엇보다 사용자의 주도적인 선택 가능성이 중심이 되었다. 이는 새로운 매체를 수용하는 방식이 전환되었다는 사실뿐만 아니라, 이와 더불어 매체를 다루는 사용자가 가지고 있는 이미지 또한 변화했다는 것을 알려주는 하나의 사건이었다.

　　　　결론부터 말하자면, 전자적 매체를 사용하는 수용자의 이미지는 매우 이상적으로 상정되었던바, 바로 우리가 얼마 전 지나왔던 지난 세기의 논의들에서 특히 그러했다. 이들에 대하여 일반적으로 퍼져나간 이미지로는, 수동적이고 조작되기 쉬운 TV 시청자 '카우치 포테이토'Couch Potato들의 바로 반대편에 서 있는 사람들이라는 것이다. 즉, 매체를 수동적으로 접하는 것이 아니라 능동적으로 대하며, 자신이 무엇을 원하는지 분명히 알고 매체를 잘 사용하는, 자의식이 뚜렷한 지식인들로 간주되었다. 그렇게 우리는 그들을 기꺼이 '탐험가'Explorer, 마이크로소프트사의 웹브라우저 혹은 '항해사'Navigator, 넷스케이프사의 웹브라우저라고 불렀다.

　　　　이렇게 멋진 사용자 이미지는 정확히 말하면 전자적 매체가 세계를 빠르게 전자 그물망으로 뒤덮기 시작한 바로 그 시기부터 시작되었다고 할 수 있다. 이때 미국의 서부해안을 중심으로 새로운 정보기술의 민주적이고 혁명적인 잠재력에 대한 믿음이 확산되었다. 앞서 언급한 '캘리포니아 이데올로기'라고 불렸던 이러한 시각은 디지털 매체가 가져올 미래상을 매우 희망적으로 바라보았다. 이미 존재하는 사회와는 전혀 다른 대안적인 사회가 기술이 마련해 놓은 가상의 공간 안에 건설되는 듯이 보였고, 이 안에서는 국적과 인종, 문화, 성별 등 실제 삶을 제약하는 경계들이 모두 사라질 수 있다고 믿었다. 사이버 스페이스에 건립될 가상의 유토피아 사회. 이 새로운 네트워크 사회 속 시민들의 관심사는 '제한 없고 독점되지 않은 정보의 흐름'이었고, 이러한 흐름 속에서 가장 강조된 것은 수없이 쏟아지는 많은 정보들 가운데 스스로 취사선택할 수 있는 주체적인 모습이었다. 바로 '결정하는 자'로서의 이미지이다. 네트워크의 사용자들은 매체가 제공하는 여러 가지 가능성 사이에서 직접 선택의 결정을 내리고, 이러한

When it comes to "e-museums" with aims beyond simply sharing images, the issue of viewer experience is closely tied to the potential for "experiences" achieved through new forms of media technology. Those experiences must be concrete; they require some kind of conscious and unconscious bond with others taking part in the same exhibition, as we would sense at an actual art exhibition. The new questions that are being asked have to do with what we are capable of offering through a technologically embodied viewer experience, and with our perceptions of those aforementioned people who are excluded from the outset. If the "face-to-face" and "non-face-to-face" can be combined— if the creation of disparate networks can be achieved anew through hyper-connections— what qualities might the resulting exhibitions have that are different from before? In addition to that question, we can also present a multidisciplinary vision for the artistic experience in these evolved media conditions and this ecological environment.

The human body, experience, performativity, and interactivity

To start off, I think I should first present a brief media culture history to explore the relationship among digital media, the human body, and experience. Bodily experience might seem to be on the wane amid our trend of non-face-to-face communication, but "interactivity"—which concerns issues of experience in digital media—is actually a central concept in digital aesthetics, one that has drawn major attention since the dawning of electronic networks. To be sure, matters of the "body" and "experience" have not always been front and center. In the early stages of the interactivity debate, the key element was the potential for users to make self-directed choices. This was an event showing not only that the ways in which people received new media had shifted, but also that the image of the media user had changed.

The long and the short of it is that the image posited for electronic media users was quite strange, particularly in the late-century discussions that we passed through recently. The image that was typically shared for them was of the polar opposite of the "couch potato," or a passive and easily manipulated TV viewer. They were seen as clearly self-conscious intellectuals, people who were active rather than passive in their use of media, people who knew what they wanted and were skilled in their media use. We referred to them as "Explorers" (web browser of Microsoft) or "Navigators" (web browser of Netscape).

Specifically, this appealing image of users can be seen as having started right at the moment when electronic media had rapidly begun sweeping the world as an electronic network. There was a growing faith in the democratic, revolutionary potential of the new information technology, particularly on the West Coast of the United States. Previously referred to here as the "California ideology," this was a very hopeful perspective on the future that digital media would bring about. It seemed as though an alternative society was being built in the virtual spaces provided by technology—a completely different society from the existing one—and people believed that all the boundaries that circumscribed real life might disappear within it, including differences of nationality, ethnicity, culture, and gender. This was the imaginary utopian society that would be created in cyberspace. What interested people about this new network society was the flow of information without limits or monopolies; the great emphasis in these trends was on an active user capable of selecting from the vast torrent of information. This was the "chooser" image. Network users, it was thought, would decide for themselves among the various possibilities that media offered, and even take part themselves in creating objects to be adopted in the process. This was the ideal "interactivity" of digital media. Some of the notable artistic forms that emerged during this period included hyperfiction, in which readers chose for themselves how stories would unfold, and interactive narrative games, where users could influence the ending.

과정을 통해 수용하고자 하는 대상의 구성에까지 직접적으로 참여할 수 있다고 믿었다. 그리고 이것이 디지털 매체에서의 이상적 상호작용성이었던 것이다. 독자가 직접 이야기 전개의 향방을 결정하는 소설인 하이퍼픽션, 사용자가 엔딩에 영향을 미칠 수 있는 인터랙티브 내러티브 게임 등이 이 시대에 시작되어 주목받은 작품 형식이었다.

그러나 이때의 상호작용성은 현재 우리가 생각하는 직접 체험으로까지는 이어지지 못했다. 그것은 이 시대의 시대정신은 결정하는 자로서의 인간의 주도력을 높이 평가하며, 반면 직접 체험의 전제가 되는 인간의 '몸'에 대해서는 다분히 경시하는 측면을 가지고 있었기 때문이다. 매체전환의 형식이 모든 하드웨어적인 것을 보이지 않는 소프트웨어로 바꾸는 방향으로 진화해 왔다는 것을 이해해야 한다. 하드웨어 중에서도 가장 하드웨어적인 인간의 '몸'은 이 과정에서 대단한 부침을 경험하게 되었다.

우선 디지털 매체기술의 '위대한 정신성'은 우리 사회를 유심론唯心論이 지배하는 현장으로 만들었으며, 이 과정에서 현실 세계에서의 인간의 몸이란 단지 벗어나야 할 대상으로 전락한다. 당시 대중문화에서 자주 등장하던 인간과 기계의 결합은 기계의 몸에 인간의 정신이 장착되는 모습으로 그려졌다. 이 결합이 가져오는 시너지 효과는 인간 본연의 육체적 허약함을 극복하는 것이었으며, 더욱이 사이버스페이스에서 그것은 그냥 잊어버려도 되는 무의미한 것이었다. 실제로 유전자 조작이나 인공신체의 이식 등의 기술은 인간의 몸을 점차 기계로 바꾸어 나가는 방향으로 발전해 왔으며, 인간의 진짜 몸은 이러한 기술의 도전에 무력하게 여겨졌다. 이러한 배경에서 근미래를 소재로 한 소설과 영화 속에서 네트워크에 자유롭게 접속할 수 있는 플랫폼을 인공두뇌에 장착한 사이보그의 등장도 드물지 않게 그려졌다. 탈인간화를 부추기는 이러한 과학기술의 발달에서 핵심적인 것은 우리의 정신은 기술적인 도움으로 언제든지 우리의 몸을 떠나 자유롭게 디지털 세계 속을 유영할 수 있다는 점이었다.

바꾸어 이야기하자면, 현실 속 고착화되어 있는 진짜 인간의 몸이란 이제 우리에게 장애로 작용한다는 것이다. 이미 귄터 안더스Günter Anders가 1950년대에 행한 진단처럼, 인간은 현대 기술매체사회에서 골동품과도 같은 '어제의 것'이며, 한마디로 시대에 뒤떨어진 '구식'이 되어 버렸다. 독일의 매체학자 노르베르트 볼츠는 고도로 복잡해진 정보의 유통에서 인간의 몸이 걸리적거리는 방해물이 되어버린 상황을 '정보사회에서 병목현상을 일으키는 인간'으로 요약한다. 기계 없이는 많은 정보를 동시에 처리할 수 없으며, 의식 속에는 아주 제한된 세계만을 담을 수 있는 인간 자체는 정보화 사회의 병목이다. 더구나 누구나 지구적으로 사고하고 세계 곳곳과 접속하며, 자유롭게 디지털 파도 위를 넘나들고자 하는 곳에서, 구체적이고 현존하는 육체는 방해요소가 되었다. 이러한 시각은 당시 소프트웨어나 하드웨어에 빗대어 육체를 다소 경멸적인 어조로 '웨트웨어'Wetware라고 불렀던 것을 이해하게 해준다. 인간의 몸은 가상 세계를 탐험하고 항해하는데 불필요한 물주머니이며, 현실 세계가 잡아놓은 인질일 뿐이다.

이렇듯 인간이 가진 한계를 구체적으로 체현해주는 몸이란 디지털 매체가 상징하는 위대한 정신성의 승전보와 함께 '무가치한 것'으로 역사의 무대에서 퇴락하는 듯이 보였다. 그러나 매체의 역사에서 그 어떤 승리도 사실 그렇게 쉽게 이루어진 적은 없었다. 몸에 대한 가치의 폄하는 곧 인간적인 것 전체가 가진 가치의 하락으로 받아들여졌으며, 이러한 위기의식의 발로는 전에 없던 강력한 반작용을 가져오게 되었다. 몸이 가진 컬트적 가치의 상승이 그것이다. 실제로 고통을 느끼고, 지각하며, 체험하고, 문화적 산물을 향유하는 유일한 주체로서의 몸이 가진 중요성이 다시 한번 부각되었다. 사실 우리 존재라는 것이 바로 우리 몸 자체인데? 우리가 우리의 몸을 떠난다고? 따뜻하고 부드러우며 고향과도 같은 우리의 몸을? 이는 매체의 전환이 빠르게 진행될수록 다시 이전 세계의 것을 그리워하는 아날로그로의 향수와도 결합되었다. 손으로 쓴 글씨, 관조, 삶의 태도로서의 느림, 이러한 것들과 함께 부상한 것이 바로 경시의

But the interactivity here did not lead to direct experiences as we think of them today. While the zeitgeist placed great stock in the initiative of the "chooser," it paid relatively little heed to the human bodies that were prerequisites for direct experience. What we need to understand here is that the forms in the media transformation had evolved in a direction where all of the hardware elements were being replaced with unseen software. As the hardest ware of them all, the human body experienced some major upheavals in the process.

To begin with, the "great spirituality" of digital media technology turned our society into one governed by idealism, during which process the real-world human body became something to be escaped from. The combinations of humans and machines that often appeared in popular culture were depicted in a way where the human spirit became invested in a mechanical body. The synergy of this mixture was enough to transcend inherent human physical frailties; in cyberspace, such things were meaningless and could simply be disregarded. Indeed, technologies such as genetic manipulation and prosthetic transplants developed in such a way as to increasingly transform the human body into a "machine," while our actual human bodies were seen as helpless in the face of this technological challenge. Against this backdrop, it was not uncommon for works of fiction and film set in the not-too-distant future to include cyborgs whose artificial brains included platforms that allowed them to freely connect with networks. The central notion of these technological advancements hastening "post-humanization" was the idea that our minds could leave our bodies behind and freely roam the digital world with the help of technology.

Conversely, this meant that actual human bodies fixed within the real world had become obstacles in our way. As Günther Andres had observed about the 1950s, humans were "yesterday," antiques in a society of contemporary technology and media; we were old-fashioned, behind the times. The German media scholar Nobert Bolz describes this situation of the human body as an obstacle to exceedingly complex information circulation as the "humanmade bottleneck in the information society." In the information society, human beings themselves are a bottleneck: unable to process large volumes of information simultaneously without machines, only capable of holding a very limited world in their consciousness. Moreover, the concrete, real-world body had become an impediment in places where people sought to think globally, connect with the whole world, and freely surf the digital waves. This perspective helps us understand the use of the somewhat sneering term "wetware" to refer to the body, drawing analogies with "software" and "hardware." The human body is a needless sack of fluids for those exploring and navigating virtual worlds—a hostage to the real world.

As a concrete embodiment of human limitations, the body seemed to be exiting the historical stage, reduced to "worthlessness" amid the triumphs of the great spirituality signified by digital media. But no victory in media history has ever been so easily attained. Disparagement of the body's value was seen as degrading the value of all that is human, and manifestations of these fears resulted in a counteraction of unprecedented force: a rise in the "cult value" of the body. Once again, people were emphasizing the importance of the body as the only subject capable of actually feeling pain, perceiving, experiencing, and enjoying cultural projects. After all, aren't our bodies how we exist? Do they want us to leave our bodies behind—the warm, soft home of our bodies? This was joined in turn by a sense of analog nostalgia, as the swift progression of the media transformation sparked longing for the world before. It was a renewed rise in handwritten letters, meditation, slowness as a lifestyle approach, and the human body itself—something that has been written off as an object of contempt. Asimov's Bicentennial Man was right: the culmination of developments in artificial intelligence was the acquisition of a living body with finite rights.

대상으로 치부되었던 인간의 몸이었다. 아시모프Isaac Asimov의 바이얼센테니얼맨이 옳았던
것이다. 인공지능 개발의 완성은 유한有限의 권리가 있는 진짜 살아있는 몸의 획득이다.

이때부터 (실은 어느 시기나 관점을 달리하며 꾸준히 진행되어 왔던) 인간의 몸에 대한
철학적 성찰이 집중적으로 주목받기 시작하고, 또한 몸이 주체가 되어 우리 사회가 보다 다양한
체험의 가능성 위에 기반을 두고 있는 형태로 진행하고 있다는 진단도 등장한다. 이러한 작용과
반작용의 상황 속에서 매체의 발달 방향도 이전과는 다르게 진행되었다. 인간의 몸으로 직접
행동해보고 체험하는 '수행성'이라는 요소가 선택만을 강조했던 '상호작용성'에 더해지게 되면서,
이로써 차가운 디지털화와 과도한 정신화를 보상하고자 했던 것이다.

이러한 작용과 반작용의 상황은 모든 영역에서 유사하게 진행되었다. 이를 이론적으로
도운 것은 인간이 행동과 관련된 '수행성' 개념이다. 미학적인 논의에서 새로이 등장한 이 용어는
독일의 연극학자인 에리카 피셔-리히테Erika Fischer-Lichte에 의해 제안된 개념이다. 에리카
피셔-리히테는 우리가 이제 문화를 하나의 퍼포먼스로 이해한다면, 그것은 우리 사회가 인간의
'행동' 개념에 주목하고, 여기에서부터 유용한 개념을 발전시키는 일로부터 시작되어야 한다고
주장한다. 지난 70년대의 '언어적 전환'이 문화를 보는 방식을 텍스트 읽기라는 은유로서
기획했다면, 이제 연구의 관심은 각각의 문화적인 사건들을 구성하고 있는 행동으로 옮겨갔다는
것이다. 여기에는 우리가 문화적 능력에 대해서 이전과는 다른 기준을 가지게 되었다는 인식이
바탕에 놓여있다. 기존의 문화적 능력이 주로 읽어내기 어려운 대상을 관찰하거나 해석하는
능력으로 이해되었다면, 이제는 진행되고 있는 사건에 능동적으로 개입하는 행동 능력이 전면에
등장하게 되었다. 바야흐로 수행적 전환의 시대다. 그리고 문화는 행동이다. 이러한 과정에서
부각되는 것은 바로 직접적인 행동의 주체가 되는 '몸'과 그 결과인 '체험'이라는 요소다. 사건을
경험하고 사건에 개입하는 인간의 몸이 다시 문화적 능력의 척도가 된 것이다.

이러한 행동이 일어나기 위한 조건으로 피셔-리히테는 행위자와 관람자가 시간과
공간의 일치 속에서 육체적으로 '공-현존'Ko-Präsenz한다는 점을 주요하게 보았다. 행위자가 직접
몸으로 한 행동에 대해 관람자가 이러한 행동을 자신의 몸으로 인지하고 여기에 반응하는 것이
전체적인 행동을 구성한다. 만약 행위자와 관람자가 여러 명이라면 이들 상호 간의 상호작용은
여러 개로 겹쳐지는 복잡한 네트워크를 이루게 될 것이다. 이것은 지금까지 디지털 미학에서
상호작용성을 규정하던 원리인 단순한 '선택과 결정'과는 큰 차이가 있다. 실제 존재하는 공간과
현존, 시간성이라는, 그동안 '순수한' 가상공간에서는 중요하게 여겨지지 않던 여러 가지
조건들을 생각해 볼 수 있을 것이다. 따라서 우리가 우리 시대의 직접 체험으로 이루어진 가상의
미술관을 구상한다면 그것은 우리가 지금까지 살펴본 짧은 미디어문화사의 경험에서 무언가를
배운 것이어야 할 것이다.

우리 집 안으로 들어온 '우리 집'에 관한 전시

이러한 의미에서 우리의 주제가 되는 전시《우리 집에서, 워치 앤 칠》은 여러 겹의 네트워크가
겹치는 체험에 대한 실험적인 시도가 된다. 이것은 현실의 전시공간에서 전시되며, 동시에
가상의 미술관으로도 구축되어 있다. 아날로그적인 실제 전시와 디지털적인 가상의 전시가
포개어져 있는 것이다. 물리적 전시는 아시아의 4개 미술관(국립현대미술관, 마닐라
현대미술디자인미술관, 치앙마이 마이암현대미술관, 홍콩 M+미술관)의 국제적 네트워크로
이루어진다. 시간적으로는 미술관-네트워크 내 각각의 미술관에서 4번의 전시가 차례대로
진행될 예정이며 공간적으로는 가상의 세계와 연동된 집의 모습들이 네 개의 공간으로 차례대로
제시된다.

At this point (as has always happened, differing only in the era and perspectives), philosophical reflections on the human body began drawing major attention, with some concluding that our society was progressing into a form based on more varied experiential possibilities with the body as agent. Within this process of action and counteraction, media developments progressed in a different way from before. With the addition of a "performativity" element of human bodies directly acting and experiencing to the "interactivity" that had previously emphasized only given choices, there was an attempt to compensate for cold digitalization and over-spiritualization.

Similar action-and-counteraction situations unfolded in every realm. This was assisted in theoretical terms by the concept of "performativity," which related people to action. Newly emerging in aesthetic discourse, the term was a concept first proposed by the German theater scholar Erika Fischer-Lichte. Fischer-Lichte claimed that if we understood culture today to be a form of performance, this should begin with society focusing on the concept of human "action," with useful concepts to be developed from that starting point. Where the "linguistic shift" of the 1970s was designed with the reading of texts as a metaphor for ways of viewing culture, the focus of research had now shifted to the actions constituting different cultural events. This was rooted in the view that we have acquired different standards from before when it comes to cultural competence. Before, cultural competence was understood chiefly in terms of the ability to observe or interpret subjects that were difficult to "read:" now, the ability to actively intervene in the events that are taking place emerged to the fore. It was the era of a "performative shift." And culture meant action. The emphasis in this process was on the "body" as a direct subject performing action, and on the "experience" as its outcome. Once again, the human body experiencing and imposing itself on events had become the measure of cultural competence.

As a prerequisite for this sort of action to occur, Fischer-Lichte assigned an important role to physical "co-presence" (Ko-Präsenz) of actor and observer amid coinciding time and space. The overall action takes shape as the actor performs some action with their body, and the viewer perceives that action with their own body and responds to it. If there are numerous actors and observers, the interactions among them come to form a complex, multiply overlapping network. This is quite different from the simple "choices and decisions" that had hitherto defined interactivity within digital aesthetics. One can consider various conditions that were not viewed as important in "pure" virtual spaces—namely actually existing spaces, presentness, and temporality. If we can envision a virtual museum consisting of direct experiences in our times, it must be something that we have learned from our experience with the brief history of media and culture that we have been examining here.

An exhibition on "our homes" comes into our homes

Viewed in this sense, the exhibition we are focusing on here, *Watch and Chill: Streaming Art to Your Homes*, is an experiment with an experience in which various network layers overlap. It is presented in a real-world exhibition space and also constructed into a virtual museum; the analog "real" exhibition is juxtaposed with a digital "virtual" exhibition. The physical exhibition takes the form of an international network linking four Asian art institutions: the National Museum of Modern and Contemporary Art, Korea in Seoul (MMCA), the Museum of Contemporary Art and Design in Manila (MCAD Manila), the MAIIAM Contemporary Art Museum in Chiang Mai, and M+ in Hong Kong. In temporal terms, four separate exhibitions are to take place in sequence as each of the museums in the network; in spatial terms, "homes" linked to the virtual world are to be presented in turn as four different spaces.

국립현대미술관의 예를 들면 다음과 같다. 입장객들을 처음 맞이하는 방은 '거실의 사물들'Things in My Living Room이며, 매우 긴 심연으로 내려가는 듯한 지하 계단을 통해 나머지 3개의 방이 층을 바꾸어 연결된다. 첫 번째 방과 이후 진입하게 되는 '내 곁의 누군가'By the Other Being의 방에서는 가장 내밀한 공간 안에 반드시 함께 있을 수밖에 없는 낯설고도 친숙한 타자와 사물-객체의 존재가 부각되어 제시된다면, 이러한 언캐니한 상황은 다음 공간인 '집의 공동체'Community of Houses와 '메타-홈'Meta-Home에서 점차 그 외연을 확장해 나간다. 전시되는 개별 작품은 모두 영상이지만, 그 작품들의 수용방식 및 구성 자체가 새로운 조건 하에서 '우리 집'을 은유하는 이번 전시의 큰 축을 이루고 있다.

4개의 기본 네트워크는 인터넷의 탄생 신화의 아르파넷을 연상시키며, 공간적 배경은 모델하우스와도 같은 견본주택이다. 그렇지만 동시에 어디서라도 플랫폼에 접속할 수 있는 사적 공간 내 데스크 위를 반복적으로 보여주고 있기도 하다. 우리 시대의 '우리 집'이란 다시 말하면 그 자체가 전시되는 견본주택이자 데스크 위의 모니터인 것이다. 공공장소와 사적인 공간이 겹쳐진다. 몇 겹의 은유가 새로운 미디어 조건에서의 '우리 집'을 표상한다. 전시를 방문한 사람들은 실제 공간 속에 배치된 영상작품들을 관람할 수 있으며, 작품과 동등한 비중으로 전시된 태블릿 기기와 헤드폰으로 즉석에서 해당 전시의 온라인 플랫폼으로 들어갈 수도 있다. 즉, 현실의 전시 속에 가상적 전시의 플랫폼도 혼재되어 있다. 이러한 겹침이 더 촘촘해지는 지점은 QR코드를 통해 전시장 안의 관람자가 사적인 디바이스로도 온라인 플랫폼에 참여할 수 있다는 점이다. 안과 밖이 연결되어 있는 클라인의 병처럼 현실의 전시 안에서 가상의 전시가 포섭되고, 포섭된 가상의 전시는 현실의 전시 밖으로 뒤집혀 뻗어 나간다. 물리적 전시의 관람자는 현실의 전시 공간과 가상의 전시 플랫폼 안을 동시에 '로그-인하여' '돌아다니며' 작품을 수용한다. 같은 공간을 각자의 디바이스를 들고 돌아다니며 영상을 관람하는 동료 행위자들과는 수행적인 공감대가 형성되며, 여기서 행위자이자 동시에 관람자인 이들의 관람행위는 분명 새로운 '체험'이 된다.

또 하나의 흥미로운 지점은 현실의 공간을 떠난 온라인 플랫폼에서의 참여의 방식이다. 앞서 도서관의 예에서처럼 현존하는 '몸'을 통해 전시를 관람하는 관람객보다 분명 훨씬 많은 숫자의 관람객이 방문하게 될 이 가상의 온라인 플랫폼은 구독형 아트 스트리밍 방식을 채택했다. 구독자는 플랫폼 구동 기간 매주 금요일 새로이 업로드되는 작품에 대한 알림 이메일을 받는다. 이것은 처음부터 모든 작품을 시간과 관계없이 언제라도 관람할 수 있도록 전면 오픈하기보다는 일정 시간과 관람의 범위에 대해 제약을 둠으로써 물리적 전시와의 연계를 강화하고 현장성을 지키고자 함이다. 마치 상업적 온택트 공연의 대표적인 예인 비욘드 라이브 공연 등이 철저히 관리된 회차의 단독 송출로 ─ 그동안 온라인 공연에 대해 우려했던 것와는 달리 ─ 참여자들에게 강렬한 일회적인 체험으로 남을 수 있도록 하는 전략과도 같다. 시간과 공간의 제약을 뛰어넘는다는 온라인의 최대 강점을 일부 포기한 이러한 방식의 채택으로 무엇보다 일정 시간 단위 안에서 마치 물리적 전시를 함께하는 관람자들 사이에서 발생하는 것처럼 무의식적 유대관계가 발생한다. 구독자들은 동일한 이메일을 수신하고 매주 새로운 작품을 이 시간의 단위 속에서 함께 공유하게 되는 것이다. 같은 시간대 내의 '공-현존'. 이와 함께 발생하는 다양한 경로의 공식적이며 비공식적인 부산물(이 글을 포함하여)들은 이러한 체험을 강화한다. 한가지 토픽을 둘러싼 수용자들의 하위문화가 거미줄처럼 짜여지면서 전방위적으로 활성화되는 것은 온라인 소통의 최대 강점 중 하나이며, 이론적으로 이러한 거미줄은 끝없이 뻗어 나갈 수 있다.

'워치 앤 칠' 온라인 플랫폼의 콘텐츠는 구독을 '신청'한 구독자에 한해 접근이 가능하다. 가상 전시의 첫 페이지에서 우리는 구독 신청을 할 수 있으며, 이를 위해서는 본인 인증이라는 절차를 거친다. 이것은 최근의 미디어 이용에서는 매우 표본적인 것이지만, 우리의

In the case of MMCA, visitors are first greeted by a room titled "Thing in My Living Room." Along an underground staircase that seems to take them down a long chasm, the remaining three rooms are connected across different floors. In the first room and the following "By the Other Being" room, the emphasis is on the "other" and the "thing/object"—familiar yet strange entities that always exist with us in our most intimate spaces. That sense of uncanniness expands to a broader scope in the next spaces, "Community of Houses" and "Meta-Home." The individual artworks on display are all video-based, but a major component of the exhibition lies in how the way they are encountered and constituted serves as a metaphor for "our homes" in these new conditions.

The four basic networks evoke parallels with ARPANET and the origin myth of the internet. The spatial backdrop is similar to a model home. At the same time, visitors are also repeatedly shown a desktop in a personal space, where a user might access the platform from anywhere. In other words, "our homes" today are model homes—that are exhibited in and of themselves—and desktop monitors. Public and private spaces overlap. These layers of metaphor express "our homes" under the new conditions of media. People visiting the exhibition can view the video works arranged in actual space, and they can also visit the corresponding online platform then and there with the tablets and headphones that are presented as items with equal weight to the art. In this way, the virtual exhibition platform exists intermingled with the real-world exhibition. This layering is made denser by the fact that visitors to the exhibition venue can also take part in the online platform with personal devices by means of QR codes. Like Klein's bottle, where the inside and outside are interconnected, the virtual exhibition is incorporated into the real-world exhibition, and the incorporated virtual exhibition stretches beyond the real-world exhibition in inverted form. Visitors to the physical exhibition "log in" and "browse" the real-world exhibition space and virtual exhibition platform at the same time that they view the artwork. A performative bond is formed with fellow actors traveling the same spaces, viewing the videos with their own devices, and the resulting act of viewing—being both actor and viewer—is without question a new kind of "experience."

Another interesting element concerns the way in which users participate on the online platform beyond the real-world space. As with the aforementioned library example, the virtual online platform will clearly be visited by many more people than those who come to see the exhibition with their existing "bodies." The approach adopted here is a subscription-based art streaming method. While the platform is operating, subscribers receive email alerts about new artwork that is uploaded every Friday. Rather than being fully opened up so that users can view every work from the beginning, regardless of time, this approach is meant to strengthen the linkage to the physical exhibition and preserve the sense of immediacy by limiting the scope of viewing and imposing specific times on it. It's a similar strategy to something like the "Beyond Live" performance, a representative type of commercial "online non-face-to-face" performance involving carefully rationed, exclusive transmissions, which—contrary to what many feared about online performances—leaves participants with the sense of a powerful one-time experience. While this choice of approach forgoes the greatest strength of the online environment with its transcendence of temporal and physical constraints, it results first and foremost in an unconscious bond within a particular unit of time, much like the one that forms among the people viewing a physical exhibition together. Subscribers all receive the same email and share in each week's new work around the same time—"co-presence" in the same time frame! The experience is reinforced by the official and unofficial byproducts produced through different channels alongside it (this essay included!). One of the great advantages of online communication is the ways in which user subcultures radiate in all directions like a spider web around a certain topic; in theory, this sort of web can continue on without end.

맥락에서는 이러한 인증을 통해 구독자가 '현실의 자신으로서' 관람의 공동체에 참가하게 된다는 점이 중요하다. 현실에 있는, 웨트웨어로서의 나와의 연계가 계속되기 때문에. 가상의 공간에 접속하는 2021년의 나는 지난 세기 캘리포니아 이데올로기에서 예언한 현실 속 나를 벗어난, 모든 현실의 제약을 벗어버린 정신적인 존재가 아니다. 물리적 현실에 몸을 두고 있는, 본인 인증을 마친 원래의 '나'로서 나는 기꺼이 가상의 집 안으로 입장한다. 이러한 배경에서 홈페이지 상단에 있는 '집의 공동체'의 배너는 매우 의미심장하다. 그곳에는 나의 계정 정보와 내가 담아놓은 작품의 리스트가 있다. 보통 다른 경우라면, '나의 페이지' 정도로 명명될 이 버튼을 전시 섹션 중 하나의 이름이기도 한 '집의 공동체'로 표기함으로써 현실 속 구독자를 가상적으로 구현된 이 '집'의 공동체 일원으로서 초대하고 있는 것이다.[1] 여기에서 관람객으로서의 우리는, 공-현존하는 존재로서, 서로에게 친밀한 공간 내 존재하는 낯선 타자가 되어 준다.

그렇지만 이미 언급한 대로, 본인 인증의 절차가 굳이 아니라도, 디지털 미디어 그 자체가 무조건 열려 있는 것은 아니다. 전자적 네트워크가 아직 실험실 안에서 개발단계에 있었을 때는 하이퍼텍스트로 이루어진 우주, 즉 언제든지 텍스트를 검색하여 스스로 작업하고 원본과 수정본을 모두 저장할 수 있는 자나두Xanadu 체계와 같은 것이 도래할 것이라는 기대가 있었지만, 실제로 실현된 것은 사용자 자신이 방문한 페이지를 읽을 수만 있고 바꿀 수는 없도록 한 월드와이드웹이었던 것이다. 물론 우리 사회의 풍경을 모두 바꾸어버린 1990년대의 월드와이드웹은 위대했다. 그렇지만 이것을 구상한 팀 버너스-리Tim Berners-Lee의 희망처럼 월드와이드웹이 전자적 메멕스Memex, 인터넷 구루 중 하나인 바네바 부쉬Vannevar Bush가 꿈꾸었던 인류를 위한 이상적 기계가 되어준 것은 아니었다. 지금까지 구현된 기술적 미디어는 사실 모두 닫힌 체제다. 특히 디지털 매체가 그렇다. 디지털 매체를 향유하기 위해서는 미디어가 사용자에게 강제하는 형식에 기꺼이 동의해야 한다는 사실은 새로운 미디어의 지지자들 사이에서 즐겨 이야기되지는 않는다. '누구나 자유롭게 접속하여 정보의 바다를 항해'한다는 사이버스페이스의 캐치프레이즈는 사실은 많은 세목을 생략하고 있다. 우선 전자적 네트워크에 접속하기 위해서 우리는 무엇보다 충전되어 있거나 충전 중인 디바이스를 소유하고 있거나 적어도 이에 접근 가능해야 한다. 모든 것이 비물질화되어 한없이 가벼워 보이지만 실상은 이런 하드웨어가 없으면 접속은 아예 불가능하다는 것이다. 또한 디바이스를 가지고 있거나 사용할 수 있어도 다시금 누락되는 존재들이 발생한다. 지역 자체에 통신망이 없다거나. 부르디외Pierre Bourdieu의 의미에서 문화 지식을 소유하지 못했다거나. 최근 이슈화되기 시작한 QR코드나 전자 키오스크 등에 있어 미디어 이용의 소외 계층에 대한 논의는 디지털 테크놀로지의 역사에 있어서 아주 새로운 것은 아닐 것이다.

그다음 관문은 역시 정보를 얻기 위해서 기꺼이 개인정보를 자발적으로 내놓는 절차이다. 작동되는 이메일 주소를 충실히 적는다거나(가짜 메일은 종종 이메일 인증을 통해 걸러진다), 사적인 핸드폰 번호까지 공공재로 내놓는다거나. 그렇지 않고서는 인터페이스를 통과할 수 없는 경우가 많다. 초연결사회의 가장 큰 공포 중의 하나는 이렇게 작성된 개인정보가 적절하지 않은 곳에서 부정적으로 이용되는 것이다. 이러한 공포감은 참여작가 중 김희천의 작품 〈썰매〉(2016)에서 이슈화되어 있다. 김희천의 이 작품에서는 3D, 게임, 가상현실 등의 소재를 활용하여 여러 겹의 서로 다른 서사를 층층이 겹쳐 놓으며, 현실의 무엇과 이에 상응하는 가상의 것을 융합적으로 연결하는 전시의 주제를 예술적 감각으로 재현한다. 이것은 이번에 함께 전시/ 스트리밍되는 같은 작가의 〈나홀로 '멈블'

[1] 편집자 주   '워치 앤 칠'에 가입하는 과정에서 계정 정보를 완성하기에 앞서 구독자들은 개인의 성향에 관한 간단한 질문에 답하게 되는데, 그 결과에 따라 네 가지 전시 챕터 중 한 가지 테마가 구독자 계정 아이콘이 된다.

Content on the *Watch and Chill* online platform is only accessible to those who have "requested" a subscription. Subscriptions are available on the first page of the virtual exhibition, requiring the user to go through identity verification procedures. It's a quite commonplace feature of media use today, but in our context, the key thing is that this authentication leads the subscriber to take part in the viewing community as their "real-world self"—due to the ongoing connection with the wetware self who exists in reality. The "me" accessing the virtual space in 2021 is not some spiritual entity who has shed their real-world self and all practical constraints, as the California ideology predicted last century. I willingly enter the virtual home as the original "me," someone who possesses a body in the physical world and completed identity verification procedures. In that context, the "Community of Houses" banner at the top of the homepage is quite significant. It contains my account information and my list of works. In other cases, this sort of button might be called "My Page" or something like that; by naming it "Community of Houses," which is also the name of one of the exhibition sections, they are inviting the real-world subscriber as a member of this virtually realized "home."[1] As viewers and as "co-present" entities, we become unfamiliar "others" to one another, existing within an intimate space.

As I mentioned before, however, digital media itself is not necessarily open, even without the identity verification procedures. When electronic networks were still being developed in the laboratory, there was hope that they might bring about a universe of hyperlinks—a "Xanadu" system where people could search for texts and work whenever they wanted, saving copies of their originals and revised versions. What actually came about was the World Wide Web, which was designed so that users could only read the pages they visited but were unable to alter them. The World Wide Web was, of course, immense in the 1990s, transforming the very landscape of our society. But it never became the electronic "Memex" sought by Tim Berners-Lee, the man who conceived it, or the ideal system for humanity envisioned by internet guru Vannevar Bush. In truth, the technological media realized to date represent a closed system—especially in the case of digital media. The fact that those hoping to enjoy digital media must willingly agree to the forms those media impose on the user is not something new media supporters like to talk about. The cyberspace catchphrase—the idea that anyone can freely access and surf a sea of information—omits quite a lot of particulars. To begin with, connecting with an electronic network requires us to own a device that is charged or charging, or at least to have access to one. Everything is dematerialized, seemingly weightless, yet we cannot actually connect at all without the hardware. There are also people who own or have access to devices but still get left out. Maybe their region doesn't have a communications network. Maybe they don't possess cultural knowledge in the Bourdieuian sense. The debate about the "media-alienated" class that has recently emerged as an issue with QR codes and electronic kiosks is not all that new a development in the history of digital technology.

The next gateway is a procedure where we voluntarily present our personal information to acquire information. Perhaps we diligently enter a working email address (fake mail is often filtered out through email verification), or we offer up our personal mobile phone number as a public good. Many times, we cannot get through the interface without doing so. One of the biggest fears of the hyper-connected society is that this personal information will end up in unsuitable places, where it is used for unsavory ends. That fear is the theme in one of the participating artist's works: *Sleigh Ride Chill* (2016) by Kim Heecheon. Kim's work uses 3D,

[1] **Editor's note**   Before completing the subscription, (s)he has to answer a simple question about one's personality. The result determines the theme of subscriber's account, which is one of the four chapters of *Watch and Chill: Streaming Art to Your Homes*, as a profile image.

보기〉(2020)에서도 마찬가지이다. 어머니와 반려견, 정서 치료를 받는 화자, 가상의 개 레이스 경기 등 서로 다른 서사가 겹쳐지는데 종종 이들 상호 간의 내러티브 내 연결점이 하이퍼링크처럼 만들어지기도 한다. 흥미로운 것은 전시장의 화면을 다시 촬영한 액자 구성으로 만들어진 이 비디오아트 작품을 관람하면서, 스트리밍하는 관람자조차 또 하나의 외부 액자가 되어버린다는 것이다. 그것도 진짜 우리 집에서! 실제의 전시관에서 집 안의 공간처럼 구현된 '우리 집'은 이제 실제 구독자의 집 안에 가상적으로 펼쳐진다. 아니, 〈나홀로 '멈블' 보기〉에서 언급된 대로, (전시장이라는) 큰 공간이 (내 방 안이라는) 작은 공간 안으로 들어오는 것이니, 펼쳐지는 것이 아니라 "구겨져 들어온다." 전체 미술관이라는 공간이 내 방 안으로 구겨져 들어와 있으며, 우리는 트라우마에 빠진 시각 장애인 안내견처럼 현실에서는 한 발짝도 움직이지 않은 채 가상의 미술관 속을 빠르게 산책한다. 뛰어난 동체 시력으로 말이다.

마지막으로 서두에 언급했던 캘리포니아 이데올로기에 대해서 다시 한번 언급하고 싶다. 모두에게 장밋빛 미래를 약속했던 새로운 기술에 대한 믿음은 우리 시대 어디로 향해 가고 있을까? 1990년대 중반 월드와이드웹과 함께 인터넷이 빠르게 성장하고, 또 빠르게 상업화되고 나서, 가상 세계라는 곳도 실제 세계와 마찬가지로 수없이 많은 제약과 경계, 암호들, 그리고 거기에 더해 온갖 버그와 악의적 바이러스로 가득한 곳이라는 것을 깨닫기까지는 그리 오랜 시간이 걸리지 않았다. 새로운 전자매체에 대한 기대가 가장 증폭되었던 시기를 지나, 2000년이라는 새로운 밀레니엄과 함께 도래한 것은 인터넷에 대한 차가운 각성이었다. 디지털 매체기술 자체로는 전자적 유토피아는 실현되지 않았다. 무엇보다 인터넷은 여러 면에서 우리를 편리하게 만들어주었지만, 동시에 우리가 잃어버리게 되는 것도 많았던 것이다. 처음 예를 들었던 도서관의 전자화만 해도, 우리는 물리적인 도서관에서만 가능했던 많은 체험의 기회를 상실하게 되었다. 매캐한 향을 내뿜던, 그 많던 옛 신문들의 묶음은 어디로 갔을까?

그렇지만 흥미로운 것은 이러한 각성이 무색하게, 2010년이 되자 소셜 네트워크 붐이 일어나면서, 적어도 국내에서는 1990년대 초반 나왔던 전자적 네트워크에 대한 희망적 담론들이 무비판적으로 재생산된 바 있다. 말하자면 캘리포니아 이데올로기의 때늦은 부활이었다. 동일한 패턴으로, 이번에는 '재스민 혁명'으로 명명된 감동적인 전자 민주주의의 가능성이 이야기되었으며, 중심이 해체된 탈위계적 구조가 강조되었다. 수용자의 생산자적 전환, 아래로부터의 민주주의, 1인 미디어의 시대 등 모두 한 번쯤 들어본 듯한 익숙한 캐치프레이즈가 마치 새것인 양 등장했다. 실제로 그때그때 등장하고 또 사라져간 소셜 네트워크는 각각의 개성 넘치는 프레임을 만들어 수용자에게 제공해 왔다. 이들이 이 프레임을 사용하여 올리는 많은 '콘텐츠'에 대하여, 이것을 과연 생산적인 행위로 봐야 하는지 아니면 잘 만들어진 상품의 소비 행위로 봐야 하는지는 생각해볼 문제다. 소셜 네트워크라는 것도 마찬가지로 보이지 않는 권력 관계에 의해 움직이며, 뛰어난 확산 도구는 될 수 있을지언정 상호 평등한 소통 도구는 되기 어렵다는 인식은, 언제나 그렇듯 한 박자 늦게 출현했던 것이다. 수용자를 생산자로 고무시키는 문제는 새 매체가 등장할 때마다 논의되는 화두이지만, 우리 시대의 주도 매체인 디지털 기반의 커뮤니케이션 매체가 이를 온전히 실현하리라는 것은 지난 1990년대 후반의 경험을 무색하게 하는, 때를 잘못 찾아 들어온 환상에 불과했다.

그렇지만 소셜 네트워크에 대한 반성적 성찰이 마무리되기도 전에, 우리 시대에 또 유사한 담론이 찾아와 유령처럼 떠돌고 있다. 그것은 이번에는 '메타버스'라는 이름을 달고 있다. 또 한 번 우리의 물리적인 세계가 모두 이 안으로 빨려 들어가 버릴 것처럼, 우리의 모든 사회적 경제적 문화적 행위가 단기간 내에 오로지 이 안에서만 이루어질 것처럼 이야기하는 논의가 공공연하게 제시된다. 그 어떤 가상공간도 현실과 포개지고 연결될 때만이 의미가 있다는 것, 그리고 그곳에서 우리의 실제 '몸'이 여전히 현존하고 있다는 사실은 또다시 생략되었다. 독자적

40

video games, and virtual reality to layer multiple different narratives, using an artistic sense to represent the exhibition's theme connecting something "real" with its "virtual" counterpart in a convergent way. The same is true for another work by Kim that is also being exhibited/streamed, *Watching 'Mumbling in Hell, Tumbling Down the Well' Alone* (2020). It layers different narratives about a mother, a pet dog, a narrator undergoing emotional therapy, and a virtual dog race; at times, their interconnections within the narrative are presented like hyperlinks. The fascinating thing is that as the streaming viewer watches this work of video art, which adopts a frame composition as it shows virtually constructed scenes of the exhibition venue, the viewer finds themselves becoming another outside "frame"—in their actual home, no less! The "your home" presented in the actual exhibition setting as if it were a space at home is now unfolding virtually within the actual subscriber's home. Or, as *Watching 'Mumbling in Hell, Tumbling Down the Well' Alone* puts it, it is "folding into" the home rather than "unfolding," since it is a large space (the gallery) entering a smaller space (our room). The entire museum space is folded into our room, and we become like the traumatized guide dog for the visually impaired, walking briskly through the virtual museum without taking a step in reality. All of this with tremendous visual acuity.

In closing, I'd like to return once again to the "California ideology" mentioned in the introduction. Where is it heading today, that faith in new technology that promised everyone a rosy future? After the rapid growth and commercialization of the internet with the World Wide Web in the mid-1990s, it did not take all that long for us to learn that the virtual world was just like the real world: filled with all sorts of constraints and borders, codes, and various bugs and viruses on top of all that. After hopes for the new electronic media passed their peak, the new millennium arrived in 2000 with a rude awakening for the internet. The electronic utopia could not come about through digital media technology alone. The internet has made things more convenient for us in various ways, but we've also lost a great deal. Even if we just look at the first example with the computerization of libraries, we've lost the opportunities for a lot of experiences that were only possible at physical libraries. Where have all those bundles of old newspapers gone, with their acrid smell?

The interesting thing, however, is how that awareness ended up giving way to those hopeful electronic network discourses of the early 1990s being uncritically reproduced—in Korea at least—with the arrival of the social network boom in 2010. It was an unexpected revival of the California ideology. Following the same pattern, there has been talk of the potential for a stirring form of electronic democracy known as the "Jasmine Revolution," emphasizing a post-hierarchical structure where the center has been broken down. Familiar catchphrases reappeared as though they were something new: the shift from consumers to producers, democracy from below, an era of one-person media. In fact, the social networks that arrived and vanished in their turn has provided users with frames that abounded in originality. When it comes to all the content that they present through these frames, it is worth considering whether that should actually be viewed as a productive act, or as an act of consuming well-made commodities. As is always the case, the perception that the workings of social networks are similarly based on unseen power relationships—and that while they can be outstanding tools for dissemination, they are not suited to being tools for equal communication—had emerged a bit belatedly. Inspiring users to become producers is a topic that always comes up whenever new media appear, but the idea that this could be fully achieved through the digitally based communication media that are the chief media of our times was simply an anachronistic illusion, one that made a mockery of our experience in the late 1990s.

Yet before we have even finished reflecting on social networks, a similar kind of discourse has arrived like a phantom in our era. This time around, it goes by the name of "Metaverse." People are speaking openly once again as though our physical world is going

화폐단위를 가지고 체험할 수 있는 가상공간은 그 영역을 계속 확대해 나갈 것은 분명하지만, 그 화폐단위는 여전히 현실에서 호환 가능할 때만 의미가 있을 것이다. 체험의 시작과 귀환은 여전히 우리의 아날로그적 몸이기 때문에.

유현주 ⓘ
연세대학교 교수

유현주는 연세대학교 독문학과와 같은 과 대학원을 졸업한 뒤, 독일 훔볼트대학교 독문학과에서 박사학위를 받았다. 현재 연세대학교 독문과 교수로 재직 중이다. 독일현대문학 연구와 함께 매체철학 및 문화이론에 대한 비평작업도 하고 있다. 저서로『프리드리히 키틀러』(공저),『텍스트, 하이퍼텍스트, 하이퍼미디어』,『하이퍼텍스트: 디지털 미학의 키워드』 등이 있으며, 옮긴 책으로는『축음기, 영화, 타자기』(공역),『보이지 않는 것의 경제』,『예술·매개·미학』(공역) 등이 있다.

to be sucked into it wholesale, as though all of our social, economic, and cultural actions will shortly be taking place entirely inside of it. Overlooked once again is the fact that all virtual spaces only hold meaning when they are layered and connected with reality, and the fact that our actual bodies will still exist there. A virtual space that can be experienced with independent monetary units will obviously continue to expand its reach, but those units will only hold meaning when they can be exchanged in reality. All experience still starts from and returns to our own analog bodies.

Yoo Hyunjoo

Professor, Yonsei University

Yoo Hyunjoo earned a bachelor's degree in German language and literature from Yonsei University and a graduate degree from the same institution before receiving her doctorate in German language and literature from Humboldt University of Berlin. She is currently a professor of German language and literature at Yonsei University. In addition to her studies of contemporary German literature, she is also a media philosophy and cultural theory critic. Her books include *Friedrich Kittler* (co-authored), *Text, Hypertext, Hypermedia*, and *Hypertext: A Keyword in Digital Aesthetics*. She has also translated *The Economy of the Invisible* and co-translated *Grammophon, Film, Typewriter* and *Aesthetic of Mediality*.

Watch & Chill

거실의 사물들
Things in My Living Room

By the Other Being
내 곁에 누군가

집의 (공동체)
Community of Houses

Meta-Home
메타-홈

우리 집에서, 워치 앤 칠

«우리 집에서, 워치 앤 칠»은 미술관과 예술가, 그리고 관객이 미술을 공유하는 새로운 방식을 탐색하고자 기획되었다. 국립현대미술관은 마닐라 현대미술디자인미술관, 치앙마이 마이암현대미술관, 홍콩 서구룡문화지구 M+와 협력하여 구독형 아트 스트리밍 플랫폼 '워치 앤 칠'(https://watchandchill.kr)을 구축했다. 디지털 시대의 행동 양식 변화에 대응하며 이를 탐구의 대상으로 삼는 이번 프로젝트는 온라인 플랫폼을 통해 아시아 지역 주요 작가들의 영상 작품을 송출하고, 이를 물리적인 공간에서 전시의 형태로도 함께 구현하여 독특한 작품 감상의 기회를 제공한다.

«우리 집에서, 워치 앤 칠»을 통해 아시아 지역의 네 미술관은 각자의 소장품을 중심으로 선별한 영상 작품을 선보인다. 본 프로젝트는 네 가지 소 주제로 구성된 챕터를 통해 미디어 환경으로 변화한 집의 다층적 연결성을 사유하고자 한다.

첫 번째 주제인 '거실의 사물들'은 집을 이루는 물건과 이들의 배치, 나열, 순환의 장면을 펼친다. 작가들은 사물 사이의 관계뿐만 아니라, 사물과 인간, 나아가 사물과 사회의 관계로까지 그 의미를 확장시킨다. '내 곁에 누군가'는 안식처로서의 집이 다른 존재들의 개입과 침입으로 인해 영향을 받는 물리적, 정신적 측면을 고찰한다. 반려자, 반려 동·식물, 로봇, 손님 혹은 침입자와 같이 일상의 시공간을 공유하는 존재들과 이들을 둘러싼 허구적 서사를 제시한다. '집의 공동체'는 전통적인 이웃 공동체와는 다른 대안적 군집의 형태를 제안한다. 각기 다른 지역, 세대, 유형의 공동체가 마주한 환경의 변화와 이를 나름의 방식으로 적응하며 나타난 여러 삶의 유형을 보여준다. '메타-홈'은 집 이상의 집, 가정의 초연결성을 다룬다. 가상의 세계와 연동된 집의 모습과 기술적 연결 너머의 정신적, 영적 연결 등 다양한 메타적 상상을 펼친다.

"도시는 점차 침대로 오고 있다."[1] 전례 없는 규모의 데이터 송수신으로 우리의 집은 거주의 사적 기능을 넘어 공적인 영역으로 진입했고, 팬데믹은 집의 그러한 현실을 더욱 드러나게 했다. '워치 앤 칠' 플랫폼은 미술관이 된 집과 집이 된 미술관에서 펼쳐지는 미디어 풍경을 활성화하며, 변화하는 매체 소비 습관에 대응하는 미술관의 유동적 가능성을 시험대에 올린다.

1
Beatriz Colomina, "The Bed in the Age of Covid-19," *Vitra Magazine*, 2020년 6월 19일. https://www.vitra.com/en-de/magazine/details/the-bed-in-the-age-of-covid-19.

일러두기

'워치 앤 칠' 온라인 플랫폼에서 영상의 포맷이 균일해지는 문제를 입체적으로 고려하여 각 작품 고유의 촬영 및 상영 포맷을 표시하지 않고, 단채널 비디오로 상정했다. 따라서 이후 작품 캡션에서 특정한 경우를 제외하고는 비디오 포맷이나 설치 사양 등을 따로 표시하지 않는다.

Watch and Chill: Streaming Art to Your Homes

Watch and Chill: Streaming Art to Your Homes seeks to explore ways to bring international art institutions, artists, and audiences together around a carefully curated selection of moving image artworks. The National Museum of Modern and Contemporary Art, Korea (MMCA) collaborated with Museum of Contemporary Art and Design (MCAD) in Manila, MAIIAM Contemporary Art Museum in Chiang Mai, and the M+, West Kowloon Cultural District in Hong Kong in launching the subscription-based art streaming platform *Watch and Chill* (https:// watchandchill.kr). Responding to and examining the changing behavioral patterns of the digital era, the exhibition shares video works by major artists active in Asia through its online platform. Presentation of this platform is not limited to the virtual space but also as physically embodied as a travelling exhibition.

The four museums in Asia introduce selected video works from their individual collections as well as their regional art communities. Staging the "home" as a primary site for consuming the *Watch and Chill* platform, the four sub-topics consider the multilayered connections of homes that have transformed into media environments.

"Things in My Living Room" presents items from the home and scenes of their placement, arrangement, and circulation. Looking beyond the relationships among objects, the artists broaden their sense to encompass relationships between objects and people and between objects and society. "By the Other Being" reflects on the physical and mental aspects of the home as a safe haven, being influenced by the interventions and intrusions of other beings. It shows those who share our time and space of the everyday— such as partners, animals, plants, robots, guests, and intruders—as it weaves a fictional narrative around them. "Community of Houses" proposes alternative forms of living together that differ from the traditional community of neighbors. Presented here are the changes in environment experienced by communities of various regions, generations, and typologies, along with the different forms of living that emerge as they adapt in their own ways. "Meta-Home" focuses on "homes beyond homes," i.e., the hyper-connectivity of our domestic spaces. It reveals varied forms of metaphysical imagination, including homes connected with the virtual world as well as mental and spiritual connections that transcend technological ones.

"The city has moved into the bed."[1] Linked via an unprecedented amount of data transmissions, our homes have gone beyond the mere private function of "dwelling" and have long entered into the public realm. The pandemic has only exposed this reality even more. Activating a media landscape that takes place in both home-as-museum and museum-as-home, the *Watch and Chill* platform will serve as a test bed for the museum to experiment with the fluid possibilities of responding to our changing habits of media consumption.

1
Beatriz Colomina, "The Bed in the Age of Covid-19," *Vitra Magazine*, June 19, 2020. https://www.vitra.com/en-de/magazine/details/the-bed-in-the-age-of-covid-19.

Editor's Note

Concerning the issues of the video format being "flattened" when streamed via the *Watch and Chill* online platform, the works' own filmed and/or screening formats are intentionally omitted in each caption as they are considered single-channel videos, with a few exceptions of specific cases.

47

거실의 사물들

의자, 빨래집게, 청소기, 바닥 타일, 장난감… '거실의 사물들'에서는 집을 이루는 물건과 이들의 배치, 나열, 순환의 장면을 담은 작품들을 소개한다. 이 챕터에서 작가들은 사물을 단순한 대상으로 보지 않고, 고유한 활기가 있는 물질이자 그 자체로 역량을 가진 것으로 간주하며 사물 사이의 관계, 그리고 이들이 인간과 사회에 미치는 정동적 효과를 탐색한다. 감염병의 유행으로 집에서 보내는 시간이 길어지면서 물건과 친밀함이 생기는 현상을 은유하며, 가정을 구성하는 물질과 이들이 나타내는 개인과 집단의 경험, 무의식, 정체성의 문제를 다룬다.

오민	‹에이 비 에이 비디오›, 2016	MMCA 소장
위안 광밍	‹주거›, 2014	작가 소장, M+ 제공
코코이 럼바오	‹무제(일식 I, II)›, 2013	작가 소장, MCAD 제공
카위타 바타나즈얀쿠르	‹어머니와 나(진공청소기 III)›, 2021	MAIIAM 소장
왕 공신	‹브루클린의 하늘—베이징에서 구멍파기›, 1995	M+ 소장

Things in My Living Room

Chairs, clothespins, vacuums, floor tiles, toys… "Things in My Living Room" shares artworks that include items from the home and scenes of their placement, arrangement, and circulation. Viewing items not simply as "objects" but as substance with its own vitality and capabilities, it explores the relationships among them and their affective impacts on people and society. As a metaphor that reflects on the intimacy that people have come to experience with "things" as the pandemic forces them to spend more time at home, this chapter focuses on the material that makes up the home and the issues of individual and collective experience, unconsciousness, and identity that it represents.

Oh Min	ABA Video, 2016	MMCA collection
Yuan Goang-ming	Dwelling, 2014	Courtesy of the artist, provided by M+
Cocoy Lumbao	Untitled (Eclipse I, II), 2013	Courtesy of the artist, provided by MCAD
Kawita Vatanajyankur	My Mother and I (Vacuum III), 2021	MAIIAM collection
Wang Gongxin	The Sky of Brooklyn—digging a hole in Beijing, 1995	M+ collection

| 오민 | ‹에이 비 에이 비디오›, 2016 | 컬러, 사운드, 12분 50초. | MMCA 소장 |

오민은 사물을 특정 정보나 구조를 이루는 일종의 모듈로 다룬다. 피아노를 전공한 작가는 음악적 구조를 시각 패턴과 리듬으로 번역하며 퍼포먼스와 영상 등 시간을 기반으로 한 형식을 통해 여러 감각이 어우러진 공감각적 체계를 구축한다. ‹에이 비 에이 비디오›는 비디오의 시간 구조를 만드는 방식에 대한 실험이다. 이 작업은 오민이 오랜 시간 정교하게 발전시킨 음악의 형식이 음악 이외 시간을 기반으로 한 매체들에 어떻게 활용되고 영향을 줄 수 있는지 연구하는 과정에서 도출된 작품이라고 할 수 있다. 음악의 구조 자체를 조형의 원리로 재배열한 작업으로, 라흐마니노프의 「피아노 소나타 2번 1악장」의 구조를 구체적인 장면으로 치환해 시각화했다. 또한 일상의 오브제들을 나열하고 조립, 구성하는 미니멀한 행위의 연속인 ‹에이 비 에이 비디오›는 팬데믹 중 살림을 정렬, 배치, 정리하는 것에 집중하는 강박을 표출하며 실내 물건들과의 새롭게 정리된 관계를 연상시키기도 한다.

Oh Min approaches objects as modules forming particular information or structures—a method that bears some connections to her own past as a piano major. Translating musical structures into visual patterns and rhythms, Oh presents her work in time-based media such as performance and video, creating synesthetic systems that combine the visual, tactile, and auditory. *ABA Video* is an experiment with ways of forming temporal structure in the video. The work emerged out of the artist's process of studying how the sophisticated musical forms can be used and influence time-based media beyond music. Here, the musical structure itself has been rearranged according to aesthetic principles: the structure of the first movement of Rachmaninov's *Piano Sonata No. 2* has been visualized through sceneries. Consisting of a series of minimal acts of arranging, assembling, and composing everyday objects, *ABA Video* also evokes the current pandemic situation with the compulsive focus on organizing and arranging the home and the new relationships we have established with interior objects.

| Oh Min | *ABA Video*, 2016 | color, 컬러, sound, 12 min. 50 sec. | MMCA collection |

Things in My Living Room
Oh Min

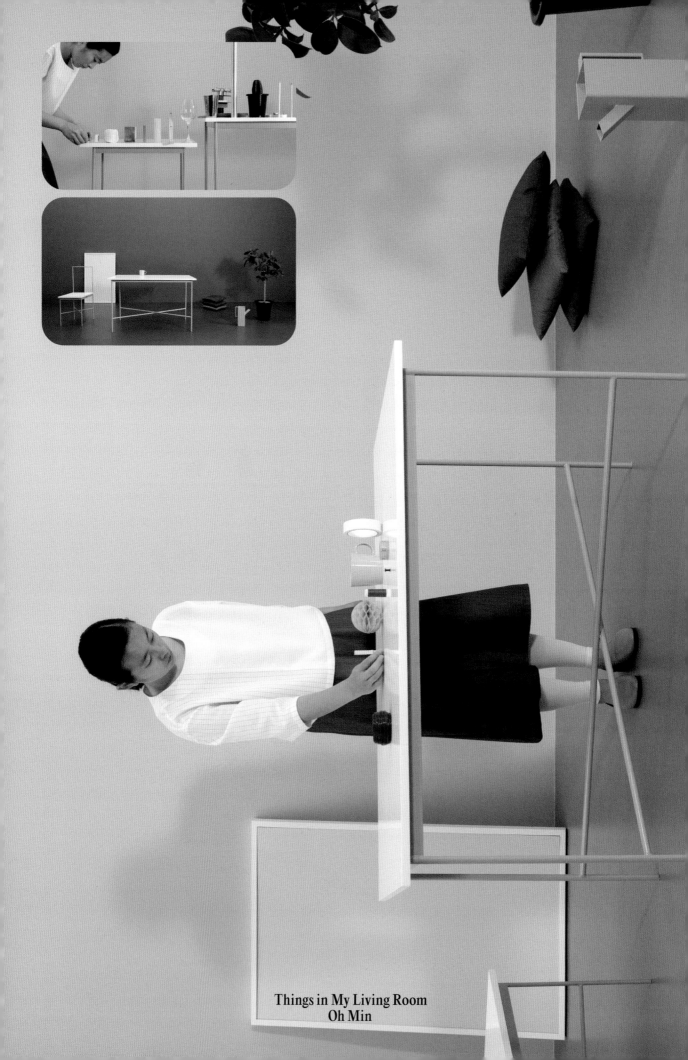

Things in My Living Room
Oh Min

| 위안 광밍 | 〈주거〉, 2014 | 컬러, 사운드, 5분 33초. | 작가 소장, M+ 제공 |

대만 비디오 아트의 선구자로서 1984년 이래 지속적으로 미디어 작품을 선보인 위안 광밍은 동시대적 존재로서의 인간의 마음과 인식을 드러내는 다양한 은유와 상징을 작품에 녹여내왔다. 〈주거〉는 물속에 조성된 평온한 거실이 한순간 거대한 폭발로 완전히 흩트러지고, 또 이내 다시 원래의 모습으로 돌아오는 장면을 담았다. 평범한 가구들로 조성된 한 거실의 일상과 그 일상을 단번에 뒤집는 과정은 바이러스로 인해 단번에 파괴된 우리의 일상과 곧 되찾을 평온의 모습을 동시에 연상시킨다.

A pioneer of Taiwanese video art who has been producing media works since 1984, Yuan Goang-ming imbues his pieces with metaphors and symbols showing the minds and perceptions of contemporary humans. *Dwelling* shows an ordinary living room that has been built in the water. A sudden, massive explosion completely disassembles it, only for it to immediately return to its original form. The process that unfolds between the everyday living room with its ordinary furnishings and the incident that suddenly turns all of that on its head makes us link both the way the pandemic has destroyed our daily lives, as well as the calm that will eventually return.

| Yuan Goang-ming | *Dwelling*, 2014 | color, sound, 5 min. 33 sec. | Courtesy of the artist, provided by M+ |

Things in My Living Room
Yuan Goang-ming

Things in My Living Room
Yuan Goang-ming

코코이 럼바오　　‹무제(일식 I, II)›, 2013　　2채널 비디오, 적외선 촬영, 무음, 6분 34초.　　작가 소장, MCAD 제공

코코이 럼바오는 시각적 대용물로서의 카메라가 지니는 가능성과 동시에 그 한계를 탐구한다. ‹무제(일식 I, II)›에서는 개기 일식의 어둠 속에서 아이에게 브라유 점자책을 읽어주는 어머니의 모습과 그녀의 손이 등장한다. 이는 곧 이질적인 환경 속에서 사물을 정보화하는 촉지의 몸짓을 의미한다.

Cocoy Lumbao explores the capabilities and limitations of the camera as an ocular proxy. *Untitled (Eclipse I, II)* shows a mother's hand as she reads a book in Braille to her child in the darkness of a total eclipse, illustrating gestures of tactile perception that convert objects into information in different environments.

Cocoy Lumbao　*Untitled (Eclipse I, II)*, 2013　two-channel video filmed with infrared camera, silent, 6 min. 34 sec.

Courtesy of the artist, provided by MCAD

Things in My Living Room
Cocoy Lumbao

| 카위타 바타나즈얀쿠르 | ‹어머니와 나(진공청소기 III)›, 2021 | 컬러, 무음, 7분 20초. | MAIIAM 소장 |

‹어머니와 나(진공청소기 III)›에서 카위타 바타나즈얀쿠르는 대기 오염의 침습이 가져온 결과를 조명하기 위해 가상의 거주 공간을 짓는다. 이 공간은 대기 오염의 현실을 다루기 위한 장소이다. 이곳에서 작가는 집은 안전하다는 가정에 이의를 제기한다. 그의 작품에서 건축 구조물은 신체의 외피를, 내부 공간은 사람의 폐와 같은 내부 장기를 닮아 있다. 작품에 나타나는 공간은 우리의 신체에 비견된다.

In *My Mother and I (Vacuum III)*, Vatanajyankur constructs a makeshift house to highlight the invasive result of air pollution which imitates the reality of 'dust' pollution. Using a living space as a factor, she challenges the idea of 'assumed' safety. The structure of the architectural space is compared to the corporeal which acts as a container; an outer skin. The interior, on the other hand, resembles the internal organs such as the human lung. In other words, the constructed house is itself the human body.

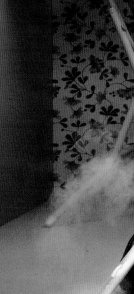

| Kawita Vatanajyankur | *My Mother and I (Vacuum III)*, 2021 | color, silent, 7 min. 20 sec. | MAIIAM collection |

왕 공신은 베이징 본가의 거실 한복판에 3.5m 깊이의 구멍을 파고, 벽돌로 벽을 두른 그 우물 바닥에 텔레비전 모니터를 놓았다. 화면에서는 그가 브루클린의 스튜디오 밖에서 촬영한 푸른 하늘 영상이 반복 재생된다. 작품은 연결과 간극을 나타내면서 세계화와 국가적 재현이라는 주제를 다루고 있다.

Wang Gongxin dug a hole 3.5 meters deep in the middle of his family's living room in Beijing and placed a television monitor at the bottom of the brick-lined well. The screen displayed looped footage of the blue-sky Wang had filmed outside his Brooklyn studio. The work represents the connections and distances, touching on the subjects of globalization and national representation.

Wang Gongxin | *The Sky of Brooklyn—digging a hole in Beijing*, 1995 | color, sound, 2min. 56sec. | M+ collection

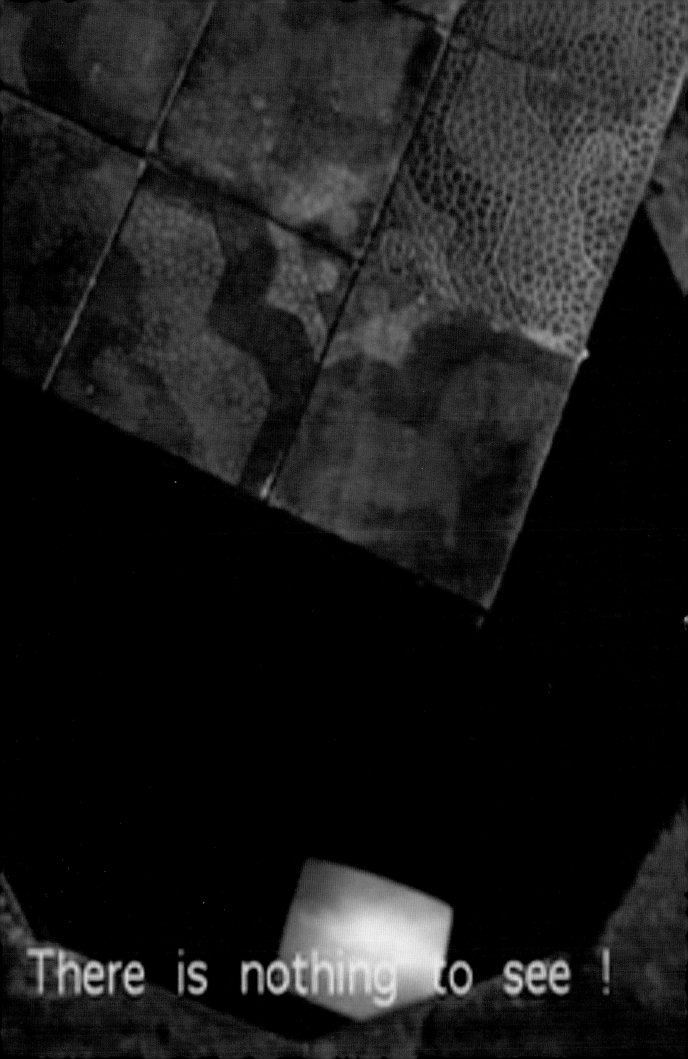

내 곁에 누군가

'반려'(companion)는 라틴어 'cum panis'에서 온 말로 한 식탁에 앉아 빵을 나누는 관계를 의미한다. 숨과 체액을 나누는 반려종과의 관계는 서로에게 안식이 되기도, 서로를 위태롭게 하기도 한다. '내 곁에 누군가'에서는 반려자, 반려 동·식물, 로봇, 손님 혹은 침입자와 같이 일상의 시공간을 공유하는 존재들과 이들을 둘러싼 허구적 서사를 제시하며 소중한 타자에 의해 영향을 받는 물리적, 정신적 측면을 고찰한다.

시린 세노	〈꽃을 따는 것〉, 2021	작가 소장, MCAD 제공
완타니 시리파타나눈타쿨	〈모든 이는…〉, 2017	작가 소장, MAIIAM 제공
차오 페이	〈아지랑이와 안개〉, 2013	M+ 소장
차재민	〈엘리의 눈〉, 2020	작가 소장
김희천	〈나홀로 '멈블'보기〉, 2020	작가 소장

By the Other Being

The word "companion" comes from the Latin cum panis, or "with bread"—indicating the sort of relationship where people sit down together at a table to share bread. As we share our breath and bodily fluids, our relationships with companions can be sources of mutual comfort or threats. "By the Other Being" considers the physical and mental aspects as we are affected by the significant "others." This chapter shows those who share our time and space of the everyday—such as partners, animals, plants, robots, guests, and intruders—as it weaves a fictional narrative around them.

Shireen Seno	*To Pick a Flower*, 2021	Courtesy of the artist, provided by MCAD
Wantanee Siripattananuntakul	*Everyone is…*, 2017	Courtesy of the artist, provided by MAIIAM
Cao Fei	*Haze and Fog*, 2013	M+ collection
Cha Jeamin	*Ellie's Eye*, 2020	Courtesy of the artist
Kim Heecheon	*Watching 'Mumbling in Hell, Tumbling Down the Well' Alone*, 2020	Courtesy of the artist

시린 세노 | ‹꽃을 따는 것›, 2021 | 컬러, 흑백, 사운드, 16분 47초. | 작가 소장, MCAD 제공

시린 세노는 마닐라를 기반으로 활동하는 현대미술 작가이자 영화감독으로 집과 관련한 기억, 역사, 이미지 생산에 대한 관심을 작업으로 도출해왔다. ‹꽃을 따는 것›에서 작가는 본인의 집에 있는 나무 식탁이 작가 자신의 나이와 같다는 모친의 말을 상기하며 식탁이 된 나무의 여정을 추적하기 시작한다. 자연의 세계와 인간의 세계 사이의 변형에 주목하는 작가는 본 비디오 에세이를 통해 미국 점령기(1898–1946) 필리핀에서 발견할 수 있었던 식물을 추적한다. 이 시기 촬영된 아카이브 사진으로 작가는 제국주의 체제하에 인간과 자연이 어떻게 얽히게 되었는지 고찰하며, 식물과 나무의 이야기를 통해 필리핀의 사진과 자본주의 발달 이면의 뒤엉킨 뿌리에 대해 사유한다. ‹꽃을 따는 것›은 반려종으로서의 식물과 지역의 식생이 역사적 맥락에서 어떻게 지역민들과 복잡하고 끈적한 관계를 맺어왔는지 조명해낸다.

Shireen Seno is a Manila-based contemporary artist and film director whose work reflects her interest in memories connected with the home, history, and the creation of images. In *To Pick a Flower*, Seno recalls her mother telling her that the wooden dining table in their home was the same age as her. The artist proceeds to begin tracing the journey of the wood that ended up being a piece of furniture. The artist's interest lies in transmutations between the world of nature and humans as she uses her video essay to follow the lives of plants found in the Philippines during the US occupation from 1898 to 1946. Using archival photographs taken at the time, she examines how human beings and nature became intertwined under the imperial system. Via the stories of plants and wood, the artist contemplates the tangled roots of photography and capitalism in the Philippines. *To Pick a Flower* examines the ways in which domesticated plants and local vegetation have formed complex and sticky relationships with local residents within their historical context.

Shireen Seno | *To Pick a Flower*, 2021 | color, b&w, sound, 16 min. 47 sec. | Courtesy of the artist, provided by MCAD

By the Other Being
Shireen Seno

완타니 시리파타나눈타쿨 〈모든 이는…〉, 2017 컬러, 사운드, 5분 5초. 작가 소장, MAIIAM 제공

완타니 시리파타나눈타쿨은 2013년 이래 작가의 반려새(아프리카 회색 앵무새) '보이스'(Beuys)와의 협업을 선보여왔다. 〈모든 이는…〉에서 '보이스'는 요셉 보이스(Joseph Beuys)의 유명한 어구인 "모든 이는 현대미술가다"라는 소리를 낸다.

Since 2013, Wantanee Siripattananuntakul has been working with "Beuys," a companion bird (African Grey Parrot). *Everyone is…* features a collaboration with Beuys the parrot who pronounces the famous words of Joseph Beuys: "Everyone is an artist."

Wantanee Siripattananuntakul *Everyone is…*, 2017 color, sound, 5 min. 5 sec. Courtesy of the artist, provided by MAIIAM

By the Other Being
Wantanee Siripattananauntakul

everyone

차오 페이는 다수의 멀티미디어 프로젝트를 통하여 사회문화적으로 급변하는 오늘날 중국의 대도시 모습과 그 속에서 보여지는 계층 구조, 문화적 다양성 및 세대 간의 간극 등을 이야기하는 작가이다. 〈아지랑이와 안개〉에서는 배달원, 청소부, 베이비시터, 경비원, 부동산 업자 등으로 분한 좀비들이 등장한다. 이들은 개개인의 특성을 지운 채 대도시의 반복적인 일상에 천착 되어 가는 현대인의 모습을 대변하고 있으며 동시에 이들이 속한 사회 속 다양한 삶의 형태를 보여준다.

Through her numerous multimedia projects, the artist Cao Fei examines the major cities of China today—which have been undergoing rapid social and cultural changes—and the things that can be discovered within them, including class structures, cultural diversity, and generation gaps. In *Haze and Fog*, zombies appear as delivery people, cleaners, babysitters, security workers, and real estate agents. With their individuality erased, they represent aspects of the modern individual that have permeated the repetitive routine in cities, while also showing the different forms of life within the societies to which they belong.

By the Other Being
Cao Fei

| 차재민 | ‹엘리의 눈›, 2020 | 2채널 비디오, 컬러, 사운드, 11분. | 작가 소장 |

차재민은 도시 개발 및 기술 발전이 급속도로 이루어지고 있는 현대 사회 속에서 개인, 집단이 마주하는 다양한 징후들을 영상으로 풀어낸다. ‹엘리의 눈›은 ‘엘리’라는 동명의 반려견과 AI 심리상담사를 통해 시감각, 눈과 시선, 투시에 대해 이야기하는 영상 에세이다. 작가는 ‘응시’에 기반하는 이러한 기술들이 그간 인간의 욕망을 반영해왔다는 점에 착안하여 종국에는 이것이 현대인들이 겪는 심리적 우울감, 정신적 문제에 개입하는 방식에 대해 반문한다.

In her video work, Cha Jaemin explores the different foretokens encountered by individuals and groups within a modern society where urban and technological development are progressing at a rapid rate. *Ellie's Eye* is a video essay that uses a pet dog and AI therapist both named "Ellie" to examine visual perception, the eye, the gaze, and the act of "seeing through." The artist questions the ways in which these technologies based on "seeing" have reflected human desires—as well as the ways in which we deal with the depression and psychological issues faced by people today.

| Cha Jeamin | *Ellie's Eye*, 2020 | two-channel video, color, sound, 11min. | Courtesy of the artist |

By the Other Being
Cha Jeamin

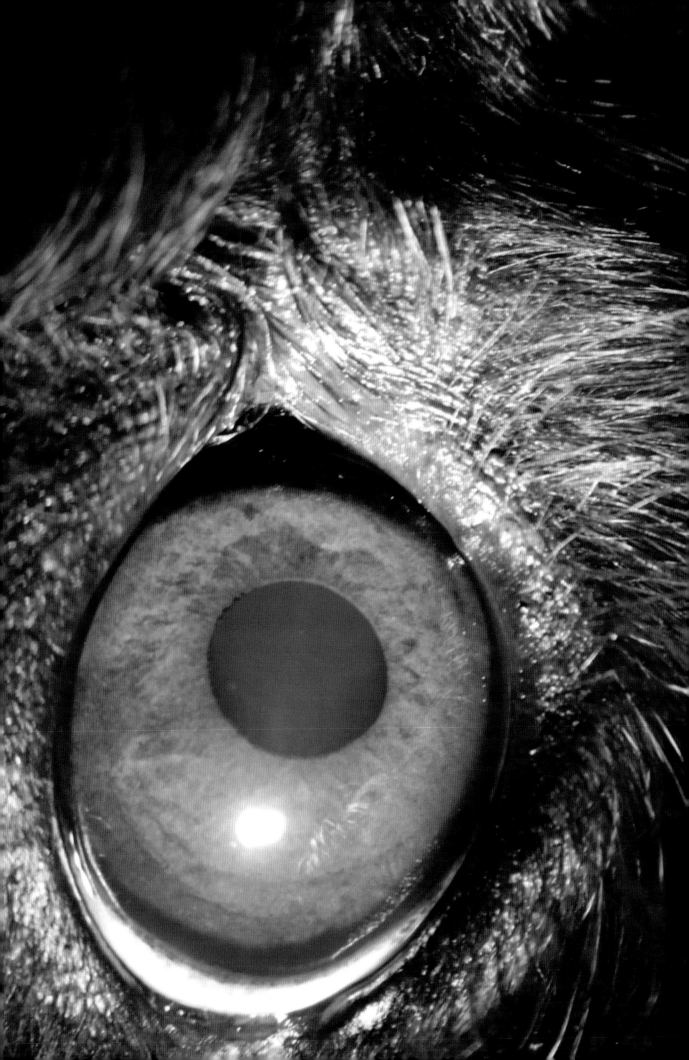

인간의 두 눈은 앞을 향해 있으며 180도 시야를 확보한다.

The human eyes both face forward,
and cover a visual field of 180°.

우리 집에서, 워치 앤 칠

김희천 | ‹나홀로 '멈블'보기›, 2020 | 유니티 웹지엘(webGL)에 임베드 된 영상, 컬러, 사운드, 24분 26초. | 작가 소장

‹나홀로 '멈블' 보기›는 도그 쇼의 형식을 차용해 작가의 자전적 이야기와 허구적 이야기를 편집해 구성한 영상이다. 가족의 반려견과 가상의 안내견, VR시점으로 공사장을 헤매는 남성의 목소리가 교차하며 서사를 전개한다. 본 영상은 작가가 조성한 가상의 공간에서 게임을 하듯 감상할 수 있도록 전시장과 온라인 플랫폼에 연동된다.

Watching 'Mumbling in Hell, Tumbling Down the Well' Alone is a video work that uses the format of a dog show to weave together the artist's own life with a fictional story. Its narrative is formed through the alternating voices of a family pet, a virtual guide dog, and a man wandering through a construction site seen from a VR perspective. The video is embedded in a game engine, again embedded on the platform so that the viewer can observe it as though playing a game in a virtual space created by the artist.

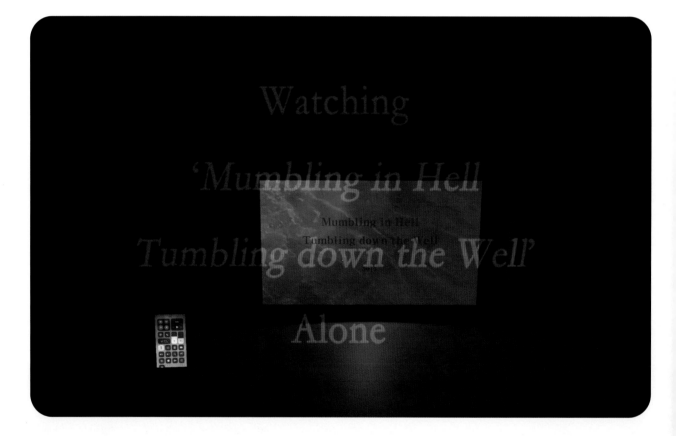

Kim Heecheon | Courtesy of the artist

Watching 'Mumbling in Hell, Tumbling Down the Well' Alone, 2020 | video embedded in unity webGL, color, sound, 24min. 26sec.

By the Other Being
Kim Heecheon

저희의 거동이 불편한 노견들을 위한 신설 리그로,

Our new league for senior pets that have physical difficulties with heavy activities,

우리 집에서, 워치 앤 칠

By the Other Being
Kim Heecheon

집의 공동체

광섬유로 연결된 우리의 집들은 아이러니하게도 고립을 야기하고 있으며, 날로 스마트화되는 도시 속에서 우리는 광활한 자연을 꿈꾸기도 한다. '집의 공동체'는 지역적 연관성을 바탕으로 한 전통적인 이웃 공동체와는 다른 대안적 군집의 형태를 제안한다. 작가들은 각기 다른 지역, 세대, 유형의 공동체가 마주한 환경의 변화와 이에 나름의 방식으로 적응하며 나타난 여러 삶의 형태들을 다룬다.

차이 시리스	‹포시즌스›, 2010	작가 소장, MAIIAM 제공
캠프	‹만에서 만을 거쳐 만으로›, 2013	M+ 소장
차재민	‹안개와 연기›, 2013	MMCA 소장
차지량	‹뉴 홈›, 2012	MMCA 소장
차지량	‹스테이›, 2021	작가소장, MMCA 커미션
마크 살바투스	‹간절히 기다리던 그 날›, 2020	작가 소장, MCAD 제공
타다 행삽쿨	‹당신은 나를 대양으로 내려가게 한다›, 2018	MAIIAM 소장

Community of Houses

Our fiber-optically wired homes ironically become an ultimate site of isolation, and we find ourselves longing for the vast wilderness as our cities grow smarter by the day. "Community of Houses" proposes alternative forms of living together that differ from the traditional community of neighbors based on physical vicinity. The artists explore the changes in environment experienced by communities of varying regions, generations, and typologies, along with the different forms of living that emerge as they adapt in their own ways.

Chai Siris	*Four Seasons*, 2010	Courtesy of the artist, provided by MAIIAM
CAMP	*From Gulf to Gulf to Gulf*, 2013	M+ collection
Cha Jeamin	*Fog and Smoke*, 2013	MMCA collection
Cha Jiryang	*New Home*, 2012	MMCA collection
Cha Jiryang	*Stay*, 2021	Courtesy of the artist, MMCA commission
Mark Salvatus	*That Day Most Eagerly Awaited*, 2020	Courtesy of the artist, provided by MCAD
Tada Hengsapkul	*You Lead Me Down to the Ocean*, 2018	MAIIAM collection

차이 시리스　　　　〈포시즌스〉, 2010　　　　컬러, 사운드, 10분 25초.　　　　작가 소장, MAIIAM 제공

차이 시리스는 개인과 사회의 역사, 국가, 젠더, 삶과 죽음 사이의 경계를 영화와 사진의 기법으로 재구성하는 작업을 해왔다. 〈포시즌스〉는 치앙마이에 이주한 건설 노동자의 거처가 된 열대 우림의 계곡과 고급 리조트 건설 현장의 운집된 기계를 비춘다. 작가는 지역 개발로 인한 환경과 인구 변화의 단면을 서정적 노래에 담아낸다.

Chai Siris's videos and photographs often deal with reconstruction of personal and social history, border conflicts between countries, gender, life and death. *Four Seasons* is a portrait of a migrant construction worker on her days off. She goes to a waterfall to rest and let her mind drift and a portrait of a construction site at night with illuminating lights from the heavy machinery.

Chai Siris　　　　*Four Seasons*, 2010　　　　color, sound, 10 min. 25 sec.　　　　Courtesy of the artist, provided by MAIIAM

Community of Houses
Chai Siris

선박은 그 자체로 많은 힘을 지닌다. 제조 과정에서 일종의 사회 집단이 만들어지고, 집이 되기도 하며, 사람과 사물, 그리고 아이디어를 운반한다. 이러한 선박의 힘은 오늘날 우리에게 그 어느 때보다도 다르게 다가온다.

‹만에서 만을 거쳐 만으로›는 인도의 컷치 지역의 선원들과 4년간의 협업으로 만들어진 결과물이다. 이 작품은 휴대전화 카메라를 포함한 다양한 녹화 장치를 활용하여 선원들이 직접 촬영한 영상들로 구성되어있다. 페르시아와 아덴만을 통해 파키스탄에서 이란 남부까지 함께 항해하는 선원들의 여정은 고국에 대한 향수와 민족주의 간의 접점 혹은 세계 무역의 논리로 쉽게 설명될 수 없는 또 다른 세계의 면면을 보여준다. 관람자는 직접 만든 배를 항해하는 선원들의 일상을 따라가면서, 선원들이 결속력을 형성하기 위해 함께 불렀던 노래를 듣기도 한다.

A boat has many powers: to gather a society in its making, to be a home, to carry people, goods, and ideas across places that, it seems to us, are more different than ever before.

From Gulf to Gulf to Gulf is a feature made in collaboration with a group of sailors from the Gulf of Kutch, India over a period of four years. The work consists of footage filmed by the seamen with a mixture of recording devices, including mobile phone cameras. Their travels, and those of co-seafarers from Pakistan and Southern Iran, through the Persian and Aden Gulfs, show us a world cut into many pieces, not easily bridged by nostalgics or nationalists, nor captured by the logistics of world trade. The work follows their daily lives as they sail the boats they make. They also make videos, sometimes with songs married to them.

Community of Houses
Camp

Looks like a new launch

Community of Houses
Camp

차재민 | ‹안개와 연기›, 2013 | 컬러, 사운드, 20분 46초. | MMCA 소장

‹안개와 연기›는 송도 신도시 일대를 소재로 한 작업이다. 구도시와 신도시의 대조적인 모습을 배경으로, 도시 개발로 인해 생업과 거처를 잃은 거주민들과 동시에 새로운 보금자리를 얻게 될 입주민 사이의 사변적인 현실을 담아냈다. 본래 어부였던 지역민의 이야기, 수직적 건축물, 공허한 밤의 탭 댄서 등이 등장하며 '국제도시' 건설의 이면을 조명한다.

Fog and Smoke focuses on the "new town" of Songdo in Incheon. Adopting the contrasting faces of the old and new city as its backdrop, it illustrates a speculative reality between the residents who have lost their occupations and homes to urban redevelopment, and the other residents who have gained a new home there. With stories from local residents who used to fish, images of vertical architecture, tap dancers appearing in empty nightscapes, and more, it shows the hidden sides behind the construction of a "global city."

Cha Jeamin | *Fog and Smoke*, 2013 | color, sound, 20 min. 46 sec. | MMCA collection

우리 집에서, 워치 앤 칠

Community of Houses
Cha Jeamin

| 차지량 | ‹뉴 홈›, 2012 | 컬러, 사운드, 83분 13초. | MMCA 소장 |

차지량은 미디어를 활용한 참여 프로젝트를 진행하며, 시스템과 개인에 초점을 맞춘 현장 작업을 이어왔다. 작가는 불특정 다수가 참여하는 방식의 퍼포먼스를 통해 참가자가 스스로 시스템의 가능성을 제안하고 상상하게 만든다. ‹뉴 홈›도 이러한 맥락에서 오늘날 주거 시스템에 무력감을 느낀 특정 세대와 함께 도시개발 이면에 남겨진 다양한 유형의 빈 집을 점거하며 불완전한 일상을 체험하는 취침 퍼포먼스이다. 작가와 참여자들은 다세대 주택, 원룸, 아파트 등 도시의 주거공간에 침입하여 하루 저녁을 보낸다. 참여자들은 입주 후 공간을 둘러보고 각자의 방에서 시간을 보낸 뒤, 새벽이 오면 모든 흔적을 지우고 도망치듯 떠나는 유사한 패턴을 반복한다.

Cha Ji Ryang carries out participatory projects involving on-site practices that focus on systems, individuals and media. Through performances with participants of unspecified many, the artist encourages them to propose and imagine their own ideas for possible alternative systems. *New Home* continues in this context, focusing on a particular generation of people who feel helpless in the face of the current housing system. It is a "sleeping performance," occupying vacant homes of different typologies—the by-products of urban development—and making imperfect life trials.

| Cha Jiryang | *New Home*, 2012 | color, sound, 83 min. 13 sec. | MMCA collection |

Community of Houses
Cha Jiryang

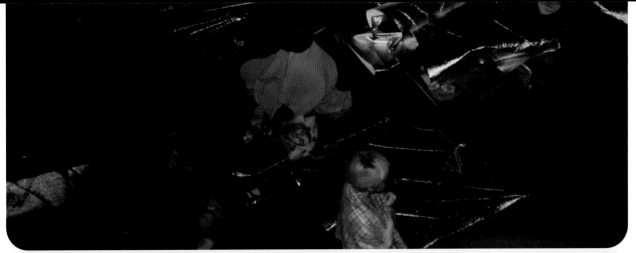

《우리 집에서, 워치 앤 칠》을 위해 작가는 근
10년만에 2012년 작품 〈뉴 홈〉에 퍼포먼스에
등장했던 참가자들을 다시 만났다. 도시와 주거
시스템에 또 다른 가능성을 추구하던 이들은 지금
어떤 모습으로 살고 있을까? 이들은 '집'이라는
개념의 물리적 공간과 사변적 현실 간의 괴리에 대해
자조하기도, 지나온 시간에 관해 소회하기도, 또 새롭게
생긴 가족들과 현재를 점검해보기도 한다. 올해 유난히
'스테이'라는 건축 유형이 유행하는 것은 코로나19
영향 때문이기도 하겠지만 십년전과는 다소 달라진
도시와 지역 간의 관계를 드러낸다. 도시를 벗어나
바다의 경관을 배경으로 '살아보기'는 또 다른 사변적
환상일까?

For this newly commissioned piece on the
occasion of *Watch and Chill, Streaming Art to
Your Homes*, the artist met with the participants
who appeared in the performance for *New
Home* (2012) again in nearly ten years. Back
then, they pursued other possibilities in the city
in an attempt to challenge the housing system
via "sleeping performance." How are they living
now? Some lament about the gap between the
physical space and the speculative reality of
"home," some reflect upon the time past, and
some examine the current situations with new
families. "Stay" being the particularly popular
architectural typology this year may be due to
the influence of Covid-19, but it also reveals
the newly formed relationship between cities
and regions that have changed somewhat from
a decade ago. Is escaping the city and staying
against the backdrop of the ocean view another
speculative fantasy?

horizontal and vertical

수평과 수직

NEW HOME

2021. 9. 12.
HNW

‹간절히 기다리던 그날›은 작가의 고향에 있는 산에 관한 영상이다. 자석처럼 사람들을 끌어들이는 바나하우 산은 여러 종교 분파를 비롯해 필리핀 공산당 무장 진영인 신인민군의 피난처이자, UFO의 연료 재보급지로 여겨지기도 하는 곳으로, 새로운 세상과 경이로운 현상을 만들어낸다. 생물 다양성이 풍부한 이 산은 상류 사회 사람들과는 달리 통치 받길 원치 않으며 혁명을 고대하는 이들을 위한 보금자리로도 여겨진다. 작품은 코로나로 인한 의한 이동 제한 조치가 시행되던 시기에 제작된 것으로, 이를 본래 가지고 있던 예전 비디오 파일들과 결합하여, 다시 세상이 자유롭게 숨쉬기 안전해질 날과 연결 짓는다. 여전히 험난한 시절의 와중에서 장차 모두와 다시 만나길 고대하는 작가의 염원을 담았다.

That Day Most Eagerly Awaited is a video about the mountain in the artist's hometown, Mt. Banahaw which acts as a magnet, a refuge to various communities as a safe ground for religious and spiritual sects, The New People's Army, the armed wing of The Communist Party of the Philippines, and a supposed site for UFO's to refuel, creating new worlds and prodigies. With rich biodiversity, the mountain was conceived as a place for people who don't want to be governed, different from those of the better classes of society and are longing for a revolution waiting to happen. He made this during the lockdown and combined it with the old video files that he has and connected it to the day when the world is safe to breathe again. The video contains the artist's longing to meet everyone passing through the tough times.

Community of Houses
Mark Salvatus

타다 행삽쿨은 사진과 비디오, 설치 등 다양한 매체를 통해 현상 이면에 쉽게 드러나지 않은 실체를 사유하는 작가이다. 〈당신은 나를 대양으로 내려가게 한다〉에서 작가는 태국 남부 지역의 나라티왓 주 인근의 깊은 바다에 잠식된 탱크를 비춘다. 이 30T69-2 탱크는 1987년 태국군이 중국에서 구입한 전차 24대 중 하나로 태국-베트남 국경인 카오 프라 위한에서 10년 이상 지속된 분쟁 중 베트남에 대항하기 위하여 사용되었다. 태국 왕실의 시리킷 여왕은 바다의 생식력을 회복하고 태국 관광을 촉진하기 위해 이 탱크를 태국 만에 방류했다. 태국의 군부 정치 상황을 대변하는 이 탱크는 본 전시에서 바다 속 다양한 어종의 서식지로서 기능한다.

Tada Hengsapkul uses a wide range of media such as photography, video, and installations to speculate upon existence that does not readily reveal itself beneath the surface. *You Lead Me Down to the Ocean* shows a tank being corroded by the deep sea near the province of Narathiwat in southern Thailand. The 30T69-2 tank is one of 24 purchased vehicles from China by the Thai army in 1987. It was used against Vietnam during a conflict that lasted for over a decade at Khao Phra Wihan on the Thai-Vietnamese border. The Thai royal family—specifically Queen Sirikit—had the tank thrown into the Gulf of Thailand to help restore the sea's fertility and promote tourism. The artwork is a metaphor for the political situation in Thailand, which is still controlled by a military government that is impeding progress: in the exhibition, the tank is shown in the depths of the sea as an object that has left behind its original purpose and serves now as a habitat for different marine species and a setting for those non-human populations to assemble.

Community of Houses
Tada Hengsapkul

메타-홈

'메타-홈'은 집 이상의 집을 의미한다. 여기에서는 보이지
않는 네트워크로 치밀하게 얽혀있는 거대한 연쇄 속의 집,
즉 가정의 초연결성(hyperconnectivity)을 다룬다.
가상의 세계와 연동된 집의 모습, 디지털 시대의 존재 방식,
여러 차원으로의 공간 확장 가능성, 또한 기술적 연결
너머의 정신적, 영적 영역의 연결 등 다양한 메타적 상상을
펼친다.

지앙 지	‹날아, 날아›, 1997	M+ 소장
구동희	‹타가수분›, 2016	MMCA 소장
구동희	‹타가수분 코멘터리›, 2021	작가 소장, MMCA 커미션
김희천, 전효경	인터뷰: ‹썰매›, 2021	MMCA 제작
씨씨우	‹유만혼의 미완된 귀환›, 2019	M+ 소장
차이 시리스	‹오십만 년›, 2016	작가 소장, MAIIAM 제공
사룻 수파수티벡	‹보안원의 CCTV›, 2019	작가 소장, MAIIAM 제공

Meta-Home

The "Meta-Home" is a home beyond a home. This
chapter examines the hyperconnectivity of homes
situated within a vast chain of minutely intertwined
invisible networks. It presents various forms
of metaphysical imagination, including homes
connected with the virtual world; ways of existing
in the digital era; possibilities for spatial expansion
into different dimensions; and mental, spiritual
connections that transcend technological ones.

Jiang Zhi	*Fly, Fly*, 1997	M+ collection
Koo Donghee	*CrossxPollination*, 2016	MMCA collection
Koo Donghee	*CrossxPollination Commentary*, 2021	Courtesy of the artist, MMCA commission
Kim Heecheon, Jeon Hyo Gyoung	*Interview: Sleigh Ride Chill*, 2021	Produced by MMCA
Cici Wu	*Unfinished Return of Yu Man Hon*, 2019	M+ collection
Chai Siris	*500,000 Years*, 2016	Courtesy of the artist, provided by MAIIAM
Saroot Supasuthivech	*CCTV of Security Guard*, 2019	Courtesy of the artist, provided by MAIIAM

지앙 지는 이주와 신체의 정치, 중국의 도시화, 미디어의 문화적 위치 등에 관해 다루는 작가로, 〈날아, 날아〉는 좁은 아파트에서 비상하는 새처럼 날갯짓하는 누군가를 비추며 갇힌 도시 거주공간 너머의 가능성을 꿈꾸는 작품이다.

Jiang Zhi addresses the politics of migration and the body, China's urbanization, and the cultural status of the media. *Fly, Fly* evokes the situation of city dwellers who long to escape their tiny, cramped apartments, this work shows a hand mimicking the movements of a bird soaring in flight.

Meta-Home
Jiang Zhi

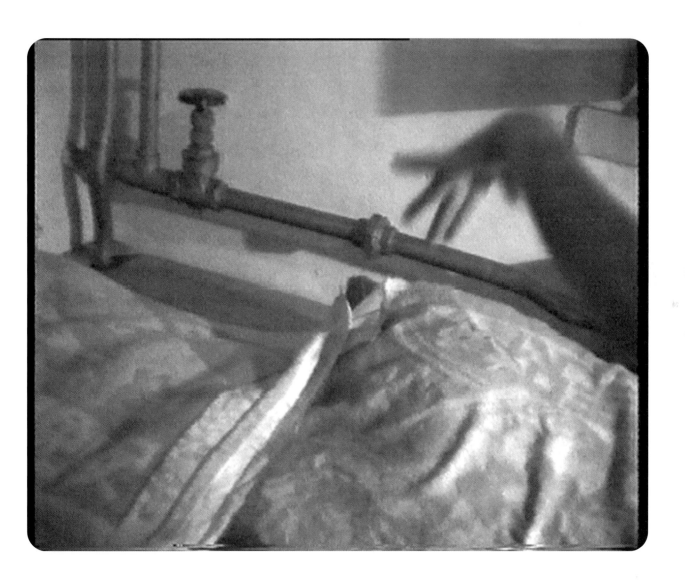

구동희는 주변에서 발생하는 사건들에 주목하여 그것들과 관련된 다양한 시각자료를 수집한다. 작가는 이미지를 반복하거나 해체하는 것과 같은 추상적 태도를 취하며 작품에 달리 해석할 수 있는 여지를 남긴다. 〈타가수분〉의 배경은 '프린스 호프'라는 동네 주점과 욕실전문기업 '로얄&컴퍼니'(구 로얄 TOTO)의 제품 전시장이다. 일반적으로 욕실은 사적인 공간으로 폐쇄적이고 호프집은 공공에게 개방된 장소이지만, 이 작업에서는 욕실은 개방적인 공간이, 호프집은 아는 사람만 드나드는 폐쇄된 장소가 된다. 이렇게 성격이 뒤바뀐 두 장소는 거울, 모니터(TV) 등 시각적 공통점이 존재한다. 두 공간의 일상적 행위들은 강냉이, 거품, 동물, 계곡 등의 이미지로 교차하며 공간과 시간, 실제와 가상을 엮어낸다. 작가는 이미지의 개입을 통해 서로 다른 장소와 상황 속에서 어떻게 소통이 이루어지는지 들여다본다.

Koo Donghee often focuses on everyday events, whilst assembling a wide range of related visual materials. She tends to leave room for her interpretation by deploying abstract approaches of repeating and de-constructing images. *Cross×Pollination* was inspired by a neighborhood pub called the "Prince Hof" and a showroom run by the Royal and Co. (formerly Royal TOTO), a bathroom interior company. Bathrooms are generally considered private, closed space whereas the pubs are public. Yet in this showroom, the bathroom is an open setting, while the pub is rather insular, frequented only by known patrons. With their natures thus reversed, the two settings share visual similarities with features such as mirrors and TV monitors. Everyday activities in those settings are juxtaposed with images of corns, bubbles, animals, and valleys—weaving together space and time, real and virtual. Through her interventions in the imagery, Koo examines how communication transpires in different places and situations.

Meta-Home
Koo Donghee

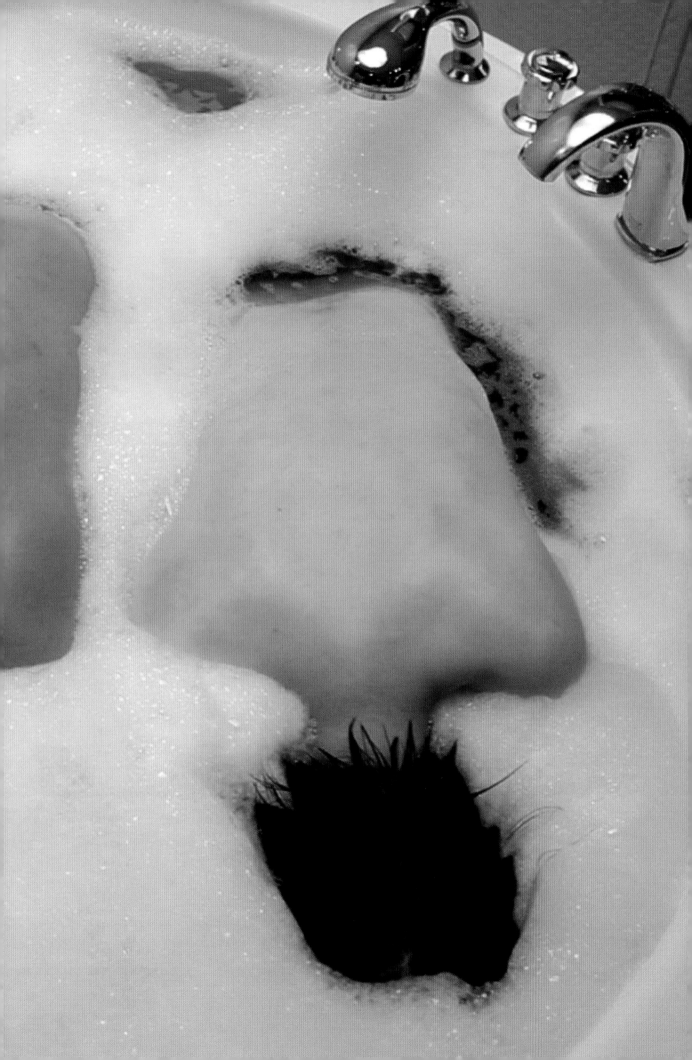

However, there Is a 'rule of 50,000 hours per 3 years'

국립현대미술관 소장품인 구동희 작가의 2016년작 ‹타가수분›은 욕실과 호프집이라는 사적이고 공공적 성격의 장소의 성격을 뒤바꾸는 일련의 행위와 이미지의 배열로 이루어진 영상이다. 작가는 '워치 앤 칠' 플랫폼을 위해 ‹타가수분 코멘터리›를 제작했다. 별도의 대사가 없던 원 영상에 작가가 연출한 상황과 시각적 모티프에 대한 주석이 음성으로 겹쳐진다. 영상에 출연했던 배우는 이 코멘터리의 화자가 되어 자칫 지나칠 수 있는 장면을 중계한다.

Koo Donghee's *Cross×Pollination* (2016) is a single-channel video composed of a series of actions and imageries that switch the characteristics of privacy and publicity between a bathroom and a pub house. Specifically for the *Watch and Chill* streaming platform, the artist produced *Cross×Pollination Commentary* adding a layer of annotations about the directed situations and visual motives on top of the original word-less video. The main actor that appeared in the work now walks through the video with the viewer, commenting on scenes that one could have overlooked.

Koo Donghee | *Cross×Pollination 코멘터리*, 2021 | color, sound, 23 min. 58 sec. | Courtesy of the artist, MMCA commission

Meta-Home
Koo Donghee

김희천, 전효경 | 인터뷰: ‹썰매›, 2021 | 컬러, 사운드, 11분 51초. | MMCA 제작

김희천은 일상 속 디지털 기술을 기반으로 한 허구적 서사를 구축하고, 이를 검증하는 방법론으로서 3D, 게임, 가상현실 등의 인터페이스를 활용한다. 작가는 여러 겹의 층위를 이루는 멀티스크린의 서사를 통해 구조적 산란을 야기하며 현실과 인터넷 세계 사이의 틈을 가시화한다. ‹썰매›는 카레이싱 게임을 생중계하는 가상의 인물이 방 안에서 서울 도심을 질주하는 것으로 시작하여 자살클럽, 퀴어 퍼레이드, 개인정보 유출 등 사회적 이슈들을 연결시키며 가상의 감각과 실재의 경계를 오간다. ‘워치 앤 칠’ 플랫폼을 위해 국립현대미술관은 작가가 직접 작품 ‹썰매›에 대해 이야기하는 특별한 비디오를 제작했다. 대담자로는 그의 미술계 동료이자 친구인 전효경(아트선재센터 큐레이터)을 섭외했는데, 이들은 작업에 등장하는 같은 길을 가상으로 또 현실에서 운전하며 대화를 이어나간다.

Kim Heecheon constructs fictional narratives based on the digital technology in our lives, using interfaces such as 3D, games, and virtual reality as a way of putting them to the test. With narratives existing in multiple layers, he induces structural disturbances to visualize the fissures between the real and online worlds. *Sleigh Ride Chill* begins with a virtual character speeding through downtown Seoul in a room of a fictional character as he narrates a car racing game. The work alternates between the real and virtual as it draws connections with social issues such as suicide clubs, queer parades, and leaks of personal information. For the purpose of the *Watch and Chill* streaming platform, MMCA produced a special video with the artist talking about *Sleigh Ride Chill*, as he makes a casual conversation with his colleague/friend Jeon Hyo Gyong (Curator, Art Sonje Center) while driving the same path that appeared in the work both virtually and in real life.

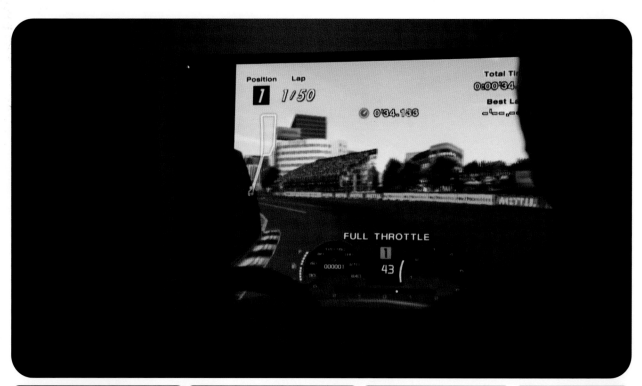

Kim Heecheon, Jeon Hyo Gyoung | *Interview: Sleigh Ride Chill*, 2021 | color, sound, 11min. 51sec. | Produced by MMCA

Meta-Home
Kim Heecheon, Jeon Hyo Gyoung

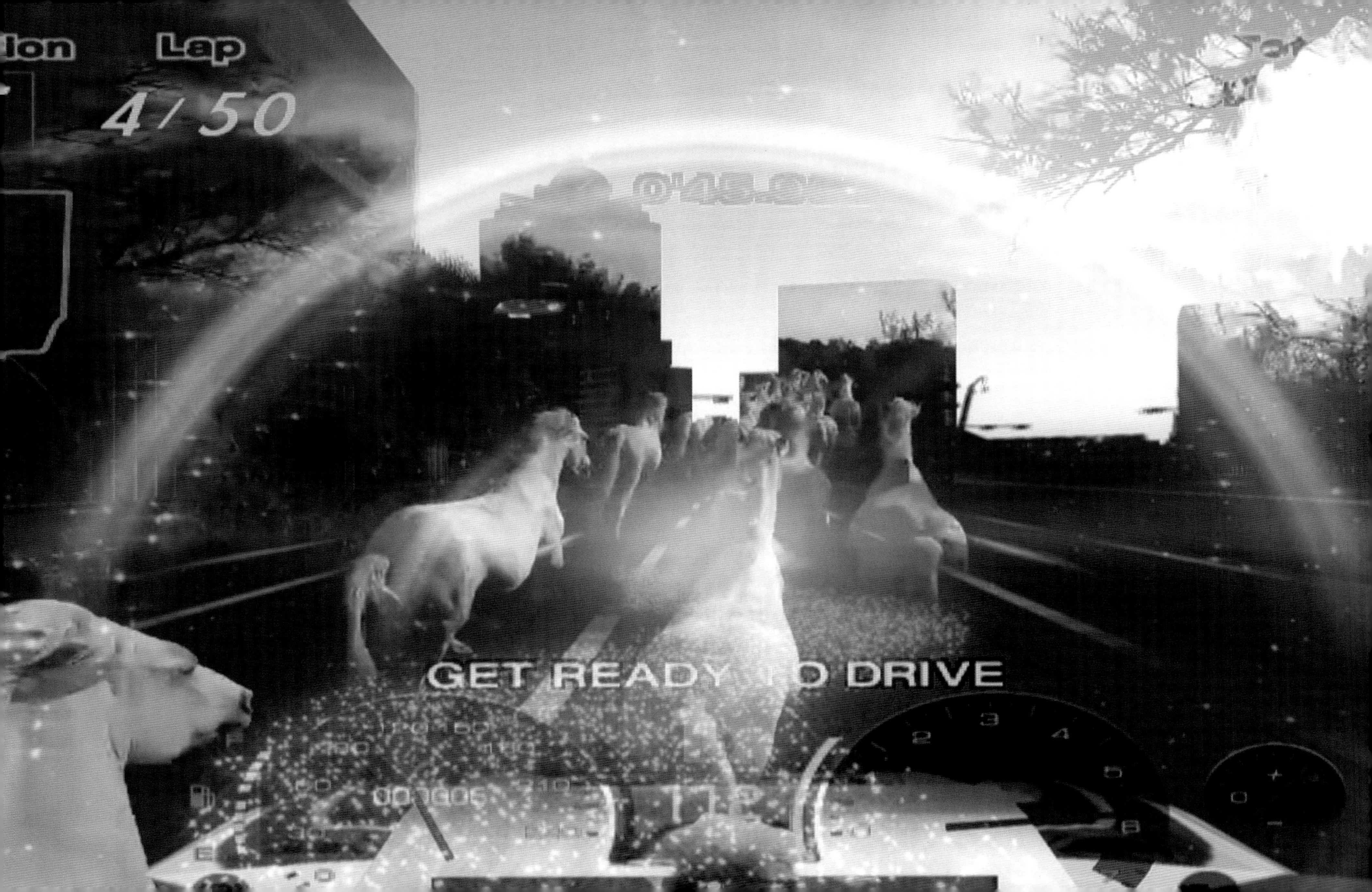
Lap
4/50
GET READY
DRIVE

〈유만혼의 미완된 귀환〉은 실제 실종 사건에서 영감을 얻었다. 2000년 자폐증을 지닌 유만혼이라는 소년이 홍콩과 선전 간의 국경을 건너다 사라졌고, 그 뒤로 다시는 나타나지 않았다. 씨씨 우는 그녀의 작업을 통해 영혼이 되어 돌아온 유만혼을 상기시킨다. 추상적인 비유로 점철된 서사 가운데서 유만혼은 잃어버렸던 자신의 실종에 관한 기억을 되살리며, 물리적인 세계로 귀환한다.

The work was inspired by the real-life disappearance of Yu Man Hon, an autistic boy who, in 2000, crossed the Hong Kong-Shenzhen border, and was never found again. In Cici's film, she reimagines the return of Yu Man-hon as an enlightened spirit. The video tells an abstract narrative in which Yu Man Hon returns to the material world, retrieving lost memories of his own disappearance.

Meta-Home
Cici Wu

Meta-Home
Cici Wu

차이 시리스는 〈오십만 년〉에서 태국 시네마 문화의 죽음과 부활을 애니미즘 사회에 접목시켜 탐구한다. 태국 여러 지역에서, 야외 상영은 '영화'를 인간을 위해 제공되는 문화적 산물에서 혼령을 위해 바쳐지는 일종의 제물의 의식으로 그 기능이 변화되었다. 이 작품을 통해 작가는 영화라는 매체가 시공간을 초월하여 스스로 살아남기 위해 본인의 기능을 변화시키는 행태와 과학적 발견이 영적 행위로 변화하는 양상을 관찰한다.

500,000 Years is an investigation of the death and rebirth of cinema culture in Thailand which engaged with animism society. In many parts of the country, the outdoor screening changed its function from a media for humans to an offering for ghosts and spirits. He would like to explore possibilities of transformation of cinema to keep itself alive here. As well as how we transform scientific discoveries into spiritual activities.

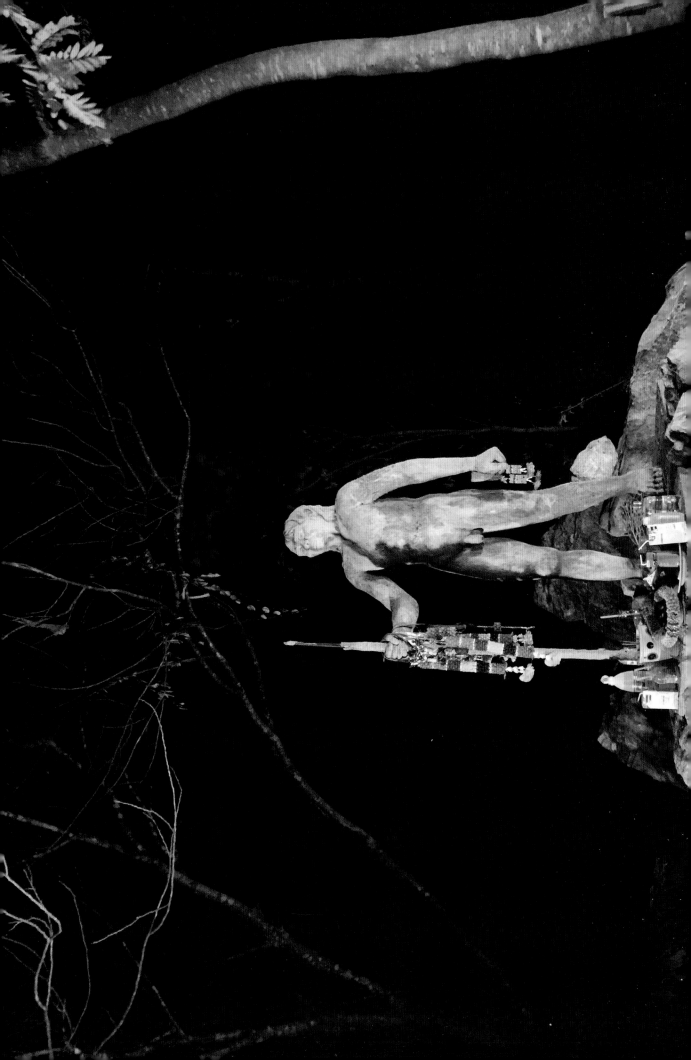

사룻 수파수티벡 ‹보안원의 CCTV›, 2019 컬러, 사운드, 8분 12초. 작가 소장, MAIIAM 제공

‹보안원의 CCTV›는 실제 CCTV 모니터와 유사한 다중 스크린의 형태로 구성되어있다. 작품 속 보안원은 그가 맞닥뜨렸던 기이한 사건에 대해 이야기하고 있으며, 그의 서술은 화면상 폐관 이후 예술센터 내 여러 구역의 모습을 담은 이미지와 겹쳐진다. 장소 특정적인 역사를 담고 있는 장소인 방콕문화예술센터의 모습은 그곳에서 누구보다 많은 시간을 보냈을 보안요원의 기억과 함께 마치 살아 있는 유기체처럼 묘사된다. 그와 동시에 CCTV 영상은 자연스레 관객을 관찰자의 시점으로 옮겨 놓는다. 방콕예술센터의 이미지는 갈 곳 없이 불확실한 상태로 검은 스크린 위를 떠돌며, 정부의 개입과 디지털 시대 속에서 부유하는 현대의 유령 이미지를 재현한다.

The footage shown in the video is divided into multiple screens, similar to a CCTV monitor. The memory of the same security guard still tells the mysterious tale he encountered, but this time with the accompanying images of the after-hour emptiness from different areas of the art centre. The coming together of the site-specific history and the memory of the security guard, who might have spent the time inside much more than other people, makes the Bangkok Art and Culture Centre look like a living organism, whereas the CCTV footage, at the same time, naturally shifts the viewer to a surveilling point of view. The rendered image of the Art Centre floats on the black screen in a limbo state with no place to go, representing the image of today's ghost in the digital age of government interference and the internet.

Saroot Supasuthivec *CCTV of Security Guard*, 2019 color, sound, 8 min. 12 sec. Courtesy of the artist, provided by MAIIAM

Meta-Home
Saroot Supasuthivec

디자인 스튜디오 워크스와의 대화
권태현(독립 큐레이터)

Design Studio WORKS in Conversation
with Kwon Taehyun (Independent Curator)

온라인 플랫폼 '워치 앤 칠'은 《우리 집에서, 워치 앤 칠》의 국제 순회전과 함께 개발된 디지털 전시 공간이다. 디자인 스튜디오 워크스(WORKS)는 '워치 앤 칠' 온라인 플랫폼의 구축 및 디자인을 맡아 미술관의 물리적 공간과 더불어 작품, 작가, 관객이 교차하는 장소로서의 인터페이스를 설계했다.
 이 책의 편집자인 권태현은 온라인 플랫폼 디자인의 전반적인 과정 및 의도를 듣기 위해 워크스와의 인터뷰를 진행했다.

 권태현(이하 권): 온라인 플랫폼과 물리적인 전시장을 아우르는 일관된 디자인 콘셉트가 눈에 띄는 프로젝트였습니다. 그런 '워치 앤 칠'의 비주얼 콘셉트가 어떻게 도출되었는지부터 이야기를 듣고 싶어요.

WORKS: '워치 앤 칠'의 디자인은 '코로나19 팬데믹 이래로 폭발적으로 늘어난 OTT 시장에 예술 스트리밍 플랫폼인 '워치 앤 칠'을 런칭한다면?'이라는 상상에서 출발했습니다. 그렇기 때문에 작가의 이름이 나열되거나, 기획적 의도, 혹은 작품의 특징 같은 요소가 디자인에 반영되는 것에 앞서 '스트리밍 플랫폼'이라는 정체성을 명확하고 효과적으로 보여주는 것에 초점을 맞추었어요.

 권: 그런 관점에서는 분명 성공적으로 작동한 측면이 있었다고 생각됩니다. 그렇다면, 스트리밍 플랫폼이라는 정체성을 명확하게 하기 위해 연구한 레퍼런스나, 구체적인 시각화 전략은 어떤 것이 있었나요?

WORKS: 넷플릭스나 왓챠 등의 OTT 서비스의 비주얼 컨셉트가 국립현대미술관 이지회 학예연구사와 워크스 모두 공통적으로 생각하고 있던 레퍼런스였습니다. 특히, 그것들의 전체적인 이미지보다는 사용자가 콘텐츠에 다다르는 단계나 효과적인 정보 전달을 위한 위계를 설계하는 구조적인 측면에서 큰 영감을 받았어요. 그러한 레퍼런스 연구를 기반으로 필수적으로 포함해야 하는 정보만을 남기고, 나머지 요소들을 소거한 뒤 개념적으로 비트는 방식으로 레퍼런스를 활용했습니다.

The online platform *Watch and Chill* is a newly developed digital exhibition space, launched with its first edition, *Watch and Chill: Streaming Art to your Homes*. Design studio WORKS created the platform as an interface that enables museums, artists, and audiences to make meaningful exchanges.
 Kwon Taehyun, editor of this catalogue, interviewed WORKS to hear the overall design process and intented interactions on the online platform.

 Kwon Taehyun(KT): In this project, the consistent design concept between the online platform and the physical exhibition venue was particularly noticeable. To begin with, I'd like to hear how the visual concept for *Watch and Chill* came about.

WORKS: The *Watch and Chill* design started with us imagining, "suppose *Watch and Chill* is being launched as an art streaming platform in a market where streaming services have grown at an explosive rate since the Covid-19 pandemic." In that sense, incorporating a list of the artists' names, reflecting elements like the curatorial intentions, or the characteristics of the artwork was the secondary concerns than showing the "streaming platform" identity in a clear and effective way.

KT: From that perspective, it seems to have definitely been a success. So were there any references you studied or any concrete visualization strategy you had in mind to make that streaming platform identity clear?

WORKS: The visual concept of a streaming service like Netflix or Watcha was something that both the Curator Lee Jihoi and WORKS considered as a reference. In particular, we were inspired less by their overall image but more by their structural aspects—the way they design the stages the user goes through to reach the content, or the hierarchies used to convey information effectively. Based on our examination of those references, we adopted an approach where we only left the information that absolutely needed to be included, while removing the other elements and conceptually tweaking it.

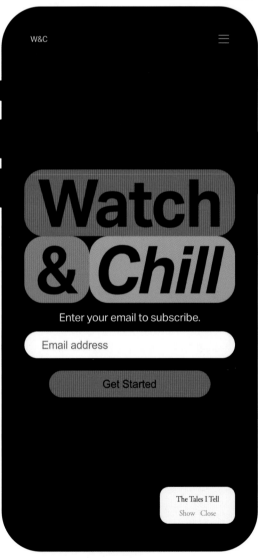

시각화의 문제에서는 '워치 앤 칠'의 런칭을 즐거운 충격으로 세상에 각인시키고 싶었어요. 그래서 다채로우면서도 분명한 표현을 중요하게 생각했습니다. 로고타입은 볼드한 색상과 블록 형태의 조형 반복, 그리고 타이포그래피의 조합으로 이루어져 있는데, 컴퓨터 운영체제에서 사용되는 기본창이나 버튼을 주요한 모티프로 삼아 디자인했습니다. 그렇게 형성된 블록들은 명령을 지시하는 버튼이 되기도 하고, 때로는 콘텐츠를 담은 하나의 블록이 되기도 합니다. 그런 블록 단위의 시스템을 만들고, 쌓아가면서 시간차를 두고 작품을 차례로 공개하는 '워치 앤 칠'의 운영 방식과 기획을 표현하기도 했어요.

또한, 플랫폼의 디자인적 요소가 작품에 섞여 들어가지 않고, 작품의 생동감이나 볼륨감을 강조할 수 있도록 초평평하게 설계했습니다. 이를테면 콘텐츠를 강조하기 위해 흔히 사용하는 그림자, 테두리 등 입체적인 효과들은 최대한 사용을 피했습니다.

　권: 세심한 디자인적 선택들에 대한 이야기를 들으니, 다시 보이는 것들이 많습니다. 간단히 언급해주셨던 타이포그래피나 색채 선택에 대해서도 더 이야기해주실 수 있을까요?

WORKS: '워치 앤 칠'의 로고타입 타이포그래피는 중립적인 서체를 사용해 메시지는 명확하게, 그러면서도 타이포그래피와 밀착한 색 체계나 기하학적인 조형은 경쾌하게 전달하고 싶었습니다. 서체로는 중립적인 서체 중에서 고딕 A1과 Aktiv Grotesk를 섞어 사용했어요. 특히, '칠'(chill) 부분은 이탤릭으로 변주를 주어서, 단어 자체가 가지고 있는 유머러스함을 표현하기도 했습니다. 또한, 각 소주제 타이포그래피 디자인은 수직 수평의 로고타입 디자인과는 대비를 주어서 렌즈를 통한 광학적인 현상을 빗댄 형태로 표현했어요. 이런 광학적인 타이포그래피에서는 과거 비디오테이프의 타이틀 디자인들을 떠올리며 노스텔지어를 자아내거나 살짝 낭만적인 분위기를 연출하고 싶었습니다.

'워치 앤 칠' 온라인 플랫폼은 미술관 전시와 같이 일시적으로, 또 정기적으로 열린다는 특성을 가지고 있습니다. 그런 점을 반영하여 스트리밍 서비스로서 역동적으로 변화하는 개방적인 모습을

In terms of the visualization issue, we wanted the impression of the *Watch and Chill* launch to be like a "pleasant shock" to the world. So It was important for us to express things in a way that was both diverse and clear. The logo is a combination of bold colors, repeated block patterns, typography. The key motifs for the design were things like the default windows and buttons in a computer operating system. The resulting blocks are buttons that deliver commands, but they can also be blocks of content. So we created a system by assembling those block units so that the design responds to the intended operation of *Watch and Chill*, presenting artworks progressively over time.

We also chose a super-flat design so that we could emphasize the vibrancy and volume of the artwork without the platform's design elements becoming entangled with the art. For example, we tried hard to avoid using the kind of three-dimensional effects that are often employed to emphasize content—things like shading and borders.

　KT: Now that I've heard you talk about these careful design choices, there are a lot of things I see in a new way. Could you talk a bit about the typography and color choices?

WORKS: With the typography for the *Watch and Chill* logotype, we wanted a neutral font to convey the messages clearly, but we also wanted to show a sense of liveliness with the geometric design and the color system, which is closely connected with the typography. For the font, we used a neutral font that was a mixture of Gothic A1 and Aktiv Grotesk. We also used Italics to vary the "chill" part in a way that also expressed the humor in the word itself. With the typography designs for the different subtopics, we created a contrast with the vertical and horizontal logotype design, presenting them in a way that's similar to optical phenomena when viewed through a lens. We wanted that optical typography to evoke a sense of nostalgia or a somewhat romantic quality, one that reminded people of the title designs on old videotapes.

One of the characteristics of the *Watch and Chill* online platform is that it takes place both temporarily and regularly, like the museum exhibitions. To reflect that, we had the color system express an open quality,

색체계로 표현했어요. 세 가지 주요색(웹을 기준으로 컬러를 선택했기 때문에 헥스 코드로 표기하면 ff4800, 009bd9, 00ffce)은 서로 다른 계열의 색상이라 다채로우면서도 비슷한 채도와 명도를 가진 색상들이기에 서로 치열하게 경쟁하며 도드라집니다. 또한, 검은 배경은 어떤 사용 환경에서도 가시성을 유지하기 위해서 기본값으로 선택했고, 대신 라이트모드도 함께 제공해 디자인 의도에서 벗어난 감각을 느낄 여지도 만들어 놓았어요.

권: 온라인 플랫폼의 디자인을 기반으로 구상되었지만, 버튼 등 요소들이 모듈화되어 온라인 플랫폼과 오프라인 전시장을 오가며 다양하게 활용되는 것이 흥미로웠습니다. 온·오프라인 교차 등 디자인 요소들의 확장된 활용 가능성에 대한 이야기를 더 듣고 싶어요.

WORKS: 스트리밍 플랫폼을 우선으로 디자인 구성을 하면서도, 그것들이 오프라인 전시공간에서도 잘 적용되기를 바랐습니다. 버튼이자 창인 이 블록은 온라인 플랫폼에서 기능, 구조, 디스플레이의 다중적인 역할을 하는 것이었고, 나아가 전시 디자인에서는 마치 플랫폼의 오프라인 런칭 이벤트의 분위기를 만들어내는 명확한 브랜드 아이덴티티로 활용할 수 있다고 생각했습니다.

한편, 온라인 플랫폼의 초평면적인 디자인을 전시 공간에서는 디자인할 대상의 활용성에 따라 다양한 물성으로 부풀려보고 싶었습니다. 그래서 어두운 화면에서 빛나고 있는 한글 로고타입 간판이나, 물리적으로 클릭하고 싶은 두께를 가진 작품 설명이 담긴 버튼, 6전시장에서 지하로 진입하는 길을 밝혀주는 영문 로고타입 간판, 집이라는 뉘앙스를 강하게 풍기는 발 매트 등 다양한 물질성을 강조하게 되었어요. 나아가 그런 아이템들은 각각의 소주제를 통과하는 기분과 함께 소장품들로부터 환대받고 있다는 초대의 메시지를 담은 것이었습니다. 영상이 많은 현대미술 전시장은 특히, 영상이 재생되고 있는 중간에 관객이 난입하는 느낌을 받는 경우가 많기 때문에, 그런 환대의 느낌을 주는 것이 필요하다고 판단했습니다.

like the dynamic changes of a streaming service. The three major colors (which were chosen based on web standards, so in hex color code terms they're "ff4800," "009bd9," and "00ffce") are different color types so they make a colorful combination, but they also have similar saturation and brightness levels, so they really stand out as they compete with each other. We opted for black as a background color to allow for visibility in every kind of user environment, while at the same time, providing a light mode option to leave some room for sensations that depart from the design intent.

KT: I found it interesting how you started out with an online focus, but with the modularization of things like buttons and other visible elements, they are used in different ways between the online platform and offline exhibition venue. I'd like to hear more about the potential for expanded uses, such as the intersection between online and offline.

WORKS: The priority in our design composition was on the streaming platform, but we also wanted these things to fit well within the offline exhibition space. As both buttons and windows, the blocks played multiple roles on the online platform in terms of features, structures, and display. In the exhibition design, we thought they might also be used as a clear brand identity, evoking an atmosphere akin to the platform's offline launch event.

At the same time, we wanted the online platform's ultra-flat design to be something that could be expanded into different kinds of materiality in the exhibition space, depending on the use of the object being designed. So we ended up accentuating the different material qualities: the Korean-language logotype signage that glows against the dark background, the buttons with the names of artworks presented with a thickness that makes you want to physically click on them, the English-language logotype signage showing the way to the basement level in Gallery 6, and the floor mat buttons that convey a strong sense of "hominess." These items were to evoke the feelings of going through the different subtopics, expressing an inviting message of being "welcomed"

권: 디자인에서 관객의 경험이 세심하게 고려되는 지점이 중요한 것으로 보입니다. 그런 관점은 온라인 플랫폼에서도 드러나는데요. 가장 먼저, 작품을 보기 위해서 독특한 질문들과 함께 회원가입을 요구하는 사용자 경험이 재미있다고 생각했습니다.

WORKS: 최근 부각되는 '개인화' 기능에 호응하기 위해 가입 절차에 질문을 넣어 사용자가 고른 선택지에 따라 다른 기본 프로필이 부여되도록 했어요. 그렇게 만들어진 프로필 이미지는 네 가지 소주제와도 연결됩니다. 그 이후에 작품을 보기 위한 절차는 가장 직관적이고 단순하게 만들었습니다. 현대미술을 개인적 공간에서 편안하게 접근하여 감상할 수 있다는 컨셉트를 잘 살리는 것이 중요했죠. '나의 리스트' 기능도 사용할 수 있는데, 방대한 양의 데이터 사이를 돌아다니는 사용자들에게 일종의 데이터 안내자 역할이 될 수 있다고 생각했습니다. '워치 앤 칠'의 데이터가 그렇게 방대하다고 할 수는 없지만, 그래도 개인 리스트 기능을 통해서 큐레이션으로 묶인 소주제 분류를 거치지 않고, 바로 원하는 작품으로 접속할 수 있도록 하는 여지를 마련한 것으로 봐주시면 좋겠습니다.

권: 온라인 플랫폼에서 시각적으로 가장 눈에 띄는 것은 역시 커다란 버튼들이었어요.

WORKS: '워치 앤 칠'은 다음 시즌을 기약하는 플랫폼입니다. 시즌마다 새로운 주제로 큐레이팅을 하기 때문에, 주제에 대한 인상적인 안내가 필요했습니다. 하나의 화면에 각 소주제를 보여주는 내용 이외의 것들은 모두 걷어냈죠. 더 나아가, 그것이 소주제를 강조하기 위한 버튼이라고 여겨지지 않을 만큼, 버튼과 전체 화면 사이의 여백을 매우 가깝게 조정했습니다. 그런 디자인을 통해 그것은 버튼으로 보일 수도, 화면 자체를 아예 소주제의 갯수에 따라 분할한 것으로 보일 수도 있지요.

권: 플랫폼과 연계된 텍스트를 읽을 수 있는 ‹나만 아는 이야기›가 하단에 팝업을 요청하는 창으로 존재하는 것도 흥미로웠습니다.

WORKS: '워치 앤 칠' 메인 프로젝트와 위성 프로젝트의 관계 설정을 시각화할 수 있는 전략이었습니다. 하단에

by the exhibited media collections. There are a lot of video works in contemporary exhibitions that make you feel like barging into the middle of a video that's already playing. So we felt like that kind of welcoming feeling was essential.

KT: I'd like to explore the online platform in a bit more detail. To begin with, I found the user experience quite Interesting—how it asks you intriguing questions before signing up, so you can view the artworks.

WORKS: The approach of including questions in the signup process and assigning a different basic profile according to the user's answers was our response to the kinds of "personalization" features that have really been emphasized these days. The resulting profile image connects with one of the four subtopics. We tried to make the following process for viewing the artwork as simple and intuitive as possible. It was important to really highlight the idea of being able to access and view contemporary art at ease in your own personal space. There's also a "My List" feature you can use, which we felt could be a kind of "data guide" for users who wander around amid all these vast volumes of data. We wouldn't describe the amount of data in *Watch and Chill* as "vast," but you can see the personal list feature as leaving room for the users to access the artwork they want right away, without going through the curated subtopic categories.

KT: Visually speaking, the large buttons were what really leaped out at me.

WORKS: *Watch and Chill* is a platform that promises to come back "next season." The curation is based on a new theme each season, so there needed to be a striking introduction to the theme. We stripped away everything from the screen but the content that shows the different subtopics. We adjusted it to make the space extremely close between the buttons and the overall screen, so that they aren't being seen as buttons to emphasize the subtopics. With that design, they could be seen as buttons, or they could be seen as dividing the screen up based on the number of subtopics.

KT: I also found it interesting how the *The Tales I Tell* part— where you can read texts related to the platform—was presented as a pop-up request window at the bottom.

위치하지만, 페이지를 로딩했을 때 우측에서 화면 안으로 들어오는 애니메이션으로 존재감을 드러냈죠. 글의 분량을 고려해 사용하고 있는 기기의 디스플레이 폭을 모두 활용할 수 있도록, 팝업창에서 벗어나 새 창으로 읽을 수 있는 기능도 포함해두었습니다.

권: 첫 번째 '워치 앤 칠'에서 파생된 데이터들을 정리하며 특별히 포착되었던 것이 사용자들의 압도적인 모바일 접근 비율이었습니다. 영상 작품을 보는 플랫폼임에도 데스크톱이나 태블릿보다 모바일 접근이 훨씬 더 많았는데, 관련해서 고려할 수 있는 지점이 있을까요?

WORKS: 모바일 접근의 비율이 높을 것이라고 짐작은 했습니다. 하지만, 사실 이 정도로 높을지는 몰랐죠. 그렇기에 이번 온라인 플랫폼에서도 모바일 사용성에 대한 고려는 당연히 주요한 과제였습니다. 그러나 영상 작품을 위한 플랫폼이기에 데스크톱에서의 웹 접속을 기본적으로 고려하여 만들긴 했습니다. 모바일 웹과 데스크톱 웹의 가장 큰 차이는 화면비 문제에 있습니다. 대부분 모바일 매체 환경에서는 세로 방향으로 보기 때문에 스크롤 등 인터페이스 구성에서 고려할 요소가 많죠. 그에 따라 세로가 긴 화면비와 상하 스크롤이 익숙한 사용자를 생각하여, 모바일에서는 인터페이스 요소들이 아래로 쌓이는 모습의 세로 방향 레이아웃을 강조했습니다. 메인 화면의 '워치 앤 칠' 로고도 화면비에 따라 세로형, 가로형을 나누어 만들어 놓았죠.

모바일은 디스플레이 기기의 물리적 크기가 작고, 사용자와 기기 간의 거리가 가깝다는 점도 큰 특징입니다. 화면 크기가 작은 만큼 글꼴 크기와 이미지를 축소하고 마진 영역을 줄여 좀 더 압축적으로 구성해야 했죠. 그럼에도 작은 화면 크기와 좁은 세로 폭 때문에 다른 방법으로 해결 방법이 필요할 때가 많았습니다. 그럴 때에는 요소들을 접거나 숨기는 방식을 사용했어요. 예를 들어, 작품 페이지에서 소주제 설명글이 너무 길어지면서 작품이 화면 아래로 내려가버리는 상황을 방지하기 위해 설명글에 '더 보기' 버튼을 넣어 글을 생략하고, 상단의 여러 기능들은 하나로 모아 메뉴바로 만들었습니다.

WORKS: That was a strategy to establish and visualize a relationship between *Watch and Chill*, the main project and the satellite project. It's located at the bottom, but we also played up its presence by using animation, where it would move into the screen from the right when the page is loaded. We also included a feature where you could leave the pop-up window and read in a new window, which would allow for the full use of the display scope of the user's device, taking into account the length of the texts.

KT: As we were going through the data produced by the first *Watch and Chill*, one thing that really stood out was the huge amount of mobile access by users. Even though it's a platform for viewing video works, there were a lot more people accessing it through mobile devices rather than desktops or tablets. Are there any aspects you might have considered in connection with that?

WORKS: We anticipated there would be a high rate of mobile access. To be honest, we had no idea it would be that high. So it was obviously crucial for us to consider mobile use for this online platform. Since it's a platform for video work, however, we considered web access on a desktop computer as the default when we were making it. The biggest difference between the mobile web and the desktop web has to do with the screen ratios. With most mobile media environments, you're looking at things vertically, so there are a lot of elements to consider in terms of the interface design, such as scrolling. So we imagined users who were used to long vertical screen ratios and scrolling up and down. That is why, for the mobile environment, we emphasized a vertically oriented layout where the interface elements accumulate toward the bottom. For the *Watch and Chill* logo on the main screen, we made vertical and horizontal forms to suit the different screen ratios.

Other big characteristics of mobile devices include the small physical size of the display device and the close distance between the user and the device. Since the screen is so small, we had to condense it a bit by reducing the size of the text and images and shrinking the margins. Even so, there were a lot of times when we needed to find other solutions due to the small screen size and narrow vertical dimensions. In those cases, we used approaches like folding or

모바일에서는 클릭이 아닌 터치라는 점도 편의성 부분에서 중요한 지점입니다. 마우스에 비해 손은 입력 부분이 넓기 때문에 링크나 버튼 사이 간격이 넓어야 해요. 그래서 메뉴와 푸터 부분을 보면 데스크톱에 비해 조금 넓은 사이 공간이 마련되어 있기도 합니다.

　권: '워치 앤 칠'이 글로벌 프로젝트였던 만큼, 사용자 통계 데이터에서 정말로 다양한 국가에서 접속한 기록이 확인되기도 했습니다.

WORKS: 온라인 플랫폼은 영문 페이지와 함께 만들어져 해외 사용자 접근성에 대한 고려가 기본에 깔려 있었습니다. 포스트 팬데믹 상황에서 물리적 한계와 국경을 넘어 예술적 교류와 네트워크를 확장하기 위한 프로젝트였기에 당연한 것이었죠. 앞으로도 이러한 요소를 고려하여 직관적인 사용자 경험이나, 더욱 다양한 번역에 대한 고려가 이루어진다면 더 좋을 것으로 생각합니다.

　권: 다채로운 관점에서 꼼꼼히 설계된 온라인 플랫폼의 디자인에 대한 이야기를 들으니, 다음 시즌이 더 기대되네요. 이렇게 이야기 나누어주셔서 정말 감사합니다.

concealing elements. For example, because the subtopic explanations on the artwork page are so long, we reduced the size by adding a "read more" button in order to prevent the sort of situation where one of the works extends down below the screen. We also created a menu bar, where we brought together the different features at the top.

Another key thing about mobile devices in terms of convenience is that they use touching rather than clicking. Compared with a mouse, fingers have a wider pressure distribution, so the spaces between links and buttons need to be large. So if you look at the menu and footer sections, there's a somewhat broader space there compared with the desktop version.

　KT: *Watch and Chill* was a global project, and our user data also showed people accessing it from a really wide range of countries.

WORKS: One of the basic considerations with the online platform was accessibility for users in different countries, since there was also an English-language version of the page. It is only natural because this was a project aimed at expanding artistic interchange and networks across physical constraints and borders in the post-pandemic era. I think it could be even better in the future to have an intuitive user experience in view of those elements, or consideration for an even broader range of translations.

　KT: Now that I've heard you talked about the online platform design and how it was so meticulously done, based on so many different perspectives, I'm looking forward even more to the next season. Thank you so much for sharing.

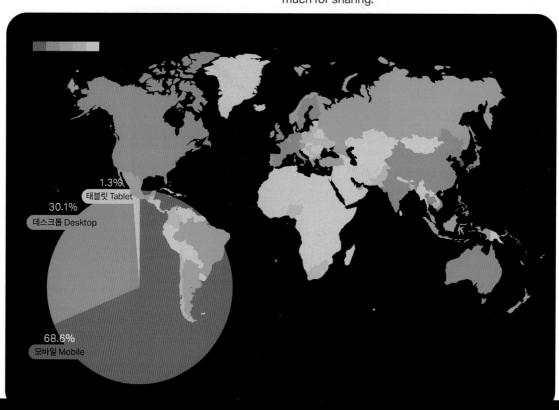

1.3%
태블릿 Tablet

30.1%
데스크톱 Desktop

68.6%
모바일 Mobile

나만
The Tales
아는
I Tell
이야기

'집'에 대한 소고
집은 아직 준비되지 않았다

윤향로(작가)

나에게 집은 집일뿐이었다. 십 대 때에는 입시 때문에 늘 새벽에 들어왔고, 이십 대에는 학교 실기실이나 작업실에서 자는 일이 많았다. 집에서 지내는 것보다 밖에서 동료들, 친구들과 시간을 보내는 것이 더 신났다. 그렇게 나에게 집은 잠을 자는 곳 이상의 의미가 없었고, 잠만 잘 수 있으면 작업실, 레지던시, 그 어디든 집으로 여겼다.

나는 2019년 결혼했고, 처음으로 내가 만드는 집에 대해 생각했다. 사실 좀 막막했다. 그때까지 원하는 집의 모습을 고민한 적 없으니까. 심지어 내가 첫 집을 고르게 되었는데, 작업실과 가까운 아파트 중에서 두 가지 기준으로 하나를 골랐다: 탁 트인 풍경. 청소하기 편한 크기. 가구를 고를 때에도 평소 의자나 조명을 수집해온 남편은 어려움을 느끼지 않았지만, 나는 어딘가 현실적이었다. 뭐랄까, 이 모든 과정이 나에겐 심즈The Sims [1]에 로그인 해 이미 지어진 집을 하나 고르는 것 같았다. 자, 집은 골랐고, 앉으려면 의자가 필요하지? 그럼 이 의자를 여기다 두자, 이렇게.

나는 그해 11월 출산을 했다. 그런데 그해 12월 31일, 중국에서 원인 불명의 폐렴이 잇따라 발병되고 있다는 기사를 보았고, 2020년 3월 11일, 세계보건기구에서 코로나19 팬데믹을 선언했다. 각국의 인사들이 외쳤다. "Stay Home. The World Was Not Prepared for Covid-19." 유아기를 제외하고, 내 인생 어느 때보다 오래 집에서 머물렀고, 이 상황이 얼마나 계속될지 알 수 없었다. 집에 갇힌 나는 스마트폰에 매달렸다. 처음 접하는 고강도 풀타임 노동 사이의 짧고 달콤한 휴식 때문일까, 나만 뒤처지는 것 같은 초조함 때문이었을까. 나는 실시간으로 업로드되는 소식들에 집착했고, 그만큼 집중력은 떨어지고 불안감은 커졌다. 내가 선택한 우리의 집에서 가족과 함께 했지만 집에서 보내는 시간이 길어질수록 괴로웠다.

나에게도 시간이 흘러 드디어 육아 선배들이 말하는 백일의 기적이 일어났고, 조금 정신을 차려 몇 개의 소셜 미디어를 탈퇴했다. 그제야 나에게 집을 둘러볼 여유가 생겼다. 가구의 위치를 바꿔보기도 하고, 고치거나 사고 싶은 것도 생겼다. 여전히 심즈의 건축물 속이지만 이제야 진심을 다해 고민해 원하는 형태로 플레이하는 것 같다. 물론 여전히 정신없다. 아이는 집안일을 끊임없이 리셋해주고, 남편과 일정이 꼬이면 공부, 회의, 강의, 심지어 작업 에스키스도 집에서 해야 한다. 집에 있는 게 답답할 때도 있지만 생의 감각을 느낄 때도 많아졌다.

나는 최근에 가족들과 우리가 살아갈 집에 대해 이야기했다. 결혼 전까지 내가 아는 이상적인 집은 도널드 저드Donald Judd의 101 스프링 스트릿 집101 Spring Street뿐이었다. 그런데 계단이 가팔라 힘들 것 같고, 1층에서 작업하면 저드처럼 기웃거리는 사람들

[1] 맥시스(Maxis)가 개발하고 일렉트로닉 아츠(Electronic Arts)가 배급한 생활 시뮬레이션 비디오 게임 시리즈

A Note on "Home"
The Home Is Not Prepared

Yoon Hyang-ro (Artist)

To me, home was just home. During my teens, I always came in at dawn because of the entrance exams, and in my twenties, I often slept at the school's or personal studio space. It was more exciting to spend time outside with colleagues and friends than to stay at home. Hence, to me, home meant nothing more than a place to sleep, and I regarded any place home as long as I could sleep in it, such as my studio and artist residency.

I got married in 2019, and thought about making a home and for the first time. I was actually at a loss, because I had never thought about what kind of home I wanted until then. As I was the one that got to choose our first house, I chose one of the apartments near my studio based on two criteria: an open view, and a size easy to clean. Even when choosing furniture, while my husband who had at times collected chairs and lighting equipment didn't have any difficulty, I was somewhat realistic. Somehow, this whole process felt like logging into The Sims[1] and choosing a pre-built house. Okay, now you picked a house, need a chair to sit on? Then let's put this chair here.

I gave birth in November of that year. But the same year on December 31st, I saw an article on consecutive cases of pneumonia of unknown cause occurring in China, and on March 11, 2020, the World Health Organization declared the Covid-19 pandemic. Figures from all over the world shouted: "Stay Home. The World Was Not Prepared for Covid-19." Besides my infancy, I was staying at home longer than at any other time in my life, without knowing how long this would last. Stuck at home, I clang to my smartphone. Was it because of the short sweet breaks between the high-intensity full-time labor that I was encountering for the first time, or was it because of the anxious feeling that I was lagging behind? I obsessed over real time online news, and this dropped my concentration and increased my anxiety. Though I was with my family in the house of my choosing, the longer I spent at home, the more painful it became.

Time passed by, and the miracle of one hundred days that parents speak of finally happened to me as well, and I came to my senses and quit some of the social media. Finally, I had time to look around the house. I tried rearranging furniture, and there came to be things I wanted to fix or buy. It seems as though while I'm still inside the Sims' architecture, I am finally giving it wholehearted thought and playing the way I want. Of course it's still crazy. The baby constantly resets the household chores, and if the schedule with my husband gets messed up, I have to do study, meetings, lectures, and even sketches for my artworks at home. It can be stifling to be home, but there are also many instances when I feel the sense of life.

[1]   Life simulation video game series developed by Maxis and published by Electronic Arts

Recently, I talked with my family about the home we will live in. Before getting married, the only ideal home I ever knew was Donald Judd's

때문에 스트레스 받을 것 같다. 창이 많아서 냉난방비도 많이 들 것 같고, 작품이 상하지 않으려면 좋은 유리가 필요하겠다. 저드처럼 침실에 친구들 작품이 많으면 이상하려나? 너무 미술가를 위한 집 같긴 하다. 그럼 또 어떤 형태의 집이 있을까? 남편은 집을 짓자고 하는데, 내가 지은 집은 어떤 모습일까? 그리고 나는 그 집에서 행복할까? 끝나지 않은 팬데믹과 함께 나의 집은 아직 준비 중이다.

W&C next available video work by Koo Donghee, 2021. 9. 17. [2021][09][17][금] ∨
오후 4시 공개 작품 Available at 4 PM KST, September 17, 2021.

작업실에 있다가 구동희의 〈타가수분〉(2016)을 관람할 수 있다는 이메일을 받았다. 2016년 가을인가, 로얄&컴퍼니 복합 문화공간에 있는 갤러리 로얄에서 열린 구동희 개인전에서 본 영상 설치와 소파가 떠올랐다. 변기 등의 욕실 관련 제품들이 전시된 쇼룸을 지나 계단으로 올라가면 등장하는 넓은 마루 한 컨 어둡게 연출된 공간에 서있는 스크린과 다인용 소파. 전시를 보다가 화장실에 갔는데, 내가 지금 욕실 전문 기업 건물 안에 있음을 확실하게 인지할 수 있었던 그곳. 생경한 모습의 전시장에서 일상과 비일상의 경계가 중요하게 여겨지지 않은 구동희의 작업을 보니, 작품 속 이미지들이 서로 조금씩 드러낸 피부를 맞대고 앉아있는 것 같았다.

　　　　나는 보수적인 관객이라서 비메오나 유튜브 같은 플랫폼에서 영상 작품을 보는 것을 좋아하지 않았다. 넷플릭스처럼 자막 언어를 선택하거나, 내가 평소에 사용하는 텔레비전이나 컴퓨터로 미술 작품을 관람하는 것을 상상한 적도 없다. 코로나19 초기부터 작품을 온라인에서 감상하는 다양한 시도가 있었지만, 작가와 기획자가 연출한 물리적 공간에서 작품을 감상하는 것이 최선이라고 믿었다. 설치 형식이 작품의 수준을 결정짓는 요소라고, 전시에 대한 물리적, 신체적 감상이 작업의 완성이라고 생각했다. 그래서 구동희의 이 전시와 작품에 대해 특별하게 기억하고 있다.

　　　　코로나19 팬데믹이 공표된 지 1년 반. 오늘 나는 생애 처음으로 새벽 다섯 시에 눈을 떴을 때 무엇이든 영상 작품을 하나 감상하고 싶다는 생각을 했다. 집안의 모든 창을 열고 멀리서 들리는 경적, 바람과 풀벌레 소리를 들으며 소파에 앉았다. 이는 요즘 내가 가장 집중할 수 있는 시공간이다. 무릎 위에 올린 맥북으로 영상 작품의 재생 버튼을 누르는 순간 영상 어딘가에서 뽑아낸 대표 이미지가 사라지고 (전시장과 달리) 작업이 처음부터 재생된다. 놀랍게도 내 안의 모든 감각들이 날카롭게 살아났고 이 감각의 총체는 작품을 너무나 입체적으로, 실감나게 경험하게 했다. 이 경험은 예상보다 훨씬 깊고 짜릿했다.

　　　　영상 작품을 전시장이 아닌 다른 방식으로 보는 내게 소설을 읽는 것과 비슷한 감각이라 느껴진다. 내가 앉아있거나 서있는 시공간이 내가 설정하는 감각과 장소로 바뀌고, 매체에 다이빙하는 것. 네트에 액세스. 그 몰입은 쉽게 깨질 수도 있고, 오랜 시간 지속될 수도 있는데, 이는 나의 경험치와 집중력 등에 따라 언제든 설정을 변경할 수 있는 종류의 감각이다. 게다가 주변 설정을 바꿔가며 다양한 경로로 진입해 감상하는 방식은 또 다른 작품의 방향성과 해석의 여지를 보여주었고, 감각을 확장하는 통로가 되었다.

　　　　모든 상황을 통제하며 한 가지 방향으로 감상의 경로와 방식을 설정해 작품을 관객에게 제시할 수 없는 것처럼, 이제 미술 작품 감상의 진입 경로를 통제하는 것은 무의미하다. 과거보다 다양해진 감상의 방식은 이제 각자의 세계에서 각자의 물아일체를

101 Spring Street. But it's stairs are too steep for comfort, and should I work on the first floor, I would be stressed out just like Judd because of people peeping in. Its many windows would raise the heating and cooling costs, and would have to be good glass to prevent damage to the artwork. Would it be weird to have a lot of artwork by friends in the bedroom as did Judd? Guess it's too much like an artist's home. So what other forms of houses are there? My husband says we should build a house, but what will such house look like? And would I be happy in that house? With the ongoing pandemic, my home is still being prepared.

W&C next available video work by Koo Donghee Fri Sep 17 2021 ∨
Available at 4 PM KST, September 17, 2021.

I received an email while I was at my studio, saying that I could watch Koo Donghee's *Cross×Pollination* (2016). The video installation and sofa I saw in Koo Donghee's solo exhibition, held at Gallery Royal in the Royal&Co multi-cultural space in the fall of 2016, came to mind. Up the stairs after passing the showroom where bathroom products such as toilets are displayed, stood a screen and a multi-seat sofa in a darkened space on one side of the wide floor. The place where, when I went to the bathroom while at the exhibition, I could clearly recognize I was inside the building of a company specializing in bathrooms. Watching Koo Donghee's work where the boundary between daily and non-daily life is considered unimportant, in an unfamiliar exhibition space, made me feel as though the images in the work were sitting close together with slightly exposed skins.

Being a conservative audience, I didn't like watching videos on platforms like Vimeo or YouTube. I have never imagined selecting a subtitle language like in Netflix or watching a work of art on a TV or a computer that I ordinarily use. Though there have been various attempts for viewing works online since the early days of Covid-19, I believed it best to view works in a physical space directed by the artists and curators. I thought that the form of installation was a determining factor of the level of the work, that the physical and bodily appreciation of the exhibition was the completion of the work. That is why I particularly remember this exhibition and work by Koo Donghee.

It's been a year and a half since the Covid-19 pandemic was declared. Today, after waking up at 5am, I felt like watching just any video work for the first time in my life. I opened all the windows in the house and sat on the sofa listening to the distant horns, the wind and the chirping of insects. This is the time and space where I can best focus these days. The moment I press the play button of the video work with the MacBook on my lap, the main picture extracted from somewhere in the video disappears (unlike at the exhibition space), and the work is played from the beginning. Surprisingly, all my inner senses sharply come to life, and the totality of these senses allow me to experience the work in a very three-dimensional and realistic way. The experience is a lot deeper and electrifying than I expected.

Viewing video works in a setting that is not the exhibition space, feels similar to reading a novel to me. Diving into the medium, with the space-time in which I sit or stand altered to the sense and place that I set up. Accessing the net. The immersion may easily break or may last for a long time, which is the kind of sense whose settings can be changed at any time according to your experience and concentration. In addition, the viewing method of entering through various paths while changing the surrounding settings showed me the possibility for different directions and interpretations of the work, becoming a way to expand the senses.

어떤 식으로 끌어낼지, 즉 어떤 조건에서도 가장 중요한 것은 관객의 몰입이라는 것이 분명해 보인다. 거대한 욕실에 들어가 그 안에 소파를 두고 전시를 보는 것 같았던 전시장에서의 〈타가수분〉 관람과 나의 집 거실 소파에 앉아 '워치 앤 칠' 웹을 통해 〈타가수분〉을 보는 경험은 마치 구동희의 작품 안에서 교차 편집되는, 이란성 쌍둥이 같은 씬scene을 보는 것 같았다. 흐릿한 경계 너머에서 대화를 주고받는 구동희의 작업처럼 어디서든 작품과 관객은 다양한 형태의 대화를 하게 되었다.

물리적 전시장이 아닌 곳에서 작품을 감상하는 50가지 방법 ［2021］［09］［24］［금］ ⌄

웹브라우저로 작품을 자막 없이 봤다.
자막을 틀고,
언어를 바꿔가며,
속도를 줄이거나 늘리고 바꾸며,
소리를 키우거나 줄이며,
음소거하고,
집에서 맥북으로,
이동 중이나 휴식 중에 아이폰으로,
스튜디오에 출근해 아이맥으로,
노이즈 캔슬링 이어폰으로,
블루투스 헤드폰으로,
컴퓨터에 내장 된 스피커로,
소파에 앉거나 누워 60인치 텔레비전으로,
스쿼트나 런지를 하며,
가정용 실내 바이크를 타며,
짐에 가서 러닝머신 휴대전화 거치대에 아이폰을 꽂고 빠르게 걸으며,
저녁 9시 아기를 재우고 아기 옆에서 소리 없이 몰래 아이폰으로,
집에서 아무도 없을 때 소리를 최대한 키워서,
중간에 멈췄던 작업을 다시 재생하고,
따뜻한 커피를 마시며, 얼음을 넣은 커피를 마시며,
점심으로 준비한 샐러드를 모니터 앞에서 먹으며,
사파리 웹 기본 화면으로 보다가 전체 화면으로 바꿔서,
화면을 최대한 작게 줄여서,
혼자 보다가 친구와 같이,
작품 링크를 친구에게 메시지로 공유하고,
작품 링크를 소셜 미디어에 공유하고,
화장실에 다녀왔다가 지나간 시간만큼 뒤로 돌려서,
산책하다가 벤치에 앉아서,
보기 싫은 마음을 억누르고 미술을 사랑하는 마음으로,
몇 번이고 반복해서,
이해가 안 되는 부분을 또 다시,
집 안의 모든 창문을 닫고,
집 안의 모든 창문을 열고,

Just as it is impossible to set a linear path and method of seeing by controlling all situations when presenting a work to the audience, it is now meaningless to control the entry point for viewing works of art. The methods of viewing that have diversified than in the past, make it clear that the most important thing is how to make each person fully absorbed from their own respective worlds, the immersion of the audience in any condition. The experience of viewing *Cross×Pollination* inside the exhibition space that felt like entering a huge bathroom with a sofa to see it, and viewing *Cross×Pollination* through the *Watch and Chill* web service while sitting on the sofa of my living room, was like watching a scene that was cross-edited inside Koo Donghee's work like fraternal twins. Just like Koo Donghee's work that converse across blurred boundaries, the works and the viewers have come to engage in various forms of conversation wherever they are.

50 Ways to View Art Outside of Physical Exhibition Space   Fri Sep 24 2021 ∨

Watched the work in a web browser without subtitles.
Turned on the subtitles,
changed the language,
slowed and fastened the speed,
increased or decreased the sound,
muted,
used MacBook at home,
and iPhone while moving or resting,
iMac when at the studio,
with noise canceling earphones,
Bluetooth headphones,
or the computer's built-in speakers,
on a 60-inch TV while sitting or lying on the sofa,
doing squats or lunges,
riding an indoor exercise bike,
or at the gym, walking fast on the treadmill with my iPhone on its phone stand,
secretly on a muted iPhone at 9pm next to the baby after putting it to sleep,
as loud as possible when no one is at home,
resuming a work on hold,
drinking hot coffee, or drinking coffee with ice,
eating the salad prepared for lunch in front of the monitor,
viewing in Safari's default web screen, then changing to full screen,
reducing the screen as small as possible,
viewing alone, then with friends,
sharing the video link with friends via text,
sharing the video link via social media,
rewinding it as much as the time that passed while at the bathroom,
sitting on a bench while taking a walk,
suppressing the urge not to see with a loving mind for art,
repeating again and again,
replaying the part that I don't understand,
with all windows closed,
with all windows open,
while watching on my iPhone, thinking I should watch this on TV,
while watching on my laptop at home, thinking I should watch it at the studio.
waiting for a better time to focus,

아이폰으로 보다가 안 되겠다, 이건 텔레비전으로 봐야겠다,

집에서 노트북으로 보다가 이건 작업실에 가서 봐야겠다,

더 집중할 수 있는 시간을 기다렸다가,

스타벅스에 앉아 마스크를 쓰고,

작업실로 돌아와 마스크를 벗고,

집에 돌아와 씻고 편한 옷으로 갈아입고,

잠자리에 들기 전 불현듯 생각나서,

아이폰에서 다른 화면으로 미러링해서,

전시에서 본 작업을 다른 매체로 다시,

화면을 바라보지 않고 소리만,

일단 틀어놓고 다른 일을 하며 슬쩍,

맥북 배터리가 나가서 다른 기기를 찾아,

다른 기기도 모두 꺼져서 충전하기 위해 기다렸다가,

영상을 보다 갑작스럽게 울린 초인종에 놀라 쏟은 커피를 수습하고,

문을 열어 세탁물을 받아 잠시 어딘가에 걸어두고,

갑작스런 방문객을 차단하기 위해 문을 잠그고 다시,

우선 어떻게든 다시.

위안 광밍, 〈주거〉(2014)　　　　　　　　　　　　　2021 09 30 목 ∨

물에 잠긴 거실의 시간이 부유한다. 벽에 걸린 시계는 제 기능을 잃고 특정 구간을
반복하며 일상의 감각이 작동하는 것을 방해한다. 물속의 청각 같다. 화면의 움직임을
좇으면 고속 카메라로 촬영했다는 것, 이케아에서 살 수 있을 법한 가구들이 실제
스케일이 아니라는 점을 발견할 수 있다. 물속에 잠긴 거실의 사물들은 부유하는 시간
속에서 유영하다 폭발한다. 그리고 폭발은 시간을 붙잡으려는 듯, 모든 일을 취소하는
것처럼 다시 사그라든다. 그렇게 물속의 거실은 폭발과 아무 일도 없었던 것처럼
돌아오기를 반복한다.

　　　　　이 작품을 보고 미켈란젤로 안토니오니Michelangelo Antonioni의 영화
〈자브리스키 포인트〉(1970)의 마지막 장면이 떠올랐다. 이야기의 흐름이나 현실과
관계없이 낭만적으로 그려지는 폭발과 그 파편의 아름다움. 내 앞의 사물이 아니라
스크린 너머라는 거리감 속에서 느끼는 어떤 희열. 화려한 시각적 효과와 어쩌면
우리에게 너무 가까워진 파괴의 미학.

　　　　　현실의 폭발은 다르다. 폭발이 일어난 장소가 환기되지 않는 곳이면 길게는
일주일까지 들어갈 수 없다. 방독면을 쓰고도 앞이 보이지 않아 그을음, 연기,
유독가스를 모두 제거해야 한다. 폭발의 원인을 모를 경우 국립과학수사연구원에서
원인을 찾을 때까지 기다려야 한다. 폭발 뒤에는 해결해야 할 일이 너무 많고 금전적
손실뿐 아니라 시간적, 정신적 손실까지 감당해야 한다. 그런데 그런 폭발을 실제로
경험한 순간에 나도 까맣게 뒤덮인 잿더미 앞에서 어떤 아름다움 느꼈다.

　　　　　영화 〈인셉션〉(2010)에서 앨런 페이지가 연기한 아리아드네가 설계한
꿈속에서 등장하는 폭발 장면은 파리에서 촬영했다. 파리 시내에서 실제 폭발물을
사용할 수 없어 고압의 공기를 이용해 폭발 장면처럼 보이도록 물건을 내뿜었다고 한다.
그래서일까, 이 영화의 폭발은 다른 어떤 영화보다 현실과 거리가 멀고, 완벽하게

Was it when we participated in *The Song of Slant Rhymes* exhibition held at the Kukje Gallery that I first saw this work? *Sleepwalkers* (2009) was your first work that I saw, and as with the *Fog and Smoke*, I was impressed by its tap dancing scene. The sense that my body temperature seems to drop lower the louder the sound of metal striking the asphalt or the building floor becomes, unlike that of the sweating dancer. The feeling of being left alone in the cold air, on a midsummer morning at 5am, when all the streetlights are out just before sunrise. I got goosebumps by the sound of tap dancing reverberating through the empty city, but I think it was closer to joy than fear. Multiple senses fit together simultaneously like pieces of a puzzle, so I came to wonder how tenaciously this artist looks at the world.

I think I began to like your work from then on. The sounds and scenes of tap dancing have become an image that often comes to mind in my daily life. Oh, and come to think of it, it is said a skilled person dancing in tap shoes can make four different sounds depending on the movement, and hearing that makes the recurring appearance of Songdo New town, the person performing a tap dance, news sounds, and the voice of the interviewee in the work each come to mind as a note.

In September, I went to the Museum of Modern and Contemporary Art, Seoul to see the exhibition, *Watch and Chill: Streaming Art to Your Homes*, and the only work I saw again multiple times was *Ellie's Eye* (2020). The two channel video installation seemed to show how technology related to visual perception develops and what kind of desire exists behind such technology, and through the two gazing eyes facing the same direction, how visual perception and awareness cannot exist separately.

Actually, while watching *Ellie's Eye*, I thought of my dog that passed away 4 years ago. Sunnie was blind for half of her 16 years with me due to cataracts. It was difficult to suppress my emotions as I remembered me and my family's failure to preserve her eyesight due to ignorance, and her sufferings from many diseases until the end.

I think I'm drawn to the kind of beauty and solidity that I'm unable to create when watching your work. A refined way of expressing anger, an effective expression that conveys emptiness, an attitude free of raw desire. Was it at TIFY in Buam-dong that we last came across? I would like to hear more about the loneliness and emptiness, cities and humans that you think of. I hope to be able to talk with you someday.

Yoon Hyang-ro ⓘ
Artist

Yoon Hyang-ro explores the possibility of abstract painting based on contemporary imaging technology. Her representative "Screenshot" work series have been presented in various medium such as painting, print, sculpture, video, furniture, and installation under the name of "pseudo painting." Recently, she is attempting works that deal with images of historical works of art in multiple layers. She's had solo exhibitions such as *Canvases* (Hakgojae Gallery, Seoul, 2020), *Surflatpictor* (P21, Seoul, 2018), and *Liquid Rescale* (Doosan Gallery, New York, 2017), and participated in group exhibitions such as *Gwangju Biennale: Imagined Borders* (Gwangju Biennale, 2018), *O philoi, oudeis philos* (Atelier Hermes, 2017). She has also co-curated exhibitions and events such as *Goods* (Sejong Center, 2015) and *Watch Yourself* (Gallery 175, 2013).

'집'에 대한 소고
발코니와 거실 사이

이기리(시인)

얼마 전부터 집이 좁다고 느껴지기 시작했다. 장소에게 잘못이나 책임을 묻고 싶진 않다. 그것은 장소의 문제가 아니라 장소에 위치해 생활하는 주체의 문제다. 내 방은 터지기 일보 직전이다. 더 이상 책을 둘 데가 없기 때문이다. 책장에 꽂혀 있는 책들 위로 또 다른 책들이 틈을 비집고 놓여 있는 것은 기본이고 무슨 책이 꽂혀 있는지 볼 수 없을 만큼 그 앞에 두꺼운 책들이 쌓여 있기도 하다. 포화 상태인 책장을 벗어나 책을 둘 자리가 필요하여 크기가 작은 책장을 하나 들였으나 이것도 순식간에 다 채웠다. 침대 밑 세 개의 서랍 중 하나의 서랍을 통째로 비워 다 읽은 책들을 집어넣었다. 그렇게 얼추 정리했다고 생각이 들었지만 아직도 침대 위엔 작업하는 원고들과 읽지 못한 책들이 널브러져 있다. 책상은 보고만 있어도 어지럽다. 내 방은 어느덧 죽은 책들의 공동묘지가 되어가고 있었다.

　　그리하여 도저히 숨을 쉴 수가 없을 때, 거실로 나온다. 창밖으로는 맑은 날씨가 펼쳐진다. 바로 앞에 뻗어 있는 나무들이 흰빛을 받으며 일렁이는 그림자를 길가에 둔 채 흔들리고 있다. 가끔 참새가 앉았다 간다. 참새를 보낸 나뭇가지는 잠깐 몸을 부르르 떨다 멈춘다. 나는 고요한 집 안에서도 바깥의 풍경을 오롯이 볼 수 있고 나무의 움직임을 보며 바람의 세기를 느낄 수 있다. 오후 두 시쯤 우리 집에서 내다보는 세계는 비현실적으로 조용해서 모든 소리가 사라져 마지막으로 남은 단 하나의 장면만이 정지된 채 멎은 것 같다.

　　사람들은 흔적도 없이 깔끔하게 사라진 것 같다. 나는 발코니와 거실 사이에서 이 세계의 유일한 생존자처럼 행동한다. 그것은 바로 음악을 하는 것이다. 노래를 부르고 연주를 한다. 발코니에 있는 전자 피아노를 연주하고 거실에 있는 기타를 연주한다. 피아노와 기타 사이에 내가 있다. 피아노를 연주하는 나와 기타를 연주하는 나 사이에 빛을 밟고 서 있는 내가 있다. 음악과 음악 사이에 텅 빈 고요가 있다.

　　집 안을 배회하는 시간이 길어지면서 내부에 배치되어 있는 사물들에 관해 관심을 갖기 시작했다. 사용자에 의해 가장 익숙한 자리에 위치되고 어느덧 한 공간을 점유하는 모습이 선연한 공포로 다가왔다. 마치 창밖으로 마주한 아무도 없는 세계처럼. 내가 이곳을 좀체 벗어나지 못하고 있다는 감각을 끌어안으며 소파에 누우면 불현듯 죽음 이후의 나를 상상해보는 것처럼.

　　또한 내부와 외부의 경계가 점점 분명해지고 있었다. 예전에는 집을 외부의 타성에 젖은 내부로 사유하곤 했는데 현 시대에서 더 이상 이 사유는 개진하기 힘들어 보인다. 왜냐하면 지금은 집이야말로 가장 안전하고 철저히 고립된 공간이기 때문이다. 그렇다. 이제는 완전한 고립을 느끼는 중이다. 소리를 하나둘 떠나보내고 있다. 나밖에 없다. 아무도 없다. 나는 누구에게도 발견되지 못한다. 그렇다면 나는 지금 어떤 존재로 이 세계를 살아가는 중인가. 졸린 눈을 반쯤 치켜든 채 발코니와 거실 사이를 떠도는 시체인가. 음악이 필요하다.

Reflecting on "Home"
Between the Balcony and the Living Room

Lee Gi-ri (Poet)

Not long ago, I started to see my home as cramped. I'm not finding fault with the place or trying to hold it to account. It's not a matter of the place, but one of the person living in it. My bedroom is just about to burst at its seams. I have no place left there to put my books. It's the norm for me to have some books in my bookcase, and then other books wedged in over top of them. There's also a pile of thick books in front, so that I can't even see which books have been shelved in the first place. I needed somewhere to put books outside of that jam-packed bookcase, so I got another smaller bookcase, but that one too filled up almost immediately. I emptied out one of the three drawers under my bed and started using it to hold the books I'd finished. I thought that might have taken care of it, but you can still see the manuscripts I'm working on and the unread books strewn out over my bed. Even the sight of my desk leaves me feeling dizzy. My bedroom is turning into a cemetery for dead books.

When I find I can't breathe in there, I head out into the living room. Outside the window, the clear skies are outstretched. In front of me are trees that sway, the white light casting their rippling shadows onto the side of the road. Sometimes a sparrow will perch in one and then fly on its way. As the branches release the birds, they quiver momentarily before coming to a stop. Even in the tranquility of my home, I can see all of the landscape outside, sensing the force of the wind as I notice the trees' movement. The world that I see from my house around two in the afternoon is unreally quiet, the sounds disappearing until it seems to like a single remaining scene that has come to a stop. It is as though the people have gone without a trace. I act as though I am the only surviving person in this world between the balcony and living room—which is to say that I perform music. I sing and play instruments. I play the electronic keyboard on the balcony, and I strum the guitar in my living room. The piano and the guitar, and me in between them. There is another "me" standing on the light in between the me who plays the piano and the me who plays the guitar. An empty stillness between music and more music.

As I spent more and more time hanging around my house, I became interested in the objects arranged inside of it. It comes as a fresh horror to me, the way they have come to occupy space, situated by their user in the most familiar of places—like the world outside my window, devoid of anyone. Like me as I embrace the feeling that I cannot escape from this place, and as I lie on the sofa and suddenly start imagining myself after I have died.

The boundary between "inside" and "outside" was growing increasingly clear. Before, I had sometimes thought of the home as an interior suffused with external habit, but it seems difficult to express that view anymore in this day and age. Today, the "home" is the safest, most thoroughly isolated place. And so it is that I find myself sensing total isolation. I send out sounds, one by one. There is only me. Nobody else. I am discovered by no one. So what have I become as I live in the world at this moment? Am I a corpse, drifting between the balcony and living room with my drowsy eyes half-raised? I need some music.

무언가를 이렇게 오랫동안 방치한 것은 처음이었다. 하물며 책상 밑 구석에 박혀 있는 사진 앨범들조차 종종 꺼내서 나의 어린 시절을 추억하고 쌓인 먼지를 닦아주는데. 거실 선반에 덩그러니 놓여 있는 기타를 계절이 세 번이나 바뀌는 동안 한 번도 치지 않았다. 그동안 내게 무슨 일이 있었던 걸까. 그래, 무슨 일이 있긴 했다. 내 입으로 얘기하긴 부끄럽지만 많은 분들이 인정할 법한 문학상을 받아 곧장 시집을 내게 되면서 본격적으로 작가 활동을 시작하게 되었다. 이전부터 작가였던 것이 아니다. 나는 그저 주변에서 '시 쓰는 학생' 정도로 불리는 상태였으니까. 물론 나는 나의 정체성을 항상 '시인'으로 상정했지만 직업적으로나 사회적 위치로나 결함을 가진 채로 이를 받아들이기엔 언제나 역부족이었다. 졸업을 했어도 학생이라고 불렸다. 배울 것이 한참 남았다는 듯이. 평생 배워야 한다는 듯이. 그리고 그 비유는 적절했다. 전 세계에 역병이 돈 지 근 일 년이 되어갈 무렵, 나는 소위 말하는 화려한 데뷔를 통해 작가로서 살아가기 시작했고, 지금은 그로부터 약 10개월이 지난 상태다.

작가로서 사는 삶에 어느 정도 적응했다고 볼 수 있다. 나는 그 어느 일을 할 때보다 열심히 살고 있다. 아이러니하게도 현재 이 세계를 위협하고 있는 바이러스 덕분에 나는 작년부터 거의 집에 콕 박혀 작업에 몰두할 수 있었다. 주변을 도사리는 병 덕분에 시인이 될 수 있었다. 요즘에도 가능하면 집에서 글을 쓰려고 몇 달 전 내 방을 아예 작업실처럼 탈바꿈했다. 사정이 이러하니 나로서는 기존에 알던 세계가 새로운 의미를 갖게 된 것은 물론이고 세계 자체가 급변했다고 생각될 수밖에 없다. 세상 앞에 책을 낸 순간부터 무척 바빴다. 나를 돌보기 위해서는 가끔 취미 생활이나 문화생활을 해주어야만 하는데 그럴 시간이 도무지 없었다. 시간을 잘 다루지 못한 탓이다. 나는 줄곧 게으름을 피우는 데 능숙하기 때문이다. 기타가 점점 맛이 가는 데에는 다 이유가 있던 것이다.

작년 겨울을 보내고 올해 봄과 여름을 보낸 후 어느덧 가을 무렵이다. 바빴던 일상 속에서도 내가 반드시 놓치지 않은 것은 꼭 시간을 내어 기타를 고치러 가겠다는 다짐이었다. 그리고 그 다짐은 결코 이번 가을을 넘겨서는 안 된다고 생각했다. 거의 죽은 거나 다름없는 나의 소중한 기타가 겨울을 맞이하게 된다면 결국 내가 아끼는 사물에 소홀한 탓에 일 년이 지나갔구나 하는 허탈함과 자신에 대한 실망감에 빠질 게 분명했으니까. 그것만은 용납할 수 없었다. 나는 내가 사랑하고 있는 사물을 내 손으로 직접 지키고 싶었다. 더 이상 나의 기타가 망가져 가는 꼴을 볼 수가 없었다.

그래서 오늘은 오로지 나의 기타를 보살피는 데 온 힘을 쏟은 날이었다. 어느 때보다 일찍 일어나 아침 식사로 간단히 시리얼을 먹고 기타 가게에 전화를 했다. 이따 낮에 가도 되나요. 언제든 오세요. 기다리고 있겠습니다. 각자의 용무만 확인하는 간단한 전화를 마치고 나는 부지런히 옷을 입고 나갔다. 양쪽 어깨에 오랜만에 기타를 메고서. 오랜만에 느끼는 감각이 왠지 낯설게 느껴져 괜히 내리쬐는 햇빛에 주머니에 손을 넣고 인상을 찌그리기도 했다. 분명 이전과는 다른 세상이다, 나조차도 계속 바뀌고 있어, 나는 잘 살아야 해, 오래 살아야만 해, 혼자 중얼거리면서 역으로 가고 지하철을 탔다.

기타는 심히 손상되었다고 했다. 넥Neck[2]이 단순히 휜 수준을 떠나 점점 기형에 도달하고 있다고 했다. 기타는 나무이기 때문에 반드시 변형이 일어날 수밖에

It's the first time I've left something alone for this long. Even the photo albums wedged under my bed I will sometimes take out to wipe off the dust and reminisce over my childhood. But I haven't played my guitar even once through three changes of the seasons; it just sits there on my living room shelf. Did something happen to me in the meantime? I guess something did. It's embarrassing to admit, but I began truly working as a "writer," publishing collections of poetry after winning the kind of literary award that many people recognize. I wasn't a writer before. I was more the kind of person that others referred to as a "guy who writes poems." I had always postulated my identity as that of a "poet," but I was always too inadequate—professionally or in terms of social standing—to accept that. Even after I had graduated, I was still referred to as "student." It was as though I still had a lot to learn—as though I would have to spend my life learning. And the analogy was a fitting one. After the pandemic had been spreading throughout the world for about a year, I made my "dazzling debut" and began working as a writer; another ten months or so have passed since then.

You could say that I've more or less gotten used to life as a writer. I'm more intense about my life than anything I've done in the past. Ironically, this virus that has been menacing the world has allowed me to devote myself to work as I've remained almost entirely confined to my home since last year. Thanks to a lurking pestilence, I've become a poet. A few months ago, I transformed my bedroom into a kind of studio so that I could write at home as much as possible. This situation has made the world I thought I knew take on a new meaning for me, leaving me with the inevitable sense that the world itself has suddenly changed. Ever since I put my book out into the world, I've been intensely busy. I sometimes need to spend time with my hobbies or with culture to look after myself, but I simply haven't had the leisure. I'm just not very good with managing my time. I'm quite proficient at procrastination. There were reasons for me losing my taste for the guitar.

I said goodbye to last winter, and to spring and summer of this year, and now we find ourselves in fall. As busy as I am from one day to the next, I have not forsaken my vow to take the time to get my guitar fixed. I insisted that I could not let this fall pass without honoring that promise. My precious guitar is already as good as dead, and if it's still in that state by this winter, I just know that I will end up disappointed in myself, despairing over the fact that I let a year pass by through my neglect of an object I treasure. That was something I couldn't allow. I wanted to personally preserve an object that I love. I couldn't just watch anymore as my guitar fell apart.

So I decided to devote all my energies today to tending to my guitar. I got up earlier than usual, had a light breakfast of cereal, and called up the guitar store. "Can I stop by sometime this afternoon?" "Sure, whenever. I'll be waiting." After this short call to confirm our business, I diligently put on my clothes and went out—the guitar hanging from my shoulders for the first time in a long while. That old feeling seemed somehow odd, and I grimaced under the warm sunshine, my hands thrust in my pockets. I walked to the station and got on the subway, murmuring to myself along the way: "Obviously it's a different world from before. I'm changing too. I need to live a good life. I need to live a long life."

The guitar was severely damaged, they told me. The neck[2] wasn't just bent, they said—it was becoming increasingly deformed. A guitar is made of wood, so some changes are going to happen, but you can slow them down a lot

없지만 관리를 잘하면 그 속도를 많이 늦출 수 있다. 예전에는 하루라도 기타를 만지지 않은 적이 없었는데 처음으로 오래 방치하고 나니 그동안 기타가 자신의 장력에 의해 얼마나 아파했을지 괜히 내 마음이 다 아팠다. 내가 진심으로 사랑하는 몇 안 되는 사물. 말하지 못하고 행동하지 못하지만 내 손길이 닿을 때 비로소 제 의미를 획득하는 사물. 나와 기타는 그런 관계에 놓여 있으므로 나는 이에 대해 일정한 책임과 복무를 느끼는 것일 테다. 가게에 있는 기타를 시연하면서 수리되고 있는 나의 기타를 봤다. 처음 집에 들여왔을 때보다 기능이 많이 떨어졌을지 몰라도 아직 나와 함께할 수 있다. 몸을 닦고 새로운 줄로 갈아준다. 헤드 머신이 뻑뻑해서 장력이 무서워 플랫 튜닝을 하고 소리를 내보았다. 괜찮다. 괜찮아. 나랑 좀 더 있자. 외로웠지. 미안해.

　　　욕조에 물을 담고 몸을 담갔다. 반쯤 잠긴 몸을 바라봤다. 물에 담겨 있지 않은 몸은 형체가 뚜렷했으나 물에 담겨 있는 몸은 일렁이는 물결에 따라 형체가 다소 일그러지기도 했다. 그렇게 눈을 감고 나른한 시간을 보내고 있으면 문득 찾아오는 불안. 이 평화가 과연 언제까지일까. 이것은 평화가 아닐지도 모른다. 나는 지금 아무에게도 목격되지 않는 나만이 거주할 수 있는 집에 살고 있다. 다시 말하면 나는 지금 집에 갇혀 있다. 다시 다르게 말하면 나는 지금 세상으로부터 방치되고 있다. 다만 인간으로서 스스로 씻을 능력이 있으므로 나는 나를 관리할 수 있을 뿐이었다. 감사하게 여기지는 못하겠다. 지독한 통증을 예고 받은 기분이다. 바깥에는 병에 걸린 사람과 병에 걸리지 않은 사람과 병이 치유된 사람과 산 사람과 죽은 사람이 마구 섞여 있다. 얼굴을 물속에 집어넣었다. 숨을 내쉬었다. 내쉬는 숨이 기포를 만들었다. 기포들은 물의 천장을 향해 솟아오르다가 깨졌다.

　　　주거는 인간의 생활 방식이고 거주는 인간의 존재 방식이다. 나는 주거한다는 감각보다 거주한다는 감각에 더 가깝게 살아가고 있다. 하이데거는 '거주'의 개념에 관해 이를 '세계 내 존재'로 치환했고 인간이 이 세계를 살아가는 시간을 '임시적'으로 사유했다. 쉽게 말하자면 나는 이 세계를 잠깐 머물다 갈 운명인 것이다. 그밖에 다른 가능성이 침투할 일은 없다. 집에 있는 시간이 길어지면 바깥과 주변이 좁아진다. 그리고 바깥과 주변이 좁아질수록 나라는 존재는 점차 소외되고 방치된다. 나를 관리하는 것은 가족도 아니고 친구도 아니게 된다. 바로 내가 지겹도록 거주하고 있는 우리 집. 그러나 정말 여기가 안전한가. 여기에 있기만 하면 병에 걸리지 않는 걸까. 기타를 관리하는 가장 좋은 방법은 틈틈이 자주 연주해주는 것이라고 한다. 악기는 주인이 지정해준 위치에 홀로 놓인 모습으로 연주를 기다린다. 음악이면 되는 것이다. 악기의 입장에서는 이 세계를 음악으로 살아가기를 원하고 있는 것이다. 음악이 없다는 것. 소리가 사라진다는 것. 악기는 사형을 선고 받은 셈이다.

　　　오랜 시간 동안 집을 안전한 공간이라고 착각한 것 같다. 집은 얼마든지 무너질 수 있다. 집은 얼마든지 파괴될 수 있다. 침대 앞에 있는 책장이 어느 날 갑자기 말도 안 되게 기울어져 잠자고 있는 나를 깔아뭉갤 수도 있다. 나의 내면은 집과 닮는다. 따라서 영화 〈데몰리션〉(2015)처럼 혼란한 내면 탓에 스스로 집을 부숴버릴 수도 있다. 집과 나는 함께 방치되고 있는 중이다. 먼지에 덮이지 않을 정도로만 살고 있다.

[2]　　　현악기의 헤드를 포함하여 지판과 프렛이 위치하는 부분

with good maintenance. Before, there hadn't been a single day that I hadn't touched my guitar. This was the first time I had left it untouched for so long, and it pained me to think of how it had been suffering under its own tension. It was one of a very few objects that I truly loved—an object that could not speak or act on its own, but acquired its own meaning when my fingers touched it. That had been my relationship with the guitar, so it was inevitable that I would feel a kind of duty to it. I strummed some of the other guitars in the shop as I watched my guitar being repaired. It may not work as well as when I first brought it home, but it can still be there with me. I wiped it down and restrung it. It has a rough machine head and worrying tension, so I tried flat tuning as I tested the sound. It's okay. That's right. Stay with me a little longer. You were lonesome, weren't you? I'm sorry.

      I filled the bathtub and lay down in it. I looked down at my own half-submerged body. The parts that were not underwater had defined shapes, while the rest of my body underneath the water was slightly warped by the ripples. When I close my eyes and bask in the languor, there is a feeling of anxiety that suddenly comes over me. How long will this peace last? Maybe this isn't peace. I'm living in my own house, somewhere where I'm not witnessed by anyone. In other words, I'm trapped in my own home. In other other words, I am now being left alone by the world. Since I have the ability as a human being to bathe myself, I can only care for me. I don't see it as something to be thankful for. It feels like I've been warned of some horrible pain to come. Outside was a mix of sick people, unsick people, people who were sick and are not cured, living people and dead people. I stuck my head under the water. I breathed out. As I breathed in, it made bubbles. The bubbles rose toward the surface of the water, where they popped.

      Residing is a human way of living; dwelling is a human way of being. The way I'm living feels closer to "dwelling" than "residing." Heidegger replaced the concept of "dwelling" with "existing in the world" and thought of time that human lives in it as "temporary." Simply put, we're fated to live briefly in this world and then pass away. There is no room for other possibilities to intrude. The longer you spend in the home, the more your exterior and surroundings contract. The narrower your exterior and surroundings become, the more alienated and neglected "you" become. It is no longer family or friends who tend to you. This is your home, where you live until you can't stand it anymore. But is it even really that safe? If I stay here, will I be free from disease? They say the best way to keep your guitar is to play it often whenever you get the chance. The instrument sits alone in the place designated by its owner, awaiting the chance to play. It just needs to be some kind of music. From the instrument's standpoint, the world is something it wants to experience through music. When there is no music, when sound disappears—that is a death sentence for the instrument.

      I seem to have long held the false belief that my home was a "safe place." A home can always come crashing down. A home can always be destroyed. The bookcase in front of my bed could suddenly fall over one day and crush me while I sleep in my bed. Inside, I am like that house. For that reason, there are times that I might destroy my own house because of the turmoil inside of me, like in the film *Demolition* (2015). My home and I are both being neglected together. We live just enough so as not to get coated in dust.

> [2]   The part of a stringed instrument
> that includes the head,
> the fingerboard, and the frets.

아무래도 사이가 좋아 보이진 않는다. 살면서 무슨 문제를 껴안고 있길래 그리 싸우는 걸까. 화해할 생각은 없는 걸까. 그만 싸우셨으면 좋겠는데 싸움은 주말 아침이 되어도 계속되는 것이다. 오늘 아침이 그랬다. 구월이지만 아직은 여름의 기운이 강하게 드는 창을 바라보면서 눈을 떴는데, 충간 너머로 싸우는 소리가 여지없이 들렸다. 아무나 우리의 문제를 좀 들여다보라는 듯이.

이번 싸움은 다행히 금방 끝났다. 이전과는 다르게 뭐라고 말하는지 잘 들리지도 않았다. 그저 두 사람이 응얼거리는 소리가 천장을 기어다니다가 어쩔 땐 섞인 말의 개체가 증가하여 사벽에 우글거렸다. 나무는 푸릇했다. 날씨가 정말 맑았다. 그래서 빛을 담은 나무가 흔들릴 때마다 벽에 나무의 그림자가 듬성듬성 그려지기도 했다. 책상 앞에 앉아 오늘 할 일을 상기하다 오른쪽을 보면 벽에 붙어 있는 영화 포스터들. "GO FOR A WALK"라는 글자가 쓰여 있고 그 밑에 어느 푸른 저녁 풀밭 사이를 걸어가는 여자와 개가 그려져 있는 카드. 올해 목표(1. 독서 100권 이상, 2. 시 50편 이상 쓰기, 3. 에세이 30편 이상 쓰기, 4. 영어 공부하기)를 적은 포스트잇. 물론 달성하지 못할 것이다. 흰 종이에 나름대로 그려본 '이기리 평일 생활계획표'는 거의 망한 계획이라고 할 수 있을 것 같다. 실패할 것이다. 나는 목표나 계획을 일부러 나의 역량보다 훨씬 높은 수준으로 세우는 사람이니까. 달성하지 않으려고. 실패하려고. 그런데 이상하게 지나고 보면 꽤 많은 일들을 했다. 말하자면 나를 벼랑 끝으로 몰아붙이는 것. 한계치에 도달하게 하여 설령 나의 허무맹랑한 목표나 계획은 실패했을지라도 내가 보낸 시간만큼은 뜨거워진다는 것. 나의 시간이 벽 속에서 이렇게 흘러가는 동안 또 다른 벽 속에서는 싸움이 있었다. 나는 오늘 아침 바로 내 방의 벽 속에는 참으로 다채로운 세계가 존재하는구나 생각하면서도 한 손을 뻗어 벽에 대니 딱딱해도 너무 딱딱하구나 금이 가거나 깨질 일은 이 집에 살면서 한 번도 없을 거라고 생각했다.

간단한 세수와 양치를 하고 잠옷에서 운동복으로 갈아입었다. 옷을 갈아입기만 했는데도 본격적으로 하루가 시작된 기분이었다. 나는 일주일 중 4일 혹은 5일을 운동한다. 그리고 되도록 평일에 계획한 운동을 다 끝내려고 한다. 그러니까 오늘처럼 주말 아침에 운동을 한다는 것은 실은 스스로에 대한 책무에 시달리는 과정에 속한다. 거실에서, 발코니에서, 뜨거운 햇볕 속에서 나를 채찍질한다. 그러게, 왜 게으르게 살아서 주말에 편히 쉬지를 못하니. 좋아하는 일을 미루고 미루다 보면 어느 순간 그것이 따분해지고 지겨운 일처럼 여겨지고 너를 고통 속으로 몰아넣는다. 이런 말들이나 되뇌면서 영혼이 탈주한 몸과 표정으로 반복 운동을 하고 있게 된다. 운동을 하다 보면 참 쓸데없는 생각을 많이 하게 되는데 오늘 한 생각은 충간 소음에 관련된 것이었다. 특히 내 방에 있으면 적나라하게 느껴질 정도로 벌어지는 두 사람의 싸움이 어떤 원인으로 발생했는지 궁금했고 그들이 싸우지 않은 날에는 어떻게 살아가는지 문득 궁금해졌다. 역시 쓸데없는 생각이었다. 남의 가정사나 궁금해하다니. 차라리 다행이다. 예전 같았으면 또 다시 불같은 화가 치밀어 올랐을 텐데. 이런 생각을 하는 것 보니 이제 두 사람이 일으키는 소음에 대해 득도한 게 아닐까.

몇 달 전 아파트 현관에 벽보를 붙인 적이 있었기에. 그 당시 나는 시시때때로 들리는 두 사람의 목소리에 화를 터뜨리기 일보 직전이었다. 나는 일상을 살다 보면 서로

They don't seem to get along very well. What kind of problems are they carrying around that make them fight like that? Don't they want to make up? I wish they would stop, but the fighting just goes on, even on weekend mornings. This morning was the same. I opened my eyes, looking at the window where it still feels very much like summer, even though it's already September. I can hear everything through the walls as they argue. It's as though our problems were out there for anyone and everyone to see.

Fortunately, this latest argument was over quickly. Unlike before, I couldn't really make out what they were saying. There were just their two muttered voices creeping over the ceiling, until suddenly mixtures of words began proliferating and swarming over the walls. The trees were green, the weather very clear. As the trees caught the light, their thin shadows appeared on the walls with every sway. I sat at my desk and thought about what I was going to do that day. Looking to my right, I saw the movie posters on the wall. "GO FOR A WALK," it read, with a card underneath showing a woman and dog walking in a grassy field one green evening. There was a little Post-It with my goals for the year (1. Read 100+ books, 2. Write 50+ poems, 3. Writing 30+ essays, 4. Study English). Obviously, I won't be reaching those. The "Lee Ki-ri weekday schedule" that I sketched out on a sheet of white paper may end up being an almost total bust—a failure. I'm someone who deliberately sets goals and makes plans that are far beyond my capabilities. It's so I don't achieve them. I'm supposed to fail. But as I pass by, I see that I've actually done a surprising amount. In a word, I'm driving myself to the brink. I've pushed myself to my limits, so that even if I failed in my wildly implausible goals or plans, I did at least spend that time intensely. While my time was passing within these walls, fights were going on inside those other walls. This morning, I found myself thinking about what a diverse world there is inside the walls of my room—yet when I reached out a hand to touch the wall, it was so very hard that I was sure it would never crack or break for as long as I live in this house.

After briefly washing up and brushing my teeth, I changed from my pajamas into my workout clothes. Even though all I'd done was to change clothes, it felt like my day had truly begun. I work out four or five days a week, and I try to do all of my scheduled exercising on weekdays. For me to be working out on a weekend morning like this, it seems like I'm really struggling with responsibilities to myself. In my living room, on my balcony, underneath the warm sunshine, I goad myself on. Why can't I just let myself go and relax on the weekend? When you keep putting off the things I enjoy, they start to seem dull and distasteful work, which plunges you into torment. Repeating this mantra, I end up doing repetitive exercises, my soul having fled my body and face. I have all sorts of odd thoughts while I'm working out; today's were about the noise I hear through my walls. I wondered what had caused the two of them to fight so loud I could hear it all from my bedroom; I suddenly became curious how they were together on the days when they weren't fighting. It was all just pointless rumination—this curiosity about other people's home life. If anything, I'm happy it wasn't like the past, when I would have flown into another rage. If I was having these kinds of thoughts, did that mean I'd gained some kind of "enlightenment" when it came to the noise the two of them were making?

A few months earlier, I'd stuck a notice on the apartment door. At the time, I was just about to explode with fury over the voices I kept hearing from the

1
2 ⋯ <u>A Note on "Home": The Home Is Not Prepared</u>
   <u>Reflecting on "Home": Between the Balcony and the Living Room</u>
   <u>Five Diary Entries on Online Platform Experiences</u>
3

153

문힐 수밖에 없는 소음을 이해할 수 있었다. 그러나 끊임없이 지속된다는 건 얘기가 달랐다. 마치 내 방에 두 명의 침입자가 발생하여 정작 주인인 내가 특정 공간에서 탈락되는 것 같은 세계. 여러 목소리가 혼재되어 방 안을 떠돌다 보면 어느새 나는 침묵을 하고 있다. 다른 목소리에 집중하고 있기 때문이다. 목소리만 내 방을 침투할 수 있는 것은 아니다. 발소리가 전형적이다. 나는 지금 굉장히 오랜 시간 동안 아랫집의 모든 생활을 방에서 받아들이고 있다. 생활 자체가 침투한 것이다. 하루는 소음이 일어나는 원인을 찾기 위해 밖에 나왔다. 우리 집은 2층이므로 대략 1층부터 4층까지가 예상 범주에 속할 수 있었다. 양해를 구해 이웃집의 문들을 두드려본 결과 잠정적으로 바로 밑에 살고 있는 1층 집이라는 결론에 도달했었다. 그때 나는 아랫집에서 들리는 발소리가 위에서 들리는 것처럼 들릴 수 있다는 사실을 처음 깨달았다. 그리고 가장 결정적인 소리는 바로 앞서 말했던 싸움이었다. 어느 날의 싸움은 거의 옆에서 보고 있다고 믿어질 정도로 선명하게 들렸다. 부엌에서 접시를 바닥에 던지는 소리가 들리면서 한 사람이 욕설을 하면 남은 한 사람이 욕하지 말라고 하는 대화. 대화라고 할 수는 없겠지만. 한 시간을 넘게 들어야만 했었다. 이 말은 한 시간이 넘도록 책도 못 읽고 글도 못 쓰고 의자에 가만히 앉아 싸움이나 듣고 있었다는 뜻이기도 하다.

혼재되는 소리들과 함께 살아가는 게 익숙해졌다. 집에만 있는 날이면 더욱 그랬다. 글을 쓰기 시작하면 타자를 치는 소리가 들린다. 음악을 켜두었으므로 방 안에 음악 소리가 울려 퍼진다. 가끔 자세를 고치면 의자가 삐걱거린다. 발끝에 휴지통이 턱 걸린다. 서랍을 열고 닫는 소리. 때마침 아랫집에서 쿵쿵대는 발소리. 곧바로 두 사람이 싸우기 시작하면 기가 막힌 심포니가 연주된다. 온갖 잡다한 소리가 방 안을 꽉 채우는 것이다. 나는 정신이 몽롱해진 채 좁은 방을 배회한다. 나의 생활도 누군가의 공간을 침범하고 있겠지. 어쩌면 생각보다 위협적인 존재로 낙인 찍혔을지도 모르겠다. 혹은 증오의 대상이 되었을지도. 의도는 전혀 없었지만 나의 생활이 일면 타인의 삶과 정신에 영향력을 끼치는 일은 딱히 유쾌하지 않아 보인다. 요즘엔 더 그렇다. 밖에 나갈 일이 손에 꼽다 보니 집에서의 생활을 최대치로 즐기고 싶기 때문이다. 조용하고 안전한 나만의 공간을 추구하게 되는 것이다.

내 곁에 누군가 있다는 것은 특정 실체만을 상정하진 않는다. 불특정 실체와도 살아가는 삶. 나에게는 반려 소리들이 있다. 대표적으로 반려 목소리를 소개했다. 이 목소리는 하나의 목소리가 아니라 두 목소리며 주로 저녁 여섯 시 반부터 일곱 시 사이에만 나를 찾아온다. 방에 데리고 있다 떠나고 나면 묻는다. 내일은 안녕하시기를. 부디 무탈한 하루를 보내시기를.

저녁에는 잠깐 편의점에 다녀왔다. 먹을 것을 들고 집으로 돌아가고 있는데 가로등이 점멸하고 있었다. 나는 휴대폰을 꺼내 그 모습을 짧은 동영상으로 남겼다. 이때만큼은 주변에 그 어떤 소리들도 들리지 않았다. 아주 침착하고 고요했다.

거푸집처럼
— 차이 시리즈 〈포시즌스〉를 보고

좋은 날씨가 계속되면 불안하다. 이러다가 갑자기 천둥과 번개를 동반한 폭풍우가 올 것만 같아서. 또 소식 없이 누군가 아프다가 세상을 떠날 것만 같아서. 좋은 것 뒤에 좋지 않은 것이 있지 않고 슬픈 것이 있어서. 그러니까 일기는 매일 느낀 불안과 공포를 기록하는 일이다. 삶을 체득하는 동시에 어떤 삶을 통째로 버리기도 해야 하는, 오롯이

154

two of them. I might have understood if it had been the kind of noise you can't help making when you're going about your life. But it was another thing for it to happen constantly. It was as though two intruders had shown up in my bedroom, and I, the actual owner, was being shut out of that space. When you have different voices mixing and roaming around the room, my own voice becomes silent—since I'm focusing on them now. It isn't just voices that infiltrate my room, either. The most common thing is footsteps. It's been quite a long time now that everything about my downstairs neighbors' life has been coming into my room. Their very life has intruded. One day, I went outside to see what was causing the noise. I live on the second floor, so I figured it could be anywhere from the first to the fourth floor. After knocking on my neighbors' doors (and begging their pardon), I came to the tentative conclusion that it was a unit on the first floor, just below mine. It was the first time I became aware that downstairs footsteps can sound like they're coming from upstairs. The most conclusive bit of noise was the aforementioned fighting. One day, I could hear the argument so clearly that I could have sworn I was standing right there watching it. I heard the sound of plates being thrown in the kitchen; one of them would curse at the other, who told them to stop cursing. You couldn't really call it a "conversation," but I had to sit through it for over an hour—which means that for over an hour, I couldn't read or write. I could only sit there in a chair listening to them arguing.

I've gotten used to living with a mixture of sounds. That's all the more true on those days when I never leave the house. As I start to write, I can hear the sound of the keyboard. I turn on the music, and the sound of music fills the room. Sometimes my chair creaks as I straighten my posture. The wastebasket catches on my foot. Drawers open and close. I hear the clomping of feet downstairs. The two of them soon start fighting, and a stupefying symphony begins to play. Every kind of noise comes together to fill my room. I wander around my cramped quarters, my mind in a haze. Maybe my way of life is intruding on someone else's space. Perhaps I've been branded as more of a threat than I realize. I may be the object of someone's loathing. I certainly haven't intended it, but it's not exactly pleasant when your life has an impact on other people's lives and minds. That's even more the case these days. Since we so rarely go out, we want to enjoy our time at home as much as possible. We're looking for our own private space, quiet and safe.

When we imagine someone there beside us, we don't just imagine a particular being. We also live with indistinct beings. For me, it's the companion sounds. As an example, I introduced you to the companion voices. It's not one voice but two of them, which come and visit me usually between the hours of 6:30 and 7 in the evening. I invite them into my room, and when they leave, I say, "I hope you have a pleasant tomorrow. May your day be free of worry."

In the evening, I stopped briefly at the convenience store. On my way back home with something to eat, I saw a street light blinking. I took out my phone and shot a brief video of it. At this particular moment, I didn't hear any noises around me. It was very quiet and still.

Like Formwork (Sun)(Sep)(12)(2021) ∨
— **Upon viewing Chai Siris's** *Four Seasons*

As nice weather continues, I start to get nervous. I get the sense that a storm is about to come, arriving suddenly with thunder and lighting. I worry that someone might sicken and die without a word. After the good things, there are things that are bad or sad. So I record my fears and worries every day in my journal. It's a

살갗으로만 하는 투쟁의 역사다. 아직 비는 내리지 않았으므로 더운 기운이 가시지는 않았다. 구월이면 류시화 시인의 「구월의 이틀」이란 시도 떠올라서, 여름의 초록이 남아 있어도 왠지 가을로 넘어가고 있는 듯한 계절감이 느껴지고, '숲', '오솔길', '나무', '새', '태양', '빙하시대' 같은 시어들이 오랫동안 가슴속에 남고, 비만 내리면, 이 모든 여름이 다 축축해지고, 움츠린 몸들을 추위 속으로 몰아넣어야 하는, 겨울이 온다는 생각에, 검은 눈동자가 자신의 색을 더 짙게 한다. 아침에 읽던 시집을 덮고서.

거실로 나와 소파에 앉아 있는 아버지에게 다가갔다. 잘 주무셨어요, 말 대신 첫 말을 다음 문장으로 뗐다. 배드민턴 치러 가실래요? 아버지는 웃으며 그러자고 했다. 원래 집에 채와 공이 없었다. 우리 집에 적어도 테니스 채와 배드민턴 채와 각각의 공들은 구비되어 있었다. 어렸을 땐 시간이 날 때마다 가족과 친구들과 공을 주고받으러 나갔다. 친구들과 놀 땐 아파트 단지에 있는 테니스장과 공원과 운동장을 갔다. 가족과는 주로 배드민턴을 쳤다. 특히 아버지랑 그렇게 많이도 쳤다. 집 앞에는 좁은 골목이 있었는데 아버지가 퇴근하고 거뭇한 저녁이 되면 그곳으로 나가 가로등 불빛에 의지하며 배드민턴을 쳤다. 아버지는 나를 혹독하게 키웠다. 초등학교, 중학생을 상대로 무자비하게 공을 몸 쪽으로 꽂았으니. 나는 절대로 공을 받을 수 없었다. 가끔 명치로 오는 공을 맞으면 잔혹한 아버지가 미웠다. 아버지는 그런 나를 보고 천진난만한 웃음으로 응수했다. 도무지 이해할 수 없는 아버지였다. 우리 자주 놀았었는데, 과거를 추억하다가 아버지와 누나랑 급작스럽게 차를 끌고 채와 공을 사러 간 것은 바로 어제였다. 문득 배드민턴이 너무 치고 싶은데 우리 집에 이제 그런 건 없었으니까. 다시 사러 나가는 기분은 설렘 그 자체였다. 어린 시절로 돌아가는 기분이었다. 중학생으로 돌아가는 것 같았다. 초등학생으로 돌아가는 것 같았다. 아버지도 그만큼 젊어질 수 있다면 얼마나 좋을까. 우리는 자연스럽게 영등포 타임스퀘어를 행선지로 설정했다. 거기에 운동 관련된 많은 기구들이 있으니 구경 겸 가보기로 했다. 영등포에 이런 거대한 건물이 생길 줄 누가 알았을까. 지금은 마치 원래부터 이 자리에 있어야 했던 것처럼 웅장한 모습으로 잘 있다. 벌써 타임스퀘어가 지어진 지도 약 12년 정도 됐으니까. 거푸집을 본 게 엊그제 같은데.

여섯 시 정도는 되어야 날씨가 선선해질 거야. 그때 누나랑 같이 가자. 나는 아버지의 말을 듣고 각자 할 일을 하며 여섯 시를 기다렸다. 얼른 배드민턴을 치고 싶었다. 오랜만에 가족과 배드민턴을 칠 수 있어서 한껏 들뜬 상태였다. 그날의 골목, 저녁 가로등 불빛 속에서 아버지와 나와 한창 신나게 배드민턴을 치고 있을 때. 둘이 어떻게 놀고 있나 궁금해서 밖으로 나오는 엄마와 누나의 모습이 생각난다. 나온 엄마와 누나는 담장 밑에 깔린 돌바닥에 앉아 두 무릎을 양팔로 모아 우리를 구경했는데. 그러다가 내가 공에 또 다시 맞으면 저녁 골목은 웃음으로 가득했는데. 언제부터 그 골목을 비워 두게 되었을까. 우리는 각자 너무 바빴다. 살기 바빴다. 꿈을 찾고 꿈을 좇느라 힘든 시간을 보내고 있었다. 가세가 기우는 집을 살리느라. 모든 마음의 모양을 어르고 달래느라. 울기 바빴다. 우는 일이 일상이었다.

동네에 있는 생태공원은 어느덧 제자리를 찾은 듯 자라난 나무들과 풀들이 흔들리며 우리를 반겨주고 있었고 자갈길을 걸으면 빗방울처럼 나는 차락차락 소리가 좋아 보폭을 냉큼 줄이기도 했다. 여기는 오면 올수록 신기해. 어떻게 군집된 건물들을 한순간에 무너뜨리고 폐허로 만들었다가 단란한 가족들과 강아지들이 따뜻한 햇볕을 받으며 뛰놀 수 있는 공원을 만들 수 있지? 마찬가지로 나는 공원의 거푸집을 또렷이 기억한다. 진입을 막는 펜스가 둘레에 쳐져 있었다. 그 안엔 아무것도 없었다. 건물들이

record of struggle through my flesh alone, where I must learn about life while also letting some lives go entirely. The rain hasn't yet started to fall, and the hot feeling doesn't subside. When September arrives, I think about the poem "Two Days in September" by Ryu Si-hwa, which gives me a sense of the season and how we are passing into the autumn even as the green of summer remains. Poetic words linger in my mind: "forest," "trail," "trees," "birds," "sun," and "ice age." When the rain starts to fall, all of that summer gets soaked in water, the huddled bodies forced into the cold. At the thought of winter coming, the black of my pupils only deepens, as I close the book of poems I had been reading that morning.

Going into the living room, I walked over to my father, who was sitting on the couch. Rather than a "How are you?" I asked him, "Do you want to play some badminton?" He laughed and said "sure." There weren't any rackets or shuttlecocks in the house before. At our home at least, we had tennis and badminton rackets with balls and birdies. As a child, I'd play catch with friends and family members whenever I had the time. If I was playing with friends, we'd go to the tennis court in our apartment complex, or to the park or sports field. With my family, it was mainly badminton. I played a lot of it with my father in particular. There was a narrow street in front of our house, and in the dim evening after my father got home from work, we would go there to play badminton under the streetlights. My father really let me have it when I was growing up. He'd ruthlessly jam me with the ball when I was just in elementary or middle school. I could never catch it. Sometimes one of them would hit me in my solar plexus, and I'd curse my father inside for his brutality. He'd look at me and give an innocent smile. I could never understand him. We often played together, but it was just yesterday that I started reminiscing over the past and suddenly decided to drive with my father and sister to get some rackets and shuttlecocks. Out of nowhere, I found myself really wanting to play badminton, and we no longer had the equipment at home. As we left to go buy some, I felt absolutely giddy. It was like I was going back to my childhood, like I was a middle school student, like an elementary school student again. I'm sure my father would love to be that much younger himself. We decided that the obvious place to go was Times Square in Yeongdeungpo. They had all sorts of exercise equipment there, and we could have a look around. Who could have imagined that such a huge building would appear in Yeongdeungpo? These days, it looks suitably grand, as though it was always supposed to be there. It's already been about 12 years since Times Square went up. It feels like only yesterday that I was looking at its formwork.

"The weather only really starts to get cool around six o'clock. We can go then with your sister," my father said. We each went about our businesses as I waited for six o'clock to arrive. I wanted to hurry up and play some badminton. I felt so excited that I was finally going to play badminton with my family. I imagined my father and I having our spirited games in the street by the evening streetlights, and my mother and sister coming outside to see what we were up to. The two of them would sit down on the stone pavement below the wall, squeezing their knees between their arms as they watched us play. I'd get hit by the shuttlecock again, and the evening street would ring out with laughter. When did we stop going out into that street? We were all too busy—busy with living. We lived through some tough times, finding and chasing dreams. Trying to save a sinking home. Trying to calm every kind of feeling. We were busy crying. Crying was a daily occurrence.

In the local ecological park, we were met by swaying trees and plants, now grown up as if they had somehow found their place. As we walked along the gravel path, I'd sometimes shorten my strides because I liked the crunching

갈리고 남은 흔적인 돌무더기와 어디서 가져왔는지 모를 흙더미가 군데군데 쌓여 있었다. 여기가 생태공원이 된다고? 친구와 나는 그 주변을 지나가면서 말도 안 된다고 대화를 나누었던 적도 있었다. 그런데 지금은 보란 듯이 물속에 사는 생물들이 있고, 하나씩 운동기구를 차지하여 어설픈 자세로 운동을 하고 있는 노년의 어르신들이 있고, 네트를 두고 배드민턴을 치는 우리 가족이 있다. 한때는 거푸집이었던 곳이 모습을 갖추게 되자 우리 가족도 오는구나. 사람들을 만날 수 있구나. 그 사실이 조금 신기해서 공을 있는 힘껏 세게 쳤다. 어항처럼 생긴 아버지의 배에 공이 꽂혔다. 맞은 공은 귀엽게 흙바닥에 떨어졌다. 옛날 생각이 많이 났다. 살아 있어서 참 좋아, 너무 좋아. 시간이 느리게 가길 바랐다.

아파트가 숲처럼 이루는 곳에 자리한 생태공원이 가끔 내 마음의 안식처가 된다. 기억난다. 지금 살고 있는 우리 집도 한때 모델하우스였지. 사람이 살고 있지 않지만 살고 싶은 사람을 위해 임시적으로 마련된 공간. 모델하우스였을 때 우리 집엔 소파 하나만 놓여 있었다. 나는 소파 위를 정신 사납게 뛰었다가 옆에 같이 있던 사촌형에게 번쩍 들어 올려졌다. 공간에게도 골격과 토대였던 시절이 있는데, 시간이라고 없을 이유는 없지 않겠는가. 말하자면 우리가 지금 살고 있는 시간에게도 거푸집이었던 시절이 있었을 것. 지금 흐르고 있는 이 시간을 맞이하기 위해 준비해야 했던 모양이 있지 않았을까. 마음도 마찬가지다. 노래도 마찬가지다. 그것들이 모두 흐르고 흘러 다 지나가기 위해 준비했어야 했을 골격과 토대가 거푸집이었을 테니. 그 안을 비우기 위해 무엇을 허물어야 했는지는 잘 모르겠다. 시간의 안과 마음의 안에는 무엇이 들어차 있었을까. 거기에 새로운 모양을 짓기 위해 무엇을 밀어버리고 무너뜨리고 또 무엇을 채우고 지어야만 했을까.

나 역시 거푸집이었다. 정확히 말하자면 온전한 육체를 갱신하다가 다시 거푸집으로 돌아가는 중이다. 나는 시간을 거푸집으로 돌아가는 형태로 받아들이고 있다. 나는 언젠가 왜소해질 것이다. 뼈만 남게 될 것이다. 피부는 축 늘어지고 얇아질 것이다. 그리고 어느 날, 약 두 시간 만에 한 줌의 가루가 되어 있을 것이다. 나는 작은 상자에 담길 것이다. 나는 사라졌으나 내가 사라지지 않았고 각자의 마음속에 남았다고 생각해줄 착한 몇몇의 사람들이 이 세상을 나보다 조금 더 오래 살아갈 것이다. 나를 허문 자리에 기왕이면 많은 사람들이 모일 수 있는 예쁜 공간을 조성해주었으면 좋겠다. 힘든 시절을 살아가는 중에, 이 방에서 쓰는 글들과 함께, 내 바람은 오직 그뿐이다. 그러기 위해 오늘 흘린 땀을 씻어내고 침대에 널브러져 있는 책들을 정리해야지. 아무렇게나 흐뜨리지 말고 깔끔하게 지내기로 약속하자. 어지럽다.

우리가 돌아가야 할 곳 2021 09 20 월 ∨
— 구동희 〈타가수분〉을 보고

이 년 만에 해남에 왔다. 해남은 우리 집 고향이다. 어머니와 아버지 모두 해남에서 태어났고 해남에서 자랐고 해남에서 같은 중학교를 나왔으며 해남에서 만났다. 해남에서부터 이어진 오랜 인연은 결실을 맺어 딸과 아들을 낳았고 그들 역시 해남과의 인연을 계속하고 있다. 나는 서울에서 태어나고 자랐지만 해남으로 갈 때만큼은 제 고향으로 돌아가는 기분이다. 이제는 코로나 때문에 어디를 갔다 오는 일 자체가 힘들어졌지만 이번만큼은 시간을 내어 조심스럽게 왔다. 올 수 있었다. 살아 있는 가족과 돌아가신 가족을 뵙고 싶었기 때문이다.

sound. The more I visited this place, the more marvelous it seemed. How were they able to simply tear down a cluster of buildings and put up a work where happy families and dogs could run about under the warm sunshine? I also clearly remember the formwork for the park. A fence surrounded it to prevent people from going inside, where there wasn't anything at all. There were only piles of stones left over from the fractured buildings, and mounds of earth brought in from who knows where. This was going to be an eco park? My friends and I talked about how absurd it was as we passed by. But these days, there are living things swimming in the water, senior citizens exercising awkwardly on the equipment, and families putting up nets to play badminton. What once was mere formwork took on its final form, and now here we were. It was a place to meet people. Marveling a bit at the notion, I struck the birdie as hard as I could. It hit my father right in his fishbowl-shaped belly. The birdie dropped sweetly to the dirt. I remembered all sorts of things from the old days. It was great to be alive. I hoped time would pass slowly.

Situated in a forest of apartment buildings, the eco park is sometimes a refuge for my mind. I can remember it. Even the house where we live today was once a model home. Nobody lived there at the time—it was just a space set up temporarily for people who might want to move in. Back when it was a model home, the only thing in our house was a sofa. I'd run wildly over the sofa, and my cousin next to me would pick me up off the ground. Spaces have their own "old days," when they were structures and foundations. Why shouldn't time have its own? In other words, even the time we are living in today had its own past when it was just formwork. Perhaps there was a shape that had to be prepared so that this current time could arrive. The same goes for minds, and for songs. All of them were once formwork, structures and foundations that had to be prepared so that they could flow by. I don't know what had to be torn down to make way inside of them. What used to fill that time and those minds? What did they have to carve away and demolish to make new forms there? What did they have to add and build?

I was once formwork myself. More precisely, I renewed a whole body, and now I am returning to the formwork. I see time as a shape that is returning to formwork. Someday, I will start to shrink. All that will be left of me is bone. My skin will droop and grow thin. One day, I'll be reduced to a handful of dust in a matter of just a few hours. I'll be placed in a little box. I will be gone, but there will be a few people who live in this world a bit longer than me. These kind people will see me as not being gone but will see me as not being gone, who will think that I live on in their hearts. I hope that in the place left behind when I am torn down, they will build a beautiful setting where lots of people can gather. That's my only wish during these difficult times, along with the things that I write in this room. To achieve that, I'll need to wash away today's sweat and clean up the books strewn over my bed. I need to promise to live more cleanly rather than letting things get scattered all around. I feel dizzy.

Where We Must Return
— Upon viewing Koo Donghee's *Cross×Pollination*

Mon Sep 20 2021 ∨

I'm back in Haenam after two years. Haenam is the town my family comes from. Both my mother and father were born and raised there; they both graduated middle school in Haenam and met in Haenam. Those ties originating in Haenam bore fruit when they had a son and a daughter, and their ties to Haenam continue to this day. I was born and raised in Seoul, but when I go to Haenam, it feels like

이틀 전 아침 일찍 서울에서 출발했는데 차가 너무 많이 막혔었다. 해남을 가기로 했다면 각오해야 할 일이었다. 서울에서 해남으로 가는 것은 하루 대부분의 시간을 도로에 쏟아야 한다는 뜻이니까. 언제 도착할지 장담할 수 없다. 그냥 도착할 때까지 가는 것. 도착해야만 이 움직임은 끝난다. 마음을 내려놓아야 한다. 여권을 챙기지 않는 게 이상할 정도다. 그렇다면 아마 도장을 잔뜩 찍고도 남았을 거다. 이제는 누나와 나 둘 다 운전을 잘할 수 있어서 아버지 혼자 모든 일을 떠안지 않아도 된다. 우리가 아주 어렸을 적, 아버지는 우릴 데리고 스물 네 시간을 넘게 운전한 적도 있다. 그때 고속도로 위에는 헬기가 떠 다녔다. 운전자들이 차에서 내려 고속도로 한가운데서 담배를 피우는 진풍경이 펼쳐지기도 했다. 헬기에선 지속적으로 사이렌이 울렸었다. 졸지 말고 안전하게 가라고 나라에서 그런 일도 했던 것이다. 아침에 출발했는데 해남에 도착하니까 다시 해가 뜨고 있는 풍경이나 저녁에 출발했는데 다시 주변이 어둑어둑해지는 풍경은 내게 꽤나 익숙한 풍경들이었다. 서해안고속도로가 생기고 난 이후부터는 이동 시간이 많이 짧아졌지만 여전히 해남은 먼 곳이다. 운전을 3교대로 했는데도 체력적으로 만만하지 않았다. 나는 고창고인돌휴게소부터 목포에 진입하여 해남까지 가는 코스를 맡았었다. 비교적 부담이 덜 되는 길을 맡았지만 책임을 가지고 성실히 운전에 임했었다.

그렇게 힘들게 도착한 해남에서 이틀째 지내고 있고 내일이면 추석이다. 하지만 우리 가족은 추석 당일에 서울로 올라갈 예정이었기에 추석에 할 일을 오늘 하고 가기로 했다. 돌아가신 할아버지와 할머니께 인사를 드리는 것. 고당리에 있는 산 중턱에는 친할아버지와 친할머니가 합장으로 모셔져 있다. 그리고 송정리 집 앞에는 외할아버지가 자신의 부모님 옆에 같이 모셔져 있다.

인사를 잘 드리기 위해서 어제는 증조외할머니가 계신 묘지에 가서 벌초를 했다. 벌초를 핑계로 오랜만에 아버지를 조수석에 태우고 트럭을 끌기도 했다. 하지만 너무 오랜만에 수동 스틱을 사용해서 그런지 운전이 어색해서 조금 하다가 그냥 다시 아버지께 운전석을 넘겼다. 기계에서 아주 작은 부품이 빠져나오자 기계가 통으로 멈추는 것처럼 머리가 돌아가질 않았다. 사실 운전을 머리로 하고 있다는 순간부터 탈락이었다. 묘지에 도착하니 정말 말도 안 되는 풍경이 우릴 압도하고 있었다. 농담 하나도 안 보태고 풀이 아버지와 내 키만큼 자라 앞이 제대로 보이지 않았다. 오죽했으면 오자마자 바로 보여야 할 입구가 어딘지를 몰라 잠깐 헤매었을 정도였다. 다행히 입구에는 나름 경계 지어진 부분이 있어서 여기서부터 풀을 치면 되겠다고 얘기했다. 기계를 쓰는 건 아버지 담당이었고 나는 옆에서 잘린 풀들을 갈퀴로 긁어 잘 모은 뒤 치우면 됐다. 아침 날씨는 선선했지만 곧이어 해가 강한 열기를 내뿜으며 우리의 뒷덜미를 위협했다. 완전 무장하여 옷을 입었는데도 시골 모기에 몇 방 물리기도 했다. 해남에 있으면 버물리를 바르고 오는 예식이라도 필요하다는 듯. 그래도 걱정했던 것과는 다르게 생각보다 훨씬 빠른 시간 내에 벌초를 끝내고 집에 돌아올 수 있었다.

그리하여 추석 연휴 동안 살아 있는 가족들에게 인사를 드렸으니 오늘만큼은 돌아가신 가족들에게 인사를 드리러 가야지. 고당리 산 중턱부터 갔다. 어머니와 아버지가 언제까지 이 길을 오를 수 있을지 모르겠다. 그만큼 올라가는 길이 험준하여 나조차도 힘을 빼면 옆으로 떨어질 위험이 있다. 나는 앞장서서 우리 가족에게 위협이 될 만한 나뭇가지나 가시 등을 치우며 갔다. 진땀을 빼고 그곳에 도착하면 봉분 두 개가 우리를 반겨준다. 하나는 할아버지와 할머니가 합장되어 있는 봉분이고 나머지 하나는 할아버지의 형인 큰할아버지가 계신 봉분이다. 우리는 두 봉분 앞에 가서 인사를 드리고

I'm going home. With the pandemic, it's become more difficult to go anywhere these days, but I took the time for extra precautions this time. I was able to do it. I wanted to see my family, both the living ones and the ones who have passed away.

I left Seoul early in the morning two days ago, and the roads were very crowded. It's something I should have been prepared for when I decided to go to Haenam. Traveling from Seoul to Haenam means having to spend the better part of a day on the highway. You can't be sure when you're going to arrive. You just travel until you get there. The movement only stops when you arrive. You have to let go of your emotions. It's enough to make it seem strange that I don't need to pack a passport. If I did, it would have been stamped all over by now. My sister and I can both drive these days, which means my father doesn't have to do it all on his own. There was one time when we were very young that my father drove us for more than 24 hours. At the time, there was a helicopter flying over the expressway. You could see drivers getting out of their cars and smoking cigarettes in the middle of the road. The siren kept blaring from the helicopter—something the state did to make sure people drove safely and didn't doze off behind the wheel. It was not uncommon for us to leave in the morning, only for the sun to already be coming up again by the time we reached Haenam, or for us to leave in the evening and only arrive when it was already getting dark again. The traveling times got a lot shorter when they built the Seohaean Expressway, but Haenam is still quite far. Even when the three of us took turns driving, it was still quite physically taxing. I was in charge of the stretch heading from the Gochang Dolmens rest area into Mokpo and on to Haenam. This was a less strenuous section, but I approached my driving diligently with a sense of responsibility.

After our difficult journey to Haenam, we spent two days ahead of the Chuseok holiday. But we were scheduled to go back up to Seoul on Chuseok day, so we decided to do everything that we would have done that day ahead of time. That meant paying respects to our late grandfather and grandmother. My father's mother and father are buried together on the middle slope of a mountain in the village of Godang. My mother's father is buried next to his parents in front of their house in the village of Songjeong.

To properly pay respects, I went yesterday to clean up my great-grandmother's gravesite. The cleanup also provided an excuse for taking the truck out, with my father riding shotgun for a change. But it had been a long time since I'd driven a vehicle with a manual transmission, which made for awkward driving until I finally just handed the wheel back over to my father. My head wasn't working—like a machine that comes to a stop when one very tiny piece comes loose. In reality, I'd lost the moment I started driving with my head. Arriving at the cemetery, we were overwhelmed by a truly staggering scene. It was no joke: the plants had grown as tall as my father and I. We could barely see in front of us. It was so bad that we ended up wandering around for a bit because we couldn't find the entrance—which should have been visible as soon as we arrived. Fortunately, the entrance had a section with some kind of a boundary, so we decided we should start trimming there. My father was in charge of the machinery, while I would stand next to him, raking up the trimmed leaves and limbs and gathering them up neatly to dispose of. The morning was brisk, but soon the sun started breathing down our necks with its intense heat. We'd come fully dressed for the occasion, but the country mosquitoes managed to get a few bites in. It was like a ritual: going to Haenam and coming home in ointment. At any rate, we were able to finish the clearing and go home much faster than I had initially feared.

주변에 소주를 뿌렸다. 그러고는 매번 앉던 자리에 앉아 펼쳐지는 풍경을 바라봤다.
고당리 마을 바로 옆에는 바다라서 할머니는 우리 가족이 온다 하면 해산물이 들어간
요리를 많이 해주셨다. 그 중에서도 나는 할머니가 해주신 굴 요리를 가장 좋아했다.
어릴 때부터 할머니가 해주셔서 그런지 굴에 대한 거부감은 전혀 없었다. 지금은
간척되어서 바다가 있어야 할 자리가 땅이 되었다. 한눈에 마을을 볼 수 있다.
할아버지와 할머니가, 그리고 우리 어머니와 아버지가, 여기서 밥도 먹고 체육대회도
하고 선생님한테 혼나기도 했겠구나. 그 시절엔 어떤 마음들이 오고 갔을까. 나는 그런
게 궁금했다. 자리에서 일어났다. 풍경을 보고 있다가 불현듯 할아버지와 할머니 앞에서
흐느꼈다. 최대한 아무에게도 눈물을 보여주지 않으려고 등을 보였지만 어깨가 주체할
수 없을 정도로 들썩였다. 너무 늦었죠. 할아버지, 할머니. 저는 작가가 되었어요. 책도
나왔어요. 보셨으면 그 누구보다 기뻐하셨을 텐데. 꼭 이 모습을 보여드리고 싶었는데.
너무 늦었어요. 죄송해요.

외할아버지에게 인사를 드릴 땐 저편으로 땅거미가 지고 있었다. 노을이
지평선처럼 가늘게 뻗어 곳곳의 기와지붕과 언덕을 비추고 있었다. 나는 속으로
가족에게 말했다. 잘 봐요, 우리에게 선물하는 풍경이에요. 나는 죽어서도 우리가 살아
있었던 시절을 잊지 않을 거예요.

집으로 돌아와서는 삼겹살을 먹었다. 어른들은 각자 취향에 맞게 술을
한잔했고 나는 음료수나 홀짝 마셨다. 나는 돌아왔다는 기분이 많이 들었다. 비로소
돌아올 수 있었다, 그렇게 말하고 싶었다. 나는 지금 살아 있기에 언젠가 내가 돌아가야
할 곳을 잘 알고 있다. 그곳이 많은 이들에게 개방된 곳일지 폐쇄된 곳일지는 반대로
살아 있어서 알 수가 없다. 아마 죽어서도 들려줄 수 없을 것이다. 하지만 당분간은 좋다.
이대로 가족과 함께 지내고 싶다. 마음껏 웃고 떠들고 싶다. 해남에는 한 번 더 돌아올 수
있겠지만, 지금 이 시간에는 돌아오지 못할 테니까.

필요한 간격으로 잘 있기 2021 10 08 월 ∨
— 오민 〈에이 비 에이 비디오〉를 보고

내가 지금 사랑하고 있는 사람은 포항에 있다. 아침에 일어나면 창밖으로 바다가
보인다고 그의 눈앞에 보이는 풍경을 사진으로 담아 보내준다. 나는 그의 옆에 있다고
상상해보면서 같은 풍경을 바라본다. 하지만 그가 바라보는 풍경은 실시간으로
움직이고 있고 내가 보고 있는 풍경은 멈춰 있다. 그가 바라보는 풍경에는 구름이
밀려오는 속도가 보일 것이고, 바람을 따라 자유로운 레이스 커튼의 찰랑임이 보일
것이고, 물이 바위에 부딪혀 여러 갈래로 쪼개지는 모습이 보일 것이다. 내가 보는
풍경에는 모든 것이 정지됐다. 더는 움직일 기분이 아니라는 듯이. 이대로 세계가 저주
받기를 바란다는 듯이. 며칠을 그와 붙어 있다가 떨어지니 간격이 느껴진다. 이것이
현재 나와 그의 간격이다. 생동하는 세계와 정지한 세계 사이에 서 있는 나는 무엇을
하고 있는가. 무엇을 할 수 있는가. 내가 있는 곳은 아직 맑은데 그가 있는 곳에서는 벌써
비가 내린다고 한다.

우리는 각자만의 시간을 보내고 있다. 그것은 필요하다. 다시 우리가 만나기
위해 지나가야 하는 시간이다. 떨어져 있어야만 또 만날 수 있다. 또 만난다는 것은
헤어짐을 전제하지 않으면 발생할 수 없는 일이니까. 또 만나자는 약속, 그것은
희망이다. 반드시 만난다는 것, 그것은 확신이다. 그리고 희망과 확신에는 언제나
불안정한 믿음이 따른다. '하지만 무슨 수로?' 같은 물음이 따라온다.

During the Chuseok holiday, I had paid respects to my living relatives, so this was a day for paying respects to the ones no longer with us. Our first stop was the middle slopes in Godang. I don't know how much longer my mother and father are going to be able to make this hike. The path up is so steep that even I might drop off to the side if I relax. I went up ahead, clearing away the branches and brambles that might pose a threat to the rest of my family. Wiping away the sweat, we arrived to find the two tombs awaiting us. One was the joint grave of my grandfather and grandmother; the other belongs to my great-uncle (my grandfather's older brother). We walked up before them, paid our respects, and poured out some soju (a distilled alcoholic beverage) around the graves. We then sat down where we usually do, looking at the sprawling landscape around us. The sea is right next to Godang, and my grandmother would often cook our family seafood dishes when we came to visit. I liked her oyster dishes best of all. I never had a problem with oysters, perhaps because my grandmother made them for us when I was very young. There's been reclamation work, and you now see land where the sea should be. You can see the entire village. Here is where my grandparents and my parents had their meals, went to athletic meets, got chewed out by their teachers. What sort of thoughts and feelings did they have at the time? These are the questions that crossed my mind. I got up, looked at the scenery for a while, and then suddenly burst into tears in front of my grandparents' tomb. I turned my back so that no one would see me cry, but my shoulders started shaking uncontrollably. It was too late. My grandfather, my grandmother··· Now I'm a writer. I even have a book out. They would have been happier than anyone to have seen it. I wished they could have seen. It was too late. I'm sorry.

As I paid respects to my mother's father, the twilight settled in the distance. The setting sun stretched out thin like a horizon, shining over tile roofs and hills. Inwardly, I told my family: "Look at that, the landscape is a gift to us. Even if I die, I will never forget when we were alive."

We went home and had some grilled pork belly. The older family members had their choice of alcoholic beverages; I swigged some water. It really felt like I had returned. "I've finally come back," I wanted to say. I'm alive now, and I know where I will have to return someday. You can't live your life in reverse to see whether it will be somewhere open to others or somewhere closed off. Probably it's not something you can share after you die. But for now it's all right. I'd like for things to continue like this with my family. I'd like to laugh and talk away. I may return to Haenam once again, but I can never return to this moment.

Doing Well at a Necessary Distance
— **Upon viewing Oh Min's** *ABA Video*

Mon Oct 08 2021 ∨

The person I love is in Pohang. When she wakes up in the morning, she sends me photographs of the seascape outside her window. I look at the same landscape, imagining myself there with her. But the landscape she is watching moves in real time, while the one I see is frozen. In her landscape, she can see how fast the clouds come moving in, the rippling of the free lace curtain in the wind, the water splitting apart as it strikes against the rocks. In the landscape I view, everything is still—like it does not feel like moving anymore. Like it wishes this curse upon the world. When the two of us are apart after spending several days together, I can feel the distance. It is the space between her and me today. What am I doing, standing here in between the vibrant world and the still one? What can I do? It's still clear where I am; she tells me it's already raining where she is.

단지 우리에게 주어진 가장 확실한 사실들은 다음과 같다. 나는 서울에 있고 내가 사랑하는 사람은 포항에 있다. 서울에서 포항까지의 거리는 약 350km다. 나는 마음만 먹으면 사랑하는 사람을 보러 가기 위해 기차표를 끊고 포항으로 갈 수 있다. 어쩌면 어느 영화의 주인공처럼 차를 끌고 비가 오는 고속도로를 질주할 수도 있다. 하지만 그렇게 하지 않고 있다. 지금은 시간을 겹칠 때가 아니다. 하여튼 멀긴 멀다.

나는 집에 혼자 있다. 집을 둘러본다. 사물들이 어질러져 있다. 소파에 있어야 할 쿠션들이 거실 바닥을 뒹군다. 식탁에 김치를 담은 통이 있다. 주방용 가위가 택배 박스 위에 있고 리모컨이 실내 자전거 안장 위에 있다. 내 방은 말할 것도 없다. 여전히 침대 위에 수십 권의 책들이 쌓여 있다. 침대는 책의 무게에 짓눌려 모양이 조금 꺼진다. 의자에도 책이 몇 권 쌓여 있고 책상에도 책이 몇 권 쌓여 있다. 나는 이러다가 책에 깔려 죽을 팔자. 벽에 붙인 포스터가 떨어지려고 한다. 마스킹테이프는 아무래도 접착력이 구린 것 같다. 예쁘기만 하고 기능을 제대로 소화한 적이 없다. 블루투스 스피커가 약간 비뚤어진 포즈로 책상 위에 있다. 이것으로 음악을 듣지 않은 지도 오래다. 전원이나 켜질지 의문이다. 나는 스피커를 제 위치에 두고 최대한 정면을 향하도록 배치한다. 측면을 바라보는 일은 있을 수 없다. 나는 그런 변화를 병적으로 의식하고 고치려는 주인이다. 사물이 내 의식에 맞게 똑바로 위치해 있지 않으면 그 변화를 잘 견디지 못한다. '예민한가?' 싶다가도 오히려 의식을 사물에 투영하여 원하는 공간감을 형성하는 것이 이 집의 안정감이 아닐까 생각해본다. 물론 의식은 사물을 해친다.

집에서 생활하다 보면 사물을 정의하게 된다. 가령 위에서 말한 주방용 가위는 실은 새로 산 옷 태그를 자르는 데 쓰이기도 한다. 그러나 이것으로 택배를 뜯진 않는다. 이러한 의미적 제약을 두기도 하는 반면 내가 진심으로 소중하게 다루는 기타는 항상 내가 원하는 시간, 원하는 장소에서 연주되어야 한다. 그 외에는 방치된다. 이것은 보편적 제약이다. 그리고 특정 사물에는 이름을 부여한다. 똑똑해 보이는 토끼 인형에게 '소크라테스'라고 부르거나 전자 피아노 아래 정갈하게 놓인 아령 여섯 개를 '건강 지킴이'라고 부르는 행위에는 자신의 애착을 의미화하는 동시에 애정하는 사물을 자신의 내면으로 귀속하여 영토화하려는 목적이 내포되어 있다. 지나친 자의식인가? 모르겠다. 하지만 나는 사물이 내가 생각하는 위치로부터 흐트러지면 즉각 발견하고 원 상태로 돌려놓는다. 사물이 인간의 손을 탈 수밖에 없는 운명이라면 차라리 좋은 주인 아래서 자리에 익숙해지는 것도 살아가는 하나의 방법이라고 여기는 걸지도.

여기서 더 중요한 것은 바로 간격이다. 나는 각각의 사물들이 딱 달라붙어 있지 않게끔 여유 있는 간격을 준다. 두 개의 리모컨을 소파에 두어도 살짝 떨어뜨린다. 쿠션들과 책들은…… 어쩔 수 없이 다다다닥 붙는다. 붙어 있지 않고 독립적으로 위치하는 사물들이 건강해 보인다. 온전한 가위, 온전한 화장품, 온전한 기타, 온전한 피아노, 온전한 신발, 온전한 손톱깎이, 온전한 셔츠, 온전한 안경…… 들로 잘 지내는 것처럼 보인다. 각자에게 필요한 간격으로 잘 있는 중이다. 그렇다면 집은 수많은 간격으로 구성되는 걸까. 또 그렇다면 이 세계 또한 수많은 간격으로 구성된 것 아닐까. 내가 지금 서울에 있고 내가 사랑하는 사람이 포항에 있듯. 이 또한 잘 있는 것 아닌가.

일기는 분명 '오늘' 있었던 일(들)을 적는 건데 왜 문장을 과거형으로 쓸까. 오늘은 현재인데 왜 과거의 문장들을 데려와 기록하게 되는 걸까. 혹시 일기란 현재와 과거를 혼동하고 착각하는 과정을 쓰는 일인가. 당연히 '있었던'에 방점을 찍어야 한다는 사실, 나도 안다. 그래서 오늘은 현재형으로 쓰고 있다. 오늘을 붙들고 싶다.

We each spend our time separately. We need that. It's time that we must pass through for us to meet again. We have to be apart for us to meet. "Meeting" cannot happen without presuming some separation. When we promise to meet again, that's hope. When we insist we will meet again, that's confidence. And with both hope and confidence, there is always a feeling of instability. There's always the question: "But how?"

The clearest facts given to us are these: I'm in Seoul, and the one I love is in Pohang. It's about 350km from Seoul to Pohang. If I decide to, I can buy a train ticket and go to Pohang to see the one I love. Like a character in a movie, I could get in my car and race down the rainy highway. But I don't do that. Now is not a moment for our times to overlap. And it is quite far.

I'm at home alone. I look around. Things are scattered all around. The cushions that should be on the sofa are on the living room floor. There's a vat of kimchi on the dinner table. Some kitchen scissors are sitting on a delivery box, and the remote control is on the seat of the exercise bike. And that's to say nothing of my room. Dozens of books are still piled up on my bed, which is starting to sag a bit under their weight. There are a few more books on the chair, and even more on the desk. At this rate, I'm going to end up crushed underneath them. The poster on the wall is about to peel away. The masking tape doesn't appear to be much of an adhesive. It's pretty enough, but it's never really served its purpose. The Bluetooth speakers sit on the desk slightly askew. I haven't used them to listen to music for a while now. I'm not even sure they'd switch on. I put the speakers back in place and orient them so they face forward as much as possible. I've got no reason to look at them in profile. I'm the sort of owner who is pathological about noticing these changes and trying to correct them. I can't bear a change unless the object is positioned the right way to suit my perceptions. "Am I being too sensitive?" I wonder, but then I think that the sense of stability in this house may come from projecting consciousness onto objects as I create the desired spatial sense. Consciousness, of course, is harmful to objects.

When you live in a house, you start to define its objects. The aforementioned kitchen scissors, for example, have also been used to clip the tags off of newly bought clothing—but not to open packages. Even as I impose those sorts of semantic constraints, however, my guitar—my most precious possession—must always be played at the time and place I desire. Otherwise, it is left alone. That's a universal constraint. I also give names to particular objects. A clever-looking stuffed rabbit is called "Socrates," while the six dumbbells neatly positioned below the electronic keyboard are called "health watchdogs." Those acts of naming signify my affection, but there's also an aim of internalizing and territorializing the objects I care for. Too self-conscious? Perhaps. But whenever an item gets away from where I think it should be, I notice it immediately and put it back in place. If it's the fate of objects to pass through human hands, then one way of living is to get used to a particular spot with a good owner.

The more important thing here is the gap. I leave ample gaps between objects so that they are not stuck close together. If I have two different remote controls on the sofa, I'll place them some distance apart. As far as the cushions and books are concerned⋯there is some inevitable closeness. Objects look healthier when they are positioned independently rather than close together. Intact scissors, intact cosmetics, an intact guitar, an intact keyboard, intact shoes, intact nail clippers, intact shirts, intact eyeglasses⋯it gives the appearance that things are going well. They are doing well, separated from each other by the necessary distance. So is the home made up of so many gaps? If so, is the world itself made up of so many gaps? Like me being in Seoul now, while the one I love is in Pohang. Is that also "doing well"?

내가 사랑하는 사람은 잘 있는가. 내 친구들도 잘 지내는가. 대전에서, 부산에서, 인천에서, 수원에서, 일산에서, 일본에서, 프랑스에서 잘 지내는가. 가족들도 목포에서, 해남에서, 춘천에서, 미국에서 잘 지내는가. 우리는 모두 다른 간격으로 지내는가. 정말 다른가. 간격은 정말 물리적 거리를 의미하는가. 오늘은 금요일이다. 금요일은 지나간다. 금요일이 다 지나갔다는 것은 오늘이 다 지나갔다는 뜻과 같다. 금요일은 돌아온다. 금요일과 다시 만날 수 있다. 오늘은 돌아온다. 오늘과 다시 만날 수 있다. 이런 착각을 거듭할수록 현재는 과거가 되고 과거는 미래가 된다. 시간이 교차된다. 나는 일기를 통해 개별적 사건들을 하루 단위로 간격을 둔다. 일기장엔 하루들이 잘 있다.

하루들이 떨어져 있다는 것, 그것은 언젠가 약속한 미래적인 만남이다. 모두 만날 날이 있을 것이다. 모두 만나게 될 것이다. 나도 사랑하는 사람을 만나기 위해 오늘을 잘해야지. 이따 전화해야겠다.

이기리 ⓘ
시인

2020년 제39회 김수영 문학상을 수상하여 작품 활동을 시작했다. 시집 『그 웃음을 나도 좋아해』가 있다. 한낮의 오후, 카페에서 햇빛 받으며 커피 마시면서 책 읽고 글 쓰는 시간을 좋아한다. 글쓰기를 통해 어디로든 갈 수 있다고 생각하는 사람. 외향적 인간. 취미 부자는 아니지만 진득한 취미를 갖고 있다. 내가 쓰는 시가 이 세계의 또 다른 외연을 보여줄 수 있기를.

In my journal, I wrote down the things that happened "today"—but why did I put the sentences in the past tense? If today is still happening, why should I have recorded it in past tense sentences? When you keep a journal, are you writing down a process of confusing past and present? I'm aware that I should obviously emphasize the "happened" part. So I write about today in the present tense. I want to hold on to today.

Is the person I love doing well? Are my friends doing well? Are they doing well in Daejeon, in Busan, in Incheon, in Suwon, in Ilsan, in Japan, in France? Are my family members doing well in Mokpo, in Haenam, in Chuncheon, in the US? Are we all separated by different distances? Are they really different? Does "distance" really just refer to physical distance? Today is a Friday. Friday is passing by. When Friday is over, that means that today is over. Friday returns. I can see Friday again. Today returns. I can see today again. The more we confuse things like this, the more present becomes past and past becomes future. Time overlaps. In my journal, I add distance by grouping individual events in daily units. In my journal, the days are doing well.

When the days are separate, that is the promise of some future meeting. All of us have the days we will meet. We will all meet. I need to get through today well so I can see the one I love. I should call her up in a bit.

Lee Gi-ri ⓘ
Poet

Lee Gi-ri began his poetry career as the winner of the 39th Kim Soo Young Literary Award in 2020. He has published the poetry collection *I Like That Laugh Too*. He enjoys spending his time reading and writing as he sips coffee underneath the sunshine in a café during the afternoon. He is someone who believes in the ability to travel anywhere through writing. An extrovert. He doesn't have a wealth of interests, but the ones he does have he pursues tenaciously—hoping the poems he writes can show a different extension of the world.

온라인 플랫폼 경험에 관한
다섯 편의 일기

조은비(독립 큐레이터)

처음 이 글 ─ "온라인 플랫폼 경험에 관한 일기" ─ 을 청탁 받았을 때 나는 관음과 노출에 대해 생각했다. 남의 일기를 읽는다는 것과 남에게 읽힐 일기를 쓴다는 것에 대해서 말이다. 이 두 가지 욕구는 잘 어울리는 한쌍 같으면서도 동시에 서로를 배반하고 있는 것처럼 여겨진다. 다시 말해, 보고 싶은 것을 보여주는 것은 만족과 함께 실망을 동반할지 모른다. 원치 않는 것을 원한다는, 그 감정의 토대를 뒤흔든다는 것. 그런 위험에도 불구하고 내가 이 제안에 응한 것은, '온라인 미술 플랫폼'이라는 장치가 그 양가성과 조응하고 있다는 예감 때문이었다. 그리고 그 반향은 내가 집이라는 공간으로부터 감지하는 고유한 진동과도 잘 어우러질 듯싶었다. 따라서 이 일기의 내용은 독자가 원하는 것과 전혀 다를 수도 있고, 어쩌면 심지어 무관한 것처럼 여겨질 수도 있다. 그러나 주지하듯 나는 이 글이 어쩔 수 없이 그렇게 될 수밖에 없는 글이라고 믿는다. 제안이 없었으면 쓰이지 않았을, 공개될 일기라는 모순이 이 글의 변치 않는 요체이기 때문이다.

      *

집에 관해 이야기하자면 별 수 없이 주위를 돌아보게 된다. 출산 이후로 지난 몇 년 간 나는 대부분의 시간을 집에서 보냈다. 네덜란드에서 지내는 2년의 시간 동안, 이국의 보육제도에 기대지 않은 채 오롯이 아기를 돌본다는 것은 곧 이동과 행위의 제약을 의미했다. 아이와 단 둘이 있을 땐 '우리'와 저 밖의 세상은 완벽히 분리되어 있는 것만 같았다. 더군다나 매 순간 돌봄이 필요한 아기를 위해 집은 놀이공간, 일터와 연구실, 만남의 장소 등으로 그 쓰임이 다양해졌다. 어쩌면 그때 나는 제약으로부터 어떤 가능성을 찾으려 했었는지도 모른다. 하지만 그것도 잠시, 팬데믹 직후 한국으로 돌아와 나는 또다른 당혹감을 느낄 수밖에 없었다. 두꺼운 매트리스 사이로 침범하는 아이의 소음은 종종 이웃 간에 긴장을 불러일으켰고, 맘충, 노키즈존 등 아이와 여성을 집단화하는 혐오와 적대적인 사회적 분위기는 외부 활동을 위축시켰다. 집은 애초부터 그저 대피소일 따름이었다. 긴급보육, 비대면 수업 등으로 전환된 교육과정은 아이들을 집으로 '가두는' 일을 반복하지만, 정작 집 안에서 "대면을 피할 공간"은 없다. 닫힌 공간 속에서 실상 불가능한 비대면은, 공적인 영역을 기준으로 마련된 '사회적 거리두기'라는 아이러니를 도드라지게 할 뿐이다. 몸과 몸이 끊임없이 부딪치고 맞닿는 양육에 물리적 거리두기란 불가능하다. 아이와 함께 가던 공공 도서관은 방역 조치를 이유로 대출만을 허용하고, 학교 운동장과 단지 내 놀이터 이용은 제한되었다. 공공 미술관은 사회적 거리두기에 따라 예약 운영을 하지만, 아이들은 애당초 환영 받는 관객이 아니었다. "집에 있으라"는 말이 공허한 것은 원래 이들에게 온전히 허락된 공간은 '집'뿐인 탓이다. 따라서 만약 우리 사회가 팬데믹 이후를 다른 방식으로 사유하고자 한다면, 나는 그 전환적 상상력을 지금, 여기의 공간-집에서부터 찾길 바란다. 집 안의 일과 집 밖의 쓰임은 분배되어야 하기에. 그리고 미술관 역시 그 분배의 책임에서 자유로울 수 없을 것이다. 팬데믹 이후

Five Diary Entries
on Online Platform Experiences

Jo Eunbi (Independent Curator)

My first thoughts, when asked to write "a diary about my experiences of online platforms," were of voyeurism and exposure. With regard to reading someone else's diary, and writing a diary to be read to someone else. I see these two desires as a well-matched yet mutually treacherous pair. In other words, I wonder if showing people what they want to see brings a combination of satisfaction and disappointment. An undermining of the emotional foundation of wanting what you don't want. The reason I accepted the proposal despite these risks was a hunch that the device of an "online art platform" corresponded with this ambivalence. It also seemed that this resonance would be well-suited to the unique affects that I felt in the space I call home. It follows that the content of this diary may be nothing like that desired by the reader, and may even seem irrelevant. But, as known, I believe that was the inevitable fate of this text. Because its immutable core is the contradiction of a public diary, one that would never have been written if it had not been proposed by someone else.

*

When you're asked to talk about your home, you unavoidably find yourself looking around it. In the last few years, since giving birth to my child, I've spent most of my time at home. During the two years I spent in the Netherlands, I did nothing but look after my child without relying on the country's foreign childcare system; this entailed limits to my movements and actions. When I and my child were alone together, it seemed as if "we" and the outside world were separated completely. Moreover, for my child, who needed looking after at every single moment, the home acquired a greater diversity of uses, from playground to workplace, research lab, and meeting venue. Perhaps, at the time, I was looking for some kind of possibility within these limits. But that was short-lived; straight after start of the pandemic, we returned to Korea and I was forced to feel yet another kind of frustration. Noise from my child, penetrating all the way through a thick mattress, caused occasional tension with our neighbors, while I found myself leaving home less often amid the hate and hostile social climate that lumped women and children together to produce labels like "mum-roach" and spaces like "kid-free zones." From the start, our home was merely a place of refuge. The educational curriculum kept on "locking kids up" at home with measures like emergency home care and contactless classes, but within the home there was no way of avoiding contact. The effective impossibility of non-contact within a confined space merely highlighted the irony of social distancing, a notion based on the public realm. In childcare, with its endless physical contact, physical distancing was impossible. The public library where my child and I used to go now only allows borrowing, as part of Covid-19 prevention measures, while school grounds and the playground in our apartment complex are closed. Public art museums are operating reservation-based systems to ensure social distancing, but children were never particularly welcome there in the first place. The emptiness of the phrase "stay at home" lies in the fact that home was the only space completely permitted to

미술관들은 제가끔 자신의 새로운 (혹은 마땅히 했었어야만 하는) 역할을 다급히 상상하고 있다. 이 플랫폼 역시 그 상상의 구현물 중 하나일 것이다. 그러므로 이어지는 일기는, 내가 그 상상 속의 누군가가 될 수 있는가, 라는 질문을 향한 내 일상의 응답이다.

오늘 오후 어린이집에서 코로나 밀접 접촉자로 분류되어 자가 격리를 해야한단 연락을 받았다. 아이를 곧바로 하원시키고 나는 네 번째 코로나 검사를 받았다. 이제부터 2주간 아이와 함께 꼼짝없이 집에 있어야할 테다. 육아는 내 시간감각을 완전히 다르게 만들었다. 양육의 일상이란 끊임없는 '반복의 반복'이라 불과 어제의 기억조차 쉽게 증발해버린다. 아이에겐 되돌릴 과거나 막연한 미래보단 '지금'이 더 중요한 탓일까. 우리는 서로와 함께 서로에 기대어 오늘만 산다. 그리고 어느날 문득, 성큼 자란 아이의 낯선 모습에서 시간은 가시화된다. 그렇게 어른과 아이의 시간은 다르게 흐른다. 작년 네덜란드에서 한국으로 귀국했을 때 네살배기는 영문도 모른 채 격리되었지만, 불과 일년 사이 아이는 이 상황을 다 이해할 수 있을 정도로 훌쩍 커버렸다. 분명한 목소리로 코로나가 빨리 사라졌으면 한다는 아이의 말엔 진심이 담겨있다. 그러나 지금 나는 아이가 겪게 될 답답함보단 당장 내 일에 대한 걱정이 앞선다. 계획된 일들을 처리하기 위해선 아이의 협조와 남편과의 역할 분담이 중요하다. 앞으로 쌓이게 될 피로에 벌써부터 고단해진다.

　　　　물론 팬데믹 이후로 일상화된 비대면 시스템이 주로 집에서 일하는 내 업무에 큰 불편을 주는 것 같진 않다. 돌이켜보면 귀국 후 지난 일 년여 간 여러 프로젝트에 참여했지만, 대부분의 업무는 주로 온라인을 통해서 진행되었다. 때로는 '사회적 거리두기'란 명분으로, 비대면의 편의성이 대면 만남을 자연스럽게 대체하기도 했다. 어느 문화재단의 심의 평가 역시 온라인으로 이뤄졌고, 평가가 종료되기까지 나는 실무자와 단 한번의 만남을 가졌을 뿐이었다. 작가성이나 작품을 둘러싼 (수치화가 어려운) 추상적인 판단은 새로운 기술과 제도에 의해 매끄럽게 합리화된다. 그리고 이 다양한 가상 회로망 속에서 내 삶은 안전하게 유지되는 듯 보였다.

　　　　여기 갇혀 있다는 것과 그렇지 않은 것의 차이를 가늠해본다. 모르겠다. 아니, 너무 잘 알겠다. 좁은 아파트 공간에서 돌봄의 '소란스러움'을 견뎌야 한다는 것. 게다가 더욱 아이러니한 것은 이 돌봄을 나누기 위한 '돌봄노동 시스템'이 연쇄적으로 작동한다는 것이다. 창밖에서는 밤낮 가릴 것 없이 택배 차량의 상하차 소음이 들려온다. 아파트 복도를 구르는 카트의 요란한 쇳소리와 분리수거 폐기물을 치우는 대형 화물차의 기계음, 팬데믹 이후로 늘어난 리모델링 공사음까지. 어떤 돌봄은 그 소란스러움으로 스스로를 가시화한다. 그러므로 코로나가 일시적으로 시장을 멈춰 세웠다 하더라도 이 시스템 아래 완벽한 멈춤은 없다. 플랫폼 경제가 이제 인간의 신체와 사고 행위 전 영역에 걸쳐 다양한 대행 서비스를 제공해주고 있기 때문이다. 식사, 쇼핑, 뉴스, 청소, 세탁, 영화, 음악, 미술작품 등에 이르기까지, 이들은 나를 대신해 내가 원하는 것을 큐레이션하고, ─당신이 지불 능력만 있다면 ─ 무엇이든 대여하고 대리해줄 수 있다고 말한다. 문득 나는 궁금해진다. 이제 인간은 스스로 선택과 결정을 할 수 있는 존재일까? 설령 그럴 수 있다해도 그럴 기회가 주어질까? 모니터 화면 안에 잘 배열된 작품들을 보면서 나는 격리된 내 처지가 그와 다를 바 없다고 생각했다. 현실과 실물로부터 유리된 채 '우리'는 절차화된 순환경제를 구성하고 있다. 그렇게 2주 간 나는 여럿의 표적이자 실적이 될 것이다.

them from the start. So if we want society to start thinking in different ways after the pandemic, I would like us to pursue these transformative imaginings in the space of here-and-now that is the home. Since we need to distinguish between the work in the home and the use outside the home. Art museums, too, bear some responsibility for this distinction. This online platform will also be one embodiment of our imaginings. The following diary entries, therefore, are daily answers to the question: Can I be considered by these imaginings as someone to take into account?

Thu Sep 09 2021 ⌄

This afternoon I got a message from the nursery that I had been classified as a close contact of a Covid-19 patient and had to quarantine at home. I fetched my child straight away and got my fourth COVID test. For the next two weeks, I'll be stuck at home with my child. Childcare has completely changed my sense of time. Its daily routine is one of repeated repetition, so that memories as recent as yesterday's are quick to evaporate. Perhaps it's because, for kids, the present is more important than a past to look back on or a vague future. Together, we rely on each other alone, and live only for today. And the sudden sight, one day, of our rapidly grown and unfamiliar looking child, gives time visible form. Time thus flows differently for adults and children. Last year, when I returned from the Netherlands to Korea, my four-year-old was quarantined without even knowing it, but, in the space of barely a year, she has grown up so fast that she understands quarantine completely. When she pronounces clearly that she wishes Covid-19 would disappear quickly, her voice is full of sincerity. But now, I am more worried about my work than about the frustration my child is going to feel. If I am to get the work I have planned done, cooperation from my child and role division with my husband are important. The thought of the fatigue that is set to build up is already wearing me down.

Of course, the contactless systems that have become part of daily life since the start of the pandemic don't seem to disrupt my work, which I generally do at home anyway, that much. Looking back, I've taken part in several projects in the year or so since returning to Korea, but most of that work has taken place online. Sometimes, the convenience of non-contact has naturally replaced in-person meetings under the pretext of social distancing. One cultural foundation conducted a jury process, and I only held one single meeting with a member of the foundation staff from beginning to end. Abstract judgments of artistic character and works (which are hard to quatify) are smoothly rationalized through new technologies and systems. And my life seemed to be safely continuing within these various virtual networks.

I try to weigh up the difference between confined here and not being so. I don't know. No, I know only too well. About having to endure the noisiness of childcare in the space of a small apartment. Even more ironic is the way the series of "childcare labor systems" that come into operation to divide this caregiving. Outside our windows comes the sound of delivery vehicles being loaded and unloaded, day and night. We hear loud metallic sounds trolleys being wheeled down the corridor outside, the mechanical sounds of big trucks taking away the sorted garbage, and even sounds of renovation work, which have become more frequent since the pandemic began. Some childcare makes itself visible through its noisiness. So even if COVID temporary brought the market to a halt, there is no complete stopping under this system. Because the platform economy now supplies diverse proxy services in all human areas, from our bodies to our thoughts. From meals to shopping, news, cleaning, laundry, films, music, and

'워치 앤 칠'에서 금요일마다 업데이트 되는 작품 공개 알림 메일이 왔지만, 벌써 두 번째 메일을 지나쳤다. 한번은 성가신 메일들 탓에 무심코 지나쳤고, 그 다음 번에는 자가 격리 해제 후 지연된 일상 탓에 확인할 겨를 없이 바빴다. 하지만 그런 상황 때문이 아니더라도, 플랫폼에 관한 글을 좀처럼 쓰기가 어렵다. "제도의 제안에 따른 제도적 경험"에 관한 글이, 왜 그 경험 자체를 서사화하는 데 실패하는가. 나는 플랫폼 속 영상을 관람하고 일기를 쓰면서도, 어쩐지 거기서 본 작품의 내용이나 플랫폼의 인터페이스에 관해 이야기하기가 어렵다. 이는 플랫폼을 구성하는 시스템의 문제만은 아닌 듯하다. 그러니까 이 실패의 원인에는 나 자신의 몫 또한 있을지 모르겠다. 말하자면, 왜 나는 이 감상에 몰입하지 못하는가.

분명 누군가는 이 플랫폼이 가진 장점들을 발견하고 확장시키며 작업들을 향유할 수도 있을지 모른다. 그러할 가능성이 다분하다. 하나 내게 이 생각은 결국 미술관이라는 제도에 대해 재고하게끔 할 따름이다. 온라인 플랫폼의 기술적인 가능성과 제약이, 특정한 개인-가령, 돌봄 노동자 또는 예술 감상에 대한 동기를 충분히 부여받지 못한 이들-을 암묵적으로 배제할 수 있다는 사실을 말이다. 지금 내게 어떤 작업이나 웹사이트에 관한 이야기는 없다. 어쩔 수 없이 지난 자가격리 기간 동안 작성한 메모로 오늘의 일기를 대신한다.

*

현재 우리는 모두 속수무책이다. 유예된 약속과 기약 없는 만남, 중단된 일상과 취소된 계획 앞에서 시간은 무력해진다. 지금 여기 가능한 것은, 결국 기다리는 일 뿐이다. 기실 우리는 그저 현재로부터 벗어나길 바랄 따름이다. 그렇게 비-현재가 현재를 말소시키고 있다. 우리는 지금을 살지 못한다. 미래를 향한 선형적인 시간배치는 근대 자본주의의 토대를 이뤘다. 과거, 현재, 미래라는 명료한 시점들은 시간을 말끔하게 재단하고, 그 위에 간격과 주기라는 친절한 범례를 새겼다. 가령 우리는 현재를 준거로 과거를 돌이켜보거나 미래를 내다보았다. 즉, 미래를 기약하는 이 위계적인 시간성은, 현재를 사는 원동력이자 다가올 시간을 대비하는 믿음직한 조건이었던 것이다. 그렇게 진보의 환상은 '어제' 보다 나은 '내일'을 상상케 했다. 예컨대, 4년마다 인체의 한계를 뛰어넘어 어김없이 기록을 갱신하던, 그 환희의 순간들을 분명 쉽사리 잊지는 못할 것이다. 그러나 오늘의 삶은 어떠한가. 균질한 간격으로 물결치던 시간의 파동이 어느새 더 이상 느껴지지 않는다. 과거의 규범과 제도로부터 울려 퍼지던 리듬은 대중없이 깨지고, 그 위계와 작위성을 뒤흔드는 진동 속에서 익숙한 템포는 서서히 잦아들고 있다. 따라서 불확실해진 것은 결국, 애초에 아직 오지 않은 하나의 '미래'가 아니라, 이를 대비하고 또 맞이하던 그 수많은 관성적인 '현재'들이다.

이 속수무책 속에서 제도의 권위는 '거리두기'의 아이러니만큼 오히려 더 강력해보인다. 과학의 견고한 체계 아래 이성과 합리를 담지하는 기술만능주의, 혹은 그 '예측'의 패러다임이 근대와는 또 다른 방식으로 개인을 통제하고 있는 것이다. 현재를 상실한 개인들은 불안 속에서 자신의 주체성을 내려놓고 제도와 권위에 의지하고, 미래에 대한 책임을 그에 전가한다. 하지만 제도나 권위는 실상 그 무엇도 책임지지 않는다. 도리어 그것들은 개인에게 그 전가의 책임을 물을 따름이다. 재작년 겨울, 공기업의 부당한 고용구조를 규탄하며 스스로 생을 마감한 이의 젊은 아내는 광화문에 분향소를 세우고 고인의 운구차를 세웠고, 이는 이내 "방역"을 이유로 강제 철거되었다.

artworks, it replaces me as curator of my own desires, telling me I can rent anything or have any service provided—as long as I can pay for it. Suddenly, I am curious. Are humans now beings that can make their own choices and decisions? And, even if they are, do they have opportunities to do so? Watching the works displayed so nicely on my monitor, it occurs to me that my own isolated situation is no different from theirs. Removed from reality and genuine objects, "we" constitute a proceduralized, circular economy. Thus, for the next two weeks, I am set to become a series of targets and results.

Fri Sep 24 2021 ∨

Every Friday, I get an email notification from *Watch and Chill* telling me about newly updated artworks. I've already missed two emails. One, I accidentally overlooked due to a load of other annoying emails, and the next time I didn't have time to read it amid my postponed daily schedule after being released from quarantine. But, even if that wasn't the reason, it's hard for me to write about the platform. Why does a text about "institutional experiences in accordance with systems and proposals" fail to create a narrative about those experiences themselves? Even as I watch the videos on the platform and write my diary, it's somehow hard for me to talk about the works I have seen there, or the platform interface. This doesn't seem to be just a question of the system that makes up the platform. Perhaps the cause of this failure is, in part, my fault. Why, you might ask, am I not becoming absorbed in the appreciation of art?

   Of course, some people might be able to discover and enlarge upon the platform's good points as they enjoy the works on display. That's more than likely. But personally, this thought just makes me end up reconsidering the art museum as an institution. The possibilities and limitations of an online platform may tacitly exclude certain individuals—those, for example, who work in caregiving or who lack the motivation to view art. Now, I have nothing to say about any artwork or website. Which leaves me with no choice but to replace today's diary entry with some notes I made during my last home quarantine period.

   *

Currently, we're all at our wits' ends. Faced with postponed appointments, meetings put off indefinitely, discontinued daily life and cancelled plans, time becomes impotent. Ultimately, the only possible thing now is waiting. To be honest, all we want is to escape reality. Thus, the non-present is erasing the present. We are unable to live. A linear arrangement of time, oriented toward the future, forms the basis of modern capitalism. The clearly-defined points of past, present and future made clean cuts in the cloth of time, superimposed with helpful legends of regular intervals and periods. We used the present, for example, as our reference point for looking back on the past and predicting the future. This hierarchical, future-promising temporality, then, was a motivation for living in the present, and a reliable condition for preparing for times to come. The fantasy of progress let us imagine a tomorrow that would be better than yesterday. I'll never forget, for example, those moments of delight every four years when we transcended the limits of the human body, setting new records without fail. But what about life today? At some point, I stopped feeling the waves of time that had rolled in with such regularity. The rhythms that had echoed out from the norms and institutions of the past have broken into inconsistency, and familiar tempos have been swallowed up by the vibrations convulsing hierarchy and randomness. As a result, what has now lost its certainty is not the single future that was always yet to arrive, but the many inert presents that prepared for and greeted that future.

나는 그가 실로 "공공의 안전"을 어떻게 위협하는지 이해하지 못했다. 그리고 그 억울함에 대한 관용이 또 다른 "불법집회"를 용인하는 알리바이가 될 수 있다는 공권력의 설명은, 더더욱 이해하지 못했다. 그러나 이보다 더 큰 문제는 이런 그럴싸한 말들에 반박할 근거를 도무지 마련할 수가 없다는 것이다. 개인의 의지와 주체성을 제한하는 공적인 힘에 대응할 마땅한 언어가 날로 사라진다는 사실을 우리는 어떻게 받아들여야할까? 개인의 왜소화를 합리화하고 오히려 긍정하게끔 만드는 이 현실의 역설을 어떻게 바라봐야할까? 공표된 기준은 타자와의 거리, "사회적 거리두기"를 명시하지만, 실상 이제 그 누구도 타인과 얼마만큼의 '간격'을 가지고 만나야하는지 확신하지 못한다. 모든 상황은 예외적이고, 그 예외상태에 대해 우리 중 그 누구도 예외가 될 수 없다.

2021 09 30 목 ∨

아이가 낮잠을 푹 잔 탓일까. 좀처럼 잠 못드는 아이를 토닥이면서 나는 아이를 재우고 나서 밤에 볼 영상작품의 목록을 떠올려본다. 하지만 아이 손이 내 손을 꽉 쥐고 놓아주질 않는 탓에, 생각을 더이상 이어가기 어렵다. 아이는 잠들기 직전이나 불안할 때 내 손가락을 쥐고 그 끝을 제 손가락으로 튕기는 버릇이 있다. 애착과 안정을 위한 습관. 그리고 그 습관은 전염성이 강해 이젠 나도 그 버릇이 종종 나오곤 한다. 아이를 토닥이기 시작한지 한 시간이 넘어가자 슬슬 속에서부터 짜증이 올라온다. 결국 나는 아이를 재우는 것을 포기하고 남편과 교대했다. 그리고 인내를 쏟아버린 수면과 비수면의 경계에서 간신히 탈출해 다시 온라인에 연결된다.

　　　아이가 태어난 직후, 나는 신생아를 키우면서 수유 텀, 수면의식, 수면패턴 등 낯선 전문 용어들을 알게 되었다. 과거엔 대체 아이를 어떻게 키웠던 걸까. 요즘 양육자들이 자주하는 소리다. 인류의 역사만큼 아이를 키워본 사람들의 수가 많다한들, 동시대 삶의 조건과 상황 속에서 개개인이 경험하는 육아는 놀라움의 항구적인 연속이다. 최근 정부가 돌봄로봇 4종을 개발한단 기사를 읽고 실소가 터져 나올 수밖에 없었던 이유다. 이는 돌봄을 직접해본 사람에 의한 발상이 아닐 것일 뿐더러 애초에 그 의도가 불순하다. 다시 말해 이 시도는, 돌봄을 여성의 타고난 자질인 것처럼 성별화 해온 사회에서 '여성의 노동'을 저평가할 뿐만 아니라 기계 기술에 의해 대체할 수 있는 것으로 간주한다는 점에서 문제적이다.

　　　독일로 이주한 케냐 출신 난민 인권 운동가 미미의 생전 인터뷰를 읽어보면, 그는 자신이 독일 정부의 난민 귀화 정책에 따라 제 의사와는 무관하게 노인병원의 간호사로 양성되었다고 밝힌다. 그는 당시의 경험을 고통스럽게 기억한다. 아프리카에서 노인은 자발적인 돌봄과 존경의 대상이었지만, 독일의 노인병원에서는 노인을 "공장의 조립라인"에 있는 부품처럼 다뤘고, "환자들은 상품 그 이상도 이하도 아니었다." 그에게 공동체의 부재를 대체하는 선진국의 의료 시스템은 이질적인 문화 충격이었고, 이를 견딜 수 없었던 그는 결국 독일 사회에 적응하지 못한다. 이처럼 소위 '문명화'된 국가의 제도가 얼마나 비인간적인지를 상기해볼 때, 돌봄로봇이라는 국가정책적 해법은 어찌 보면 인간에게 남아 있는 일말의 개인성마저 박탈하고 통제하려는 기술-자본의 교묘한 수사에 지나지 않을 것이다.

　　　나에게 있어 '돌봄'의 경험은 매순간의 상호성에 기반한다. 아이의 손가락과 내 손 끝이 만나, 우리는 서로를 돌본다. 인간의 취약성과 늙음, 의존성과 관계, 공감

Amid this helplessness, the authority of the system actually appears as strong as the irony of "social distancing." The technocracy that contains reason and rationality under the unshakable regime of science, or the paradigm of "prediction," are controlling individuals in yet another way to modernity. Individuals who have lost the present surrender their own agency amid their uncertainty and depend on institutions and authority, passing on responsibility for the future to the latter. Yet institutions and authority effectively take responsibility for nothing. On the contrary: they merely hold individuals responsible for passing on the buck to them. In the winter of the year before last, the young wife of a man who had taken his own life in protest at the unfair employment structure of a publicly-owned company set up an a memorial altar and a hearse for her late husband, but these were soon forcibly removed in the name of "Covid-19 prevention" measures. I really couldn't understand how she was threatening "public safety." Even less comprehensible was the explanation from the authorities that tolerating such injustice would in turn function as an excuse for other "illegal assemblies." But the bigger problem was that I simply could not find any grounds for arguing against such plausible statements. How must we accept the fact that suitable language for responding to public power that limits the wills and autonomy of individuals is disappearing by the day? How must we regard the paradox of a reality that rationalizes the shrinking of the individual and actually makes it a positive thing? Officially proclaimed standards clearly call for "social distancing" from others, but no one is now actually sure how much of a "distance" they must keep when meeting others. All situations are exceptional, and no one is excepted from them.

Thu Sep 30 2021 ⌄

Maybe it's because my child had a nap during the day. She is totally unable to get to sleep, and as I pat her, I think of the list of video works to watch tonight once I've put her to bed. But it's hard to continue this train of thought as she grips my hand and refuses to let go. When she is uneasy, just before falling asleep, she has a habit of grasping my fingers and flicking their ends with her fingers. It's a habit of attachment and stability. And it's a highly infectious habit, so I often catch myself doing it these days, too. When I've been patting her for more than an hour, I feel irritation slowly rising inside me. In the end, I give up trying to get her to sleep and my husband takes over. Barely escaping the boundary of exhausted patience between sleep and sleeplessness, I go online again.

After my child was born, I learned a host of specialist terms such as lactation period, sleep consciousness, and sleep patterns. How on earth did people use to raise kids? You often hear parents ask that these days. Child raising may be as old as history itself, but the personal experiences it brings every different individual within the circumstances of contemporary life and conditions is a perpetual series of surprises. That's why, when I read a recent article on how the government is developing four types of childcare robots, I couldn't help laughing. Not only could the idea not have come from anyone with actual experience of raising kids; it was based on dubious intentions from the start. It was problematic, in other words, both for undervaluing "women's work" in a gender-based society that saw childcare as the innate gift of women, and for regarding that work as something that could be replaced by machine technology.

In an interview that I read, the late Mimi, a Kenyan refugee rights activist who had been living in Germany stated that she had been trained as a nurse in a geriatric hospital, regardless of her own wishes, in accordance with the

능력과 맥락이 제도화될 수 있다는 미래주의적 낙관은 현재를 겁박하면서 제도의 '환상'을 강요한다. 돌봄은 제도나 기술 등, 절차화된 방식에 의해 대체될 수 있는 것이 아닌 모든 사람의 가치로 회복되어야 한다.

갑자기 방문이 열렸다. 잠에서 덜 깬 아이가 울면서 엄마를 찾는다.

엘레베이터에 또 다른 층에서 인테리어 공사를 시작한단 안내문이 붙었다. 벌써 몇 번째인가. 집에 오래 더 잘 머물기 위해서, 부수고 짓는 일을 반복한다. 팬데믹이 불러온 가장 큰 부작용은 어쩌면 그 원인을 성찰할 기회마저 앗아간다는 것일지 모른다. 시끄러운 소음을 이기지 못하고, 결국 나는 일거리를 들고 나와《우리 집에서, 워치 앤 칠》오프라인 전시를 본 뒤 카페에 들어가 일을 했다. 서울에 부재했던 것이 불과 3년인데, 그 사이 익숙한 동네와 거리는 제 모습을 완전히 바꿨다. 주택가 골목 곳곳에 카페가 생겼고, 늘어난 카페 수 만큼이나 고정된 일터 없이 임시적으로 일하는 젊은이들도 많아졌다. 그리고 노트북을 사이에 두고 넷플릭스를 감상하고 있는 젊은 연인들. 영화를 보면서도 서로를 끊임없이 촬영하는 그들을 보면서, 문득 이들에게 미술관이 제시한 온라인 플랫폼은 어떻게 다가올까, 궁금해졌다.

미디어를 경유한 동시대 예술 환경은 전시/작품뿐만 아니라, 관객성에도 변화를 가져왔다. 어쩌면 새로운 세대의 '관객'에게 오프라인의 전시는 온라인에서 본 것을 단지 재확인하거나 현장에서 본 것을 온라인 상에 재배열하는 일인지도 모르겠다. 미술관 안내문보다 더 자세하게 전시를 소개하고 있는 어느 블로거의 전시 후기를 읽다보니, 전시를 다시 본 것 같단 착각에 빠져든다. 나는 '워치 앤 칠'의 온라인 플랫폼과 그에 조응하는 오프라인 전시를 보며 느낀 어떤 동어반복에 대해 생각하면서 새삼 현재 전시가 처한 양가성을 떠올려 본다.

오늘날 전시는 하나의 유기적 개체로 존재하며 그 안에 설치된 작업들은 그 장기로서 서로 작용하고 보조하고 길항하고 신호를 주고받는다. 그럼으로써, 생동하는 작업의 성질과 상태는 전시를 얼마간 '살아' 있게 한다. 그리고 이 짐승은 분명 관객을 먹고 산다. 관객은 전시장 내부로 걸어들어가 그 안을 순환하며 작업에 의해 소화되고 흡수되며 궁극적으로 서로에게 변화를 준다. 이 화이트 큐브라는 종의 피부는 당연히 대개 백색이다.

하지만 어느 순간-관객들이 스마트폰을 쥐고 소셜미디어 계정에 늘 접속되어 있기 시작했을 즈음-부터 화이트 큐브는 속이 뒤집히기 시작했다. 그 맹렬한 구토는 단지 관객을 전시장 내부에서 온라인 공간으로 뱉어내게 만들었을 뿐만 아니라 그 장기를 가죽 바깥으로 내놓게 했다. 이토 준지의 어떤 만화와 같이 겉과 속이 뒤집혔다. 전시의 장기(작업)는 제가끔 절단되어 흰 피부 바깥 온라인 공간에 그야말로 '전시'되고 '유통', '판매'된다. 그러나 더 두렵고 소름끼치는 건, 그럼에도 불구하고 이 짐승이 죽지 않는다는 것이다. 속이 텅 빈 화이트 큐브가 여전히 살아 꿈틀거린다는 것.

이는 뒤집어 입을 수 있는 옷, '리버서블'reversible을 떠올리게 한다. 이 실용적인 복식은 한 벌의 옷을 두 가지 이상의 방식으로 입을 수 있게 한다. 하나의 동일한 실루엣을 지닌 두 가지 무늬의 옷. 이 안감과 겉감의 위치 전환은 드라마틱하다. 왜냐하면 리버서블 재킷은 그것을 뒤집기 전에는 그 속(혹은 겉)이 어떤 표면을 지니고 있는지 짐작할 수 없기 때문이다. 하지만 그 전환은 몇몇의 '드라마'를 겪으며 그 효과를

German government's refugee naturalization policies. In Africa, old people received voluntary care and respect from others, but in the German geriatric hospital they were traded as parts on "a factory assembly line," and "patients were products: no more, no less." To Mimi, the medical system of a developed country, standing in for absent communities, came as a culture shock. Unable to bear it, she ultimately fails to adapt to German society. When we recall this inhumanity of systems in "civilized" countries, the state policy-level solution of a childcare robot seems like no more than a piece of cunning techno-capitalist rhetoric aimed at stripping away the last drop of human individuality and achieving control.

In my experience, childcare is based on constant reciprocity. My child's fingers meet my fingertips, and we look after each other. The futuristic optimism, which holds that human vulnerability, old age, dependence, relationships and powers and empathetic powers and contexts can be institutionalized, threatens the present and forces the "fantasies" of the system upon it. Childcare must be restored through the values of all humans, which cannot be replaced though proceduralized means such as institutions or technology.

Suddenly, the bedroom door opens. My child, half asleep, is crying and looking for her mum.

Mon Oct 01 2021 ⌄

A notice has been put up in the elevator announcing interior work on another floor. Yet again. Constantly ripping down and rebuilding your home in order to stay there longer and in better conditions. Perhaps the biggest side-effect of the pandemic is the way it has snatched away even the chance to reflect on its causes. Unable to stand the loud noise, I end up taking my work, going to see the offline *Watch and Chill: Streaming Art to Your Homes* exhibition, then going to work in a café. I've only been away from Seoul for three years, but in that time the neighborhood and streets I knew have changed completely. Cafés have appeared throughout the alleyways in residential areas, and the number of young people doing temporary work without a steady job has risen just like the number of cafés. And of young lovers watching Netflix on shared laptops. Watching them take endless photos of each other as they watch their films, I suddenly find myself wondering how an online platform presented by a museum could be perceived them.

The contemporary art environment, by way of new media, has brought change both to exhibitions and works and to the nature of viewers. To the new generation of "viewers," perhaps, an offline exhibition is merely about re-confirming things seen online, or re-arranging things seen at an actual museum, via the internet. Reading a review by a blogger, which describes the exhibition in more detail than the texts at the museum, I fall under the illusion that I have viewed the exhibition again. Thinking about the sense of tautology I felt when viewing *Watch and Chill*'s online platform and its corresponding off-line exhibition once again reminds me of the ambivalence faced by contemporary exhibitions.

Exhibitions today are like single organic entities, and the artworks displayed within them are their organs, interacting, assisting, competing, and sending and receiving signals. In so doing, the life-filled character and conditions of the works bring the exhibition, to some extent, "to life." And the resulting animal is clearly one that feeds on viewers. Viewers walking into the exhibition venue and making their way around it are digested and absorbed by the works; ultimately, each changes the other. The skin of this species known as the "white cube" is, generally, white.

상실하기 마련이다. 더이상 속(혹은 겉)이 궁금하지 않은 것이다. 이처럼 전시장 바깥으로 토해져나온 작업은 철저히 이미지 자본적 기준에 따라 평가되고 세속화된다.

벤야민이 지적한, 의례 이후 예술이 아우라를 상실하는 것처럼 화이트 큐브의 가죽 바깥으로 토해져 나온 작업은 본래의 생물성을 잃는다. 적어도 그런 듯이 보인다. 이때 제도와 관객은 다시 작업을 화이트 큐브의 입 속으로 밀어넣어 이를 되살려놓곤 한다. 리버서블. 다시 뒤집힌다. 아우라/유기성을 가지지 않은 예술을 그들 또한 원하지 않기 때문이다. 그렇게 오늘의 작업은 '토끼의 간'처럼 흰 가죽을 수시로 뒤집으며 겉과 속을 왕복한다. 이는 온라인 공간이 개인의 사적인 영역을 여닫는 것을 연상시킨다. 전시라는 미적인 짐승은, 소셜 미디어에 제 은밀한 내면을 강탈 당했다가 다시 돌려받기를 반복하는 것이다. 그렇게 심미적 아우라와 자본적 세속성 사이의 환율에 따라 쉼없는 거래가 이루어진다.

이 속이 텅 빈 흰 피부의 짐승은, 주지하듯 오늘날 제도 미술/전시가 처한 상황을 은유한다. 동시대 미디어 플랫폼을 경유한 안전한 피드의 감각은, 때로 실제 전시 경험을 충족하며 현실의 경험을 대체하거나 심지어 변형시킨다. 요컨대 팬데믹 이후 전시는 왜 여전히 지속 가능하며, 작품은 왜 전시장으로 돌아와 관객과 마주하는가? 작업들은 결국 물리적 공간으로 회귀하여, 동시대 미술/전시/자본이 개념이나 상품성으로 포착하지 못하는 추상에 제 몸을 가린다.

2021 10 10 금 ⌄

───────────────────────────────

지난 여름에 이사 온 이 집은, 대규모 개발로 세워진 신축 아파트 단지에 인접한 구축 아파트이다. 우스갯소리로 신축의 인프라를 덩달아 누릴 수 있다는 점에서 나름의 편의성이 있지만, 사실 동네에서 아이와 가장 좋아하는 장소는 개발이 '덜' 된 건너편의 시장 골목이다. 아이와 함께 구립 어린이 도서관에 가기 위해선 재래시장 골목을 지나야 한다. 대규모 아파트들에 위압적으로 둘러쌓인 다가구 주택을 지나, 우린 골목 구석구석을 누빈다. 어릴적부터 봐온 아주 익숙한 골목길 풍경에서 어떤 낯선 정서가 느껴지는 건, 바로 옆 말끔한 신축 단지와의 대비에서 온 이물감 탓일 테다. 오늘날 부동산 자본은 서울 전역의 잉여공간을 샅샅이 찾아 기어코 식민화하고 만다. 이렇게 아파트의 환금성이 중산층의 주거 형식을 획일화하고 있는 상황에서, 개발에 밀려난 골목길은 이제는 낡은 노스텔지어가 아닌 위태로운 욕망을 표상한다.

아이와 함께 이 길을 걸을 땐 그저 걷기만 해서는 안될 일이다. 무조건 '달리는' 본능을 지닌 아이들에겐 서울은 위험한 도시다. '오토바이 온다! 빨리 벽으로 붙어!' 나는 아이의 걸음을 확인하고 아이는 스스로를 돌본다. 오늘은 어느 길로 갈까? 비선형적으로 가지치는 길목 앞에서 우리의 오감도 함께 열린다. 어느 집에서 들리는 라디오 속 멜로디와 노인의 목소리, 아이들이 저마다 뛰어가는 모습. 갑자기 가게 앞을 청소하던 주인장의 시선이 아이에게 향하고, 쑥스러워진 아이가 제 얼굴을 가린다. 매일 걸어도 새로울 이 길을 아이는 유심히 바라보고 경험한다. 그에 반해 신축 아파트 단지는 각 시설물 간의 '경계'가 분명히 구획되어 있어 도보 이용이 쾌적하다. 잘 정돈된 단지 내 조경은 마치 분재와 같이 익숙한 '자연 풍경'을 눈 앞에 가져다 논다. 그러나 어쩐지 우리가 그것과 마주하기 위해 더 많은 제약에 노출된 것만 같다. 조경 시설물은 만지면 안되고 인공 폭포는 정해진 시간에만 물이 흘러 나온다. 집으로 들어가기 위해선, 단지 입구의 차단기 지나, 공동 현관문을 열고, 엘리베이터를 타고 내려, 끝내 도어락을

But at a certain moment—around the time when viewers began carrying smartphones and being constantly logged on to their accounts—the white cube began to retch. Its violent vomiting not only spewed out viewers from the exhibition venue into online space, but expelled its own organs from within its skin. Inside and outside were reversed, like something from a Junji Ito manga. The exhibition's organs (artworks) are individually conveyed into the online space outside the white skin, where they truly are "exhibited," "distributed" and "sold." But even more creepy and disturbing is the fact that, despite all this, the beast does not die. That the empty white cube remains alive, wriggling around.

This calls to mind reversible clothing. Practical garments of this kind can be worn in at least two different ways. Clothes with the same silhouette but two different patterns. This switching of lining and outer fabric is dramatic. Because until a reversible jacket is reversed, there's no way of knowing what its inner (or outer) surface looks like. But after a few of its "dramas" have played out, the switch tends to lose its effect. We are no longer curious about its inside (or outside). In the same way, works vomited out of the exhibition venue are judged and deconsecrated according to image-capital standards alone.

Just like, as Benjamin noted, art loses its aura in the post-ritual age, works spewed outside the skin of the white cube lose their original animate qualities. Or at least appear to. At this point, institutions and viewers sometimes try to bring works back to life by cramming them back into the mouth of the white cube. Reversible. Turning back the other way. Because they don't want art without an aura or organic qualities, either. Artworks today thus move constantly from inside to outside and back, like a "rabbit's liver" in a folk tale, as the white skin is reversed again and again. This is reminiscent of the way online space opens and closes the private realms of individuals. The aesthetic animal that is the exhibition has its hidden inner side repeatedly plundered, then returned, by social media. Trade continues endlessly according to the exchange rate between aesthetic aura and capitalist secularity.

Within this cycle, the white-skinned beast, as everyone knows, is a metaphor for the situation faced by art and exhibitions today. The steady feed of feelings that reaches us via contemporary media platforms sometimes provides an experience akin to an actual exhibition, replacing or even transforming experiences of reality. In short, why has it been possible for exhibitions to continue since the beginning of the pandemic, and why have artworks returned to exhibition venues to face viewers? Ultimately, artworks return to physical space, and hide behind the abstraction that contemporary art/exhibitions/capital cannot capture their concepts or commercial value.

 Fri Oct 10 2021 ⌄

We moved into this home last summer. It's an old apartment located next to a new apartment complex built as part of a large-scale development project. I joke that it's convenient because we get to benefit from the facilities of the new complex, too, but in fact my child and my favorite place in the neighborhood is the streets of the "less" developed market opposite. I have to pass through the lanes of the traditional-style market each time my child and I go to the children's library run by the district council. We pass by low-rise apartment houses surrounded overbearingly by huge apartment blocks, then thread our way through the network of alleyways. The reason I feel an unfamiliar emotion amid the familiar backstreet scenes I have known since childhood is probably the feeling of strangeness produced by their contrast with the clean, new complexes right next to them.

열어야 한다. 지나야 하는 '게이트'의 수는 꾸준히 상승한다. 이뿐만이 아니다. 아파트 단지 입구 곳곳에 놓인 "외부인 출입 금지" 팻말은 아이와 함께 보기에 낯뜨겁다. 입주민들의 공동 관리비로 유지되는 아파트의 조경과 시설물들을 '외부인'이 누려선 안될 일이란 것이다. 경계는 사람과 사람 사이에도 존재한다.

　　　　내가 지극히 주관적으로 어떤 풍경들을 대비시킨 것은, 오늘날 도시적 삶의 환경과 미술의 경험 방식 역시 이와 별반 다르지 않단 사실 때문이다. 팬데믹 이후, 미술제도 기관에서 미술에 대한 접근성을 빠르게 상상하면서 과거에 비해 그 편리성과 제도성을 갖추고 있는 한편, 오히려 그것에 진입하기 위한 단계 또한 상승하고 있다. 미술관에 가서 작품을 감상하는 노력은 차라리 단순하지 않은가. 온라인 플랫폼에 접속하기 위해선 개인정보를 기입하고 '아이디'를 획득해야만 한다. 이후 각각의 작품에 접속하기까지는 몇 개의 단계를 반드시 거쳐야 한다. 아마 그 마지막은 삼각형 모양의 플레이 버튼을 클릭하는 일일 것이다. 이러한 새삼스러운 작동방식은-마치 플랫폼 자본의 의도처럼-감상자의 소비 패턴과 취향을 세분화된 카테고리로 정교화할 수도 있을 것이다. 그러나 이러한 장치들을 통해 우리가 작품과 만날 수 있는 그 '마주침'의 순간은 역설적으로 감소한다. 각각의 정해진 게이트를 통과한 내가 이웃을 만날 수 없는 것처럼 말이다.

　　　　지난해 네덜란드 헤이그에 위치한 마우리츠하위스 미술관에서 마주친 헤라르트 테르 보르흐의 〈아이의 머리를 빗는 어머니〉(1652-1653)에는 엄마가 어린 아이의 머리를 빗겨주는 모습이 담겨 있다. 그러나 미술관에서 이 평온한 실내 풍경화에게 시선을 주는 사람은 분명 많지 않을 것이다. 왜냐하면 이 작품이 요하네스 페르메이르의 〈진주 귀고리를 한 소녀〉(1665) 바로 왼편에 걸려 있기 때문이다. 명화를 보기 위해 몰려든 사람들에 둘러싸여 바로 옆에 있는 이 작품은 제대로 보기 힘들 뿐더러, 관객들의 주의 깊은 눈길을 받기엔 아무래도 어려운 처지다. 나는 이런 배치가 꽤나 얄궂다고 생각하면서, 우연히 만난 이 외면 받은 작품 앞에 한동안 서 있었다. 진주 귀고리를 한 소녀와 사진을 찍으려는 관객들로부터 비켜줄 수 있냐는 핀잔을 간간이 들어가면서 말이다. 하지만 넷플릭스식의 플랫폼에선 이러한 만남의 가능성마저 차단될 것이란 점에서, 아이의 머리를 빗는 어머니가 앞으로 맞게 될 운명은 더욱 가혹할지 모른다.

　　　　분명 관객이 제시된 '시스템' 안에서만 미술을 경험하게 된다면 개별적인 맥락화의 가능성은 현저하게 줄어들 것이다. 가이던스에 따라서 콘텐츠에 도달하는 제도적인 길에 '옆' 길이란 없다. 그리고 이 직선의 답답함은 플랫폼에서 작품을 보는 내 조건에도 영향을 미친다. 나에게 주어진 '스크롤'의 권능이 작품에 대한 무례일지 모른단 생각에도 불구하고, 나는 곧잘 원하는 시점으로 이동하기 위해 스크롤 바를 재차 끌어 당기곤 했다. 그러다 어느 순간부터는 이 스크롤의 감각에 익숙해져, 내가 시간을 적절하게 조정하고 있단 착각마저 들었다. 어쩔 수 없이 스크린을 봐야만 하는 극장의 블랙박스가 아니라면, 나는 지나치게 산만한 관객이 되고마는 것이다. 그리고 또 어느 한편으론 작가가 획정한 시간성을 깨뜨릴 수 있단 이 힘이 내게 모종의 불편한 감정을 일으키기도 했다. 그건 작품의 온전한 감상이 온전히 내 책임 하에 있단 사실에서 비롯한 어떤 부담감이었다. 그 개별적인 시간의 흐름이 내 손끝에 달렸다는 것이 그다지 달갑지만은 않았다.

　　　　그러나 이 감정은 새로운 경험을 이끌기도 했다. 즉 그 아이러니한 자율성에도 불구하고, 제작자의 의도에 순순히 따르게끔 만드는 작품을 만나기도 하는

Today, real estate capital ends up sniffing out and colonizing every last inch of surplus space in Seoul. In a situation where the cashability of apartments is bringing uniformity to the middle-class living environment, alleyways pushed aside by development represent not threadbare nostalgia but perilous desire.

When I walk through these streets with my child, we cannot simply walk. To kids, with their instinct for running at all costs, Seoul is a dangerous city. "There's a motorbike! Stand against the wall! I check my child's walking and she looks after herself. Which way shall we go today? Faced with the spreading, non-linear branches of the alleyways, our five senses come to life. Sounds of a radio and an old woman's voice coming from a house somewhere; children running around. Suddenly, a shop owner cleaning up in front of her store turns her gaze to my child, and she covers her face, overcome with shyness. She watches and experiences these streets intensely; they must seem new even though she walks them every day. By contrast, the "boundaries" between each facility in the new apartment complex are clearly defined, making it a pleasant place for a walk. The landscaping in the well-ordered complex presents you with a familiar "natural landscape" every bit as familiar as a bonsai tree. But it somehow feels as if we have been exposed to more limitations in order to experience these things. We're not allowed to touch the landscaped features, and the water in the artificial waterfall only flows at set times. In order to get home, we have to pass the barrier at the entrance to the complex, open the door to the shared lobby, get in and out of the elevator, then, finally, unlock the apartment door. The number of gates to be passed is steadily increasing. And that's not all. I feel ashamed to see the various "Outsiders Prohibited" signs around the complex while in the company of my child. Outsiders must not be allowed to enjoy the landscaped gardens and facilities maintained using the fees paid by residents, they are saying. Boundaries exist between people, too.

The reason I have contrasted these scenes with such extreme subjectivity is that the landscape of urban life today is not that different from the way we experience art. Since the start of the pandemic, institutions in the art world have swiftly re-imagined the accessibility of art, making it more convenient and systematic than before. Meanwhile, the number of stages required to gain access is also increasing. Isn't it actually easier to just go to a museum and view works there? To access online platforms, you have to enter personal information and acquire an "ID." After that, you are made to go through several more stages before you can access the artworks. Perhaps the last of these is clicking on the triangular play button. This new and unexpected mode of operation—as if intended by the financial backers of the platform—may elaborate the consumption patterns and tastes of viewers into clearly-divided categories. But, paradoxically, such devices actually decrease our moments of "encounter" with artworks. Just as I, after passing through each prescribed gateway, am unable to meet my neighbors.

Last year, I encountered Gerard ter Borch's *Mother Combing Her Child's Hair* (1652-1653) at Mauritshuis Museum in The Hague. But it's clear that few people in the museum will pay much attention to this painting and its tranquil indoor scene. That's because it hangs immediately to the left of Johannes Vermeer's *Girl with a Pearl Earring* (1665). Located just next to the famous painting and surrounded by people crowding in to get a glimpse of the latter, this work is not only hard to see properly but in a situation where it can hardly expect close attention from viewers. I stood in front of the dismissed work for some time, thinking how perverse its location was. All the while, viewers were telling me to get out of the way so that they could take photos with the girl with the pearl earring. But given that platforms like Netflix preclude even the possibility of such

것이다. 그건 일종의 항복선언이었다. '나는 스크롤을 반납한다.' 게다가 한번으론 아쉬워 나는 그 작품을 여러 차례 반복적으로 감상했고, 이는-제도가 끝내 틈입할 수 없는-작업이 가진 고유의 힘을 발견하는 새로운 방식으로 여겨졌다. 이와 같이 온라인 플랫폼은 어떤 상황에 조건 지어진 어떤 시민에게 하나의 선택지가 될 수 있다. 그러나 이는 동시에, 미술관의 온라인으로의 '이주'가 팬데믹에 대한 손쉬운 반응에 머물러선 곤란하다는 뜻이기도 하다. 대안적인 접근은 미술관 제도가 예술가와 관객 그 사이의 어떤 긴장 관계로부터 벗어나려는 시도에 다름 아니기 때문이다. 분명 미술관이 그 미래를 상상하는 데 있어, 그간 누락시키고 배제해왔던 것을 포괄하는 것이 최우선이란 사실에는 변함이 없을 것이다.

　　　이러한 점에서, 어느 재벌 기업가가 사후 미술관에 기증한 소장품의 전시가 이 팬데믹 상황에서도 연일 흥행하고 있다는 작금의 사실은 다소 의미심장하다. 관람 예약은 이미 한 달 전에 마감되었고, 이는 한국 미술을 애호하는 잠재된 관객들을 새삼 발견하게 한다. 하지만 이 아이러니한 풍경 앞에서 나는 이렇게 되묻고 싶다. 어린이가 현대미술관에 가지 않으면 미술관은 망할까? 물론 안 망할 것이다. 미술관에 외국작가가 없다면 망할까? 아주 망하지는 않을 것이다. 그렇다면 미술관에 이건희가 없으면 망할까? 아마도 망할 것이다. 이 문답은 우리가 지금부터 새롭게 상상할 미술관에 의해 '다시' 쓰여야할 것이다. 지금 여기에서 우리는 누구이며 공통의 경험은 무엇인가. 누구여야 하며 무엇이어야 하는가.
[3]

[3]　　　이 일기에 서술된 사건들은 실제일 수도 또 허구일 수도 있다. 하지만 그 어떤 경우에도 별반 차이는 없을 것이다. 겪지 않은 것을 겪은 듯한 기분이 바로 내가 이 플랫폼에서 가장 온전하게 겪을 수 있었던 것이기 때문이다.

조은비 　　ⓘ
독립 큐레이터
___

조은비는 KT&G 상상마당 갤러리, 아트 스페이스 풀에서 큐레이터로 일했다. 《아직 모르는 집》(아트 스페이스 풀, 2013), 《여기라는 신호》(갤러리팩토리, 2015), 《복행술》(케이크갤러리, 2016), 《모빌》(두산갤러리 서울, 2017) 등을 기획했고, 공동 번역서 『스스로 조직하기』(미디어버스, 2016)를 출간했다. 2022년 d/p기획지원프로그램 선정 전시 《리버서블, 우연을 기대》(가제)를 2022년 10월 d/p갤러리에서 개최할 예정이다.

an encounter, the fate awaiting the mother combing her child's hair may be even harsher.

Of course, experiencing art only within a "system" that posits the existence of viewers will markedly reduce the possibility of individual contextualization. On the institutional path that delivers us to content in accordance with guidance provided, there are no "side" streets. And this linear frustration also affects my condition when viewing works on platforms. Despite the thought that the power of "scrolling" bestowed upon me may be a discourtesy to the artworks, I kept dragging the scroll bar to jump to the points I wanted to watch. Then, at a certain moment, I got used to the sensation of scrolling, and even managed to delude myself into thinking that I was controlling time. Anywhere other than inside the black box of a cinema, where there's no choice but to watch the screen, I end up becoming an overly distracted viewer. And, on another hand, the power of the artist to rupture defined temporality also caused me a certain feeling of discomfort. It was a sense of burden, deriving from the fact that I alone was responsible for properly appreciating the works. I wasn't entirely glad to find this personal flow of time completely at the will of my fingertips.

But this feeling also brought new experiences: despite the ironic autonomy, I also encountered works that made me obediently follow the intentions of their creators. It was a kind of declaration of surrender. "I hereby return the power of the scroll bar." Once was not enough, and I found myself viewing these works several times. I saw this as a new way of discovering the unique power of works—a power upon which institutions could not encroach. In this way, online platforms can become an option for some citizens, in conditions created by some circumstances. Yet at the same time, this also means that the online "migration" by art museums should not be just an easy reaction to the pandemic. Because alternative approaches are no more than attempts by the art museum system to escape the relationship of tension that exists between artists and viewers. Clearly, when art museums imagine this future, it remains a fact that their top priority is including the things they have previously omitted and excluded.

In this sense, the fact that an exhibition of works posthumously donated from the collection of a chaebol industrialist is proving an enduring hit even amid the pandemic is deeply significant. Reservations for viewings closed a month ago, revealing new and previously hidden Korean art lovers. But, faced with this ironic scene, I want to ask: If young children don't go to contemporary art museum, will museums go under? Of course they won't. Will museums go under if they show no works by foreign artists? Not completely. Will art museums go under without Lee Kun-hee? Perhaps they will. These questions and answers will have to be re-written by the art museums that we must now newly imagine. Who, here and now, are we, and what are our shared experiences? Who do we have to be, and what do they have to be?

[3]

[3] The incidents described in this diary may be real and may be fictional. But whichever is the case, it won't make much difference. Because the thing I experienced most fully on this platform was a feeling of having experienced something I haven't experienced.

Jo Eunbi ⓘ
Independent Curator

Jo Eunbi has worked as a curator at KT&G Sangsangmadang Gallery and Art Space Pool. She has curated many exhibitions, including *A House Yet Unknown* (Art Space Pool, 2013), *Floating and Sinking* (Gallery Factory, 2015), *The Art of Not Landing* (Cake Gallery, 2016), and *Mobile* (DOOSAN Gallery Seoul, 2017). She is also a co-translator of the publication *Self-Organized* (Mediabus, 2016).

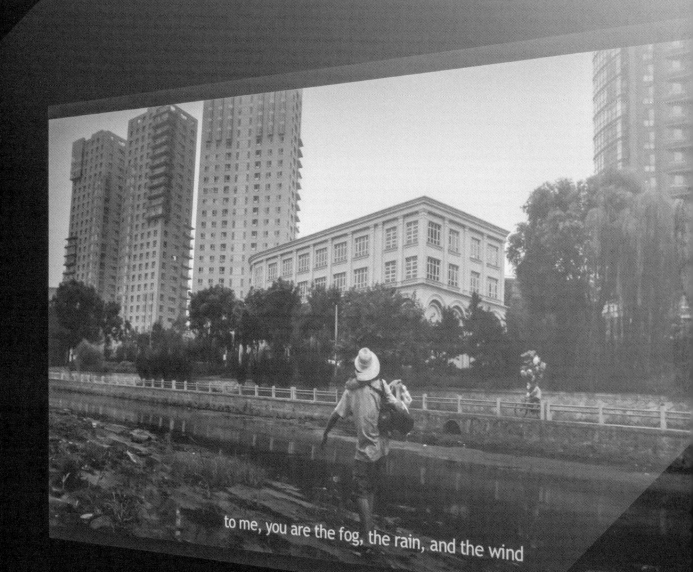

to me, you are the fog, the rain, and the wind

국립현대미술관 서울에서 열린 전시 «우리 집에서, 워치 앤 칠»은 가정 환경에서 미디어 아트를 마주하는 독특한 경험을 제안하는 일종의 견본주택이다. 건축농장(최장원)이 디자인한 ‹사물공간›은 각기 다른 크기의 방으로 이루어진 전시장 전체를 아우르는 공간의 경험에 대한 개념이 되었다. ‹사물공간›은 집의 비정형성에 대한 탐구이다. 전시장 안에서의 집은 그 전형적인 의미가 전복되며, 사물들은 미디어와의 병치를 통해 새로운 풍경으로 재정의된다. ‹사물공간›은 유연함을 통해 전시공간과 개별 작품들의 관계성에 주목하며, 파빌리온과 가구 사이의 경계에서 관람객을 위한 다양한 크기의 단위 공간을 제안한다. 동시에 장치와 부품으로서 집, 건축이 가지는 시각적인 기호, 구조와 재료에 대한 실험이기도 하다. 총 네 개의 전시 영역은 ‘재료의 파편’, ‘부유하는 방’, ‘연결된 공간’, ‘기울어진 벽’이라는 서로 다른 공간적 해석을 통해 우리에게 ‘집’은 과연 무엇인지 묻는다. 사적 공간인 집, 공적인 공간으로서의 전시장, 그리고 집의 익숙함과 낯선 재료들의 대립과 공존 속에서 관람객이 자유로운 동선과 순서로 스트리밍 플랫폼을 체험할 수 있도록 했다. 또한, QR 코드부터 각 공간의 이동식 전자기기까지 관객이 직접 ‘워치 앤 칠’ 플랫폼에 접속하도록 다양한 장치를 마련해 프로젝트가 가지고 있는 온·오프라인의 교차적 성격을 극대화했다.

Watch and Chill: Streaming Art to Your Homes at MMCA Seoul takes the form of a model house demonstrating the unique experience of encountering media art in a domestic environment. Farming Architecture (Choi Changwon) was commissioned to design the spatial experience of the gallery spaces, realized as *Space of Things*, a concept that persists throughout four differently sized rooms. *Space of Things* is an exploration of the informality of the home. Within the exhibition setting, the typical meaning of the home is subverted, while objects are redefined as a new landscape through their juxtaposition with media. With its flexibility, the focus of the object-space is on the relationship between the overall exhibition space and the individual artworks, presenting viewers with unit spaces of different sizes on the borderline between a pavilion and household furnishing. *Space of Things* is also an experiment with the home as device and component, with visual symbols, structures, and materials associated with architecture. The four areas of the exhibition that the architect has sub-themed himself—"Fragments," "Floating Room," "Connected Places," and "Slanted Walls"—render different interpretations of the "home." The spatial arrangements of *Space of Things* offer the viewers the freedom to experience the streaming platform according to their own path and sequence, amid the privacy of the home, the museum as public space, and the discord or coexistence of the familiarity of the domestic environment and the extraordinary materials. From the QR code at the entrance to portable devices in each room, the exhibition was equipped with various items for the audience to get access to the streaming platform *Watch and Chill* firsthand, either on their mobile phones or other devices.

국립현대미술관 서울, 6전시실

Gallery 6, MMCA Seoul

2021.8.24.–10.24.

Watch
& Chill

《우리 집에서, 워치 앤 칠》 전시 전경, 국립현대미술관,
2022.

Watch and Chill: Streaming art to Your Homes,
Exhibition at MMCA, 2022.

마닐라 현대미술디자인미술관은 자동차 극장에서 영감을 얻어 야외에서 물리적인 전시를 하기로 결정했다. 야외에서 영화를 상영하는 방식은 아시아 일부 지역에서 인기 있는 오락의 수단이었다. 자동차 극장은 1950년대 미국에서 인기를 얻기 시작했는데, 그것은 온 가족이 야외에서 먹고 마시며 마치 거실을 자동차 안으로 옮겨오는 것과 같았다. 필리핀은 자동차 극장의 역사에 포함되지는 않지만, 팬데믹 시기의 영상이 중심이 되는 전시를 실현하기 위한 대안으로 자동차 극장이라는 맥락을 반영할 수 있다고 보았다. 자동차 극장으로 연출한 공간에서 열린 '워치 앤 칠' 전시는 팬데믹 시기 영상 작품의 상영이 지닌 가능성과 한계를 충분히 고려해 이뤄졌다. 팬데믹으로 인해 미술관은 전시를 전혀 다른 관점에서 검토해야만 했다. 우리는 자동차 극장을 통해 시행 중인 정부의 방침을 준수하고, 공중 보건을 위협하지 않으면서도 미술관이라는 공간과 그 너머에서 실행할 수 있는 새로운 수평적 가능성들을 제안할 수 있었다. '워치 앤 칠' 자동차 극장은 관객들에게 차량에 머무는 사적인 경험과 함께 야외에서 예술 작품을 감상할 기회를 만들기도 했다. 자동차 극장에는 FM 라디오 신호로 전송되는 사운드를 통해 감염 노출 없이 작품을 감상하기 위해 기꺼이 멀리 운전해 나온 사람들뿐만 아니라, 주차장의 지역 주민들까지 함께 어우러졌다.

MCAD decided to have its physical presentation in an outdoor space and took inspiration from the drive-in theatre. The use of the outdoor for cinema has been a popular means for mass entertainment in some parts of Asia, while drive-in theatres on the other hand rose to popularity in the US during the 50s where entire families brought their living room to their vehicles with drinks and food in the open air. The Philippines did not have either historically, but these two elements fed into thinking about the drive-in as a feasible project during the pandemic for an exhibition that centered on the moving image. The presentation of *Watch and Chill* within the space of a drive-in theatre came as we thought through the possibilities and limitations of showing the moving image during a pandemic. The difficulties brought on by the pandemic for art institutions led us to examine exhibition presentation through different lenses and propose lateral possibilities that could be undertaken beyond and outside the institution's space without endangering public health, and keep within government rules that were in play during that period. MCAD's *Watch and Chill* drive-in theater gave our audience the possibility of privacy in their own cars, but also the opportunity for carefully orchestrated open-air engagement. Presented within the open-air car park of the college, and using FM radio signal for audio in keeping with original drive-in technology, *Watch and Chill* attracted those who lived further out willing to make the drive, without risk of exposure; and the local residents who lived around the college, who could simply walk into the car park, and safely see the works, in the open air.

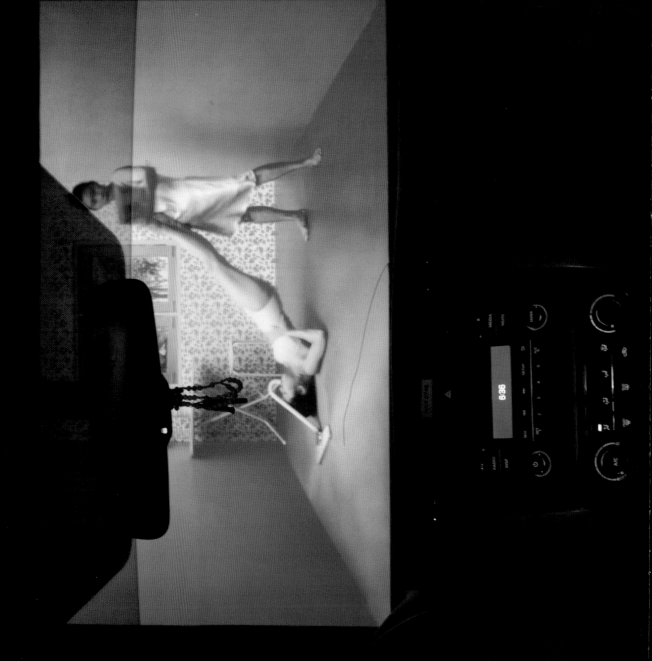

《우리 집에서, 워치 앤 칠》자동차 극장 전경,
마닐라 현대미술디자인미술관, 2021.

Watch and Chill: Streaming art to Your Homes,
Drive-in theatre at MCAD, 2021.

마이암현대미술관의 '원형 감상 공간'은 «우리 집에서, 워치 앤 칠»를 위해 특별히 시간 기반 매체의 감상을 위한 야외 공간으로 설계되었다. 미술관 현장의 상영 플랫폼 디자인은 집안의 거실과 같은 안락한 관람에 중점을 둔다. 한 번에 서른 명의 관람객을 수용하는 이 작은 감상 공간에는 푹신한 소파가 여러 줄 놓여 있고, 그 주위로 점차 높아지는 흰색의 원형 철제 구조물이 마치 안쪽의 관람객을 감싸듯 둘러싼 가운데, 큼지막한 곡면 스크린이 철제 구조물과 매끄럽게 조화를 이룬다. 설계를 맡은 건축가들은 투명한 물결 무늬 타일로 구조물의 벽체를 만들었는데, 내부와 외부를 구분하는 파티션을 닮은 이 벽체는 상영 공간만을 위한 것이라는 인상을 주는 동시에 주변 공간과 동떨어진 느낌이 들지 않게 한다. 감상 공간은 미술관의 입구에 자리하였는데, 마이암의 트레이드마크인 티크 나무가 서 있는 곳이다. 낮이면 이 극장은 관람객이 그늘 아래 앉아 미술관의 도서관에서 가져온 책을 읽는 모임의 공간이 되고, 밤이면 하늘 아래에서 영상을 감상하는 장소로 변모한다. '워치 앤 칠' 프로젝트 이후에도 마이암에서는 이 공간을 활용해 신진 미술가와 감독들이 작품을 관객들에게 선보일 수 있도록 지원할 예정이다.

치앙마이의 젊은 건축가 집단인 폼볼스튜디오가 디자인한 '원형 감상 공간'은 건축농장이 설계한 국립현대미술관 서울의 «우리 집에서, 워치 앤 칠» 전시 구조물과 스타일에서 영감을 얻었다.

The Circular Viewing Zone at MAIIAM Contemporary Art Museum is designed to be an outdoor space for viewing time-based media works specifically for the *Watch and Chill: Streaming Art to your Homes*. The design of the on-site screening platform stresses viewing comfort, like being in one's own living room. This small viewing zone, which can accommodate 30 viewers at a time, is outfitted with rows of comfortable foam sofas surrounded by white circular steel structures in gradual heights as if enveloping the audiences inside, and a large curved projection screen that strikes the unmarred harmony with the steel structures. The architects used transparent corrugated tiles to construct the building's walls, which are comparable to the partition between the indoors and outdoors, giving an impression of a dedicated animation projection space while not being too alienated from the surrounding areas. The zone is located at the museum's entrance hall and is home to an Indian oak, MAIIAM's trademark tree. During the day, this cinema serves as a gathering place for audiences to sit in the shade and read books they pick up from the museum library, while in the evening, it transforms into a venue for watching animations under the stars. Following the *Watch and Chill* project, the museum will continue to use this area in supporting emerging artists and directors by allowing them to screen their work to the public.

Designed by pommballstudio, a Chiang Mai-based group of young architects, the Circular Viewing Zone is inspired by the structure and style of Farming Architecture's *Watch and Chill: Streaming art to Your Homes* exhibition at the MMCA Seoul.

치앙마이 마이암현대미술관 원형 감상 공간   Circular Viewing Zone at MAIIAM, Chiang Mai   2021.12.10.–2022.1.3.

《우리 집에서, 워치 앤 칠》원형 감상 공간 전경,
마이암현대미술관, 2021.

Watch and Chill: Streaming art to Your Homes,
Circular Viewing Zone at MAIIAM, 2021.

M+ 미술관에서는 새롭게 문을 연 두 개의 공간에서 프로젝트를 선보일 계획을 세웠다. 소장품의 온디맨드형 도서관인 '미디어테크'에서 특별 기획 초대 프로그램으로 '워치 앤 칠'을 진행하고, 빅토리아 항이 내려다보는 '대형 계단' 오디토리움의 커다란 LED 스크린에서 작품을 상영하는 것이다. M+의 소장품을 비롯하여 다른 기관의 작품들까지 전시하기 위하여 작가들과 큐레이터들이 이번 프로젝트의 주제를 두고 일련의 계획을 발전시켜나갔다. 그러나, 준비를 모두 마치고, 광동어 자막 작업과 트레일러까지 공개된 상황에서, 결국 다섯 번째 팬데믹이 홍콩을 몰아붙이면서 상영을 취소해야 했다. 하지만 그것이 이번 프로젝트에서 우리의 구심점을 무너뜨리지는 못했고, 온라인 영상 커뮤니티도 건재했다. 나아가 M+는 처음부터 온라인으로 계획한 연계 프로그램 〈M+ 인터내셔널〉을 통해, 정확히 지금 이 상황이 제시하고 있는 디지털이라는 기회와 그 과제를 다루어낸다.

At M+, our plan was to present the project in two spaces of the freshly opened museum. The Mediatheque, our on-demand library for the collection with *Watch and Chill* as a specially curated guest program, and our spectacular LED screen at the Grand Stair auditorium overlooking Victoria Harbour. We had included a handful of additional works as loans and from the collection, and developed a series of public programs engaging artists, curators, and local writers to converse on the four themes of the exhibition. As everything was ready, the screening information published, all screening files subtitled in Cantonese, the trailer actively circulating, we had to cancel the screenings as the fifth pandemic wave holds the city at bay. But the headquarter is not lost, the online film community is alive, and we are getting ready for "M+ International," a series of events that we had wisely planned online from the beginning and that addresses precisely these digital opportunities and challenges that we need to rely on now and certainly in the future.

홍콩 서구룡문화지구 M+ 미디어테크 〉 Mediatheque at M+, West Kowloon Cultural District, Hong Kong 〉 2022.1.7.–2.28.

《우리 집에서, 워치 앤 칠》 미디어테크 전경, M+, 2022.

Watch and Chill: Streaming art to Your Homes,
Mediatheque at M+, 2022.

나만
The Tales
아는
I Tell
이야기

방구석 미술관,
머잖아 우리가 도달할 곳

백민석(소설가)

며칠 전에 라디오에서 진행자가, 옛 정취를 간직한 스페인의 도시들을 열거하면서 어서 팬데믹이 끝나 여행을 가고 싶다고 하는 이야기를 들었다. 얼마나 그리움이 담뿍 묻어나는 목소리로 소개하는지, 주방에서 늦은 아침을 준비하다 말고 나도 몇 년째 계획만 짜고 있는 산티아고 순례를 이제라도 떠나고 싶다는 생각이 들었다. 그러면서 얼핏, 진행자가 유럽 서쪽 끝에 있는 스페인을 너무 우리나라처럼 여기고 있는데 하는 느낌을 받았다. 스페인이 우리나라 영토인 것처럼, 전주나 군산처럼 언제든 떠났다가 돌아올 수 있는 우리나라의 일부인 것처럼 말하고 있다는.

스페인은 무비자 입국이 가능하니, 평범한 여행자에게는 전주나 군산처럼 출입에 아무 제한이 없는 나라다. 비행기를 타고 공항에 내려 숙소를 잡고 관광지를 돌아다니는 일에 제약이 없다. 장시간 비행기를 타야 하지만 그 정도 불편은 즐거운 여행길에 걸림돌이 되지 않는다. 저가 항공사를 이용한다면 금전적인 제약도 별것 아니게 느껴질 것이다. 이런 식으로 우리는 사라고사나 코르도바를 정서적으로, 자연스럽게 우리나라 도시처럼 여기게 된다.

해외여행이 자유로워지면서 세계 곳곳을 국경을 의식하지 않고 다닐 수 있게 되었다. 21세기는 여행이 자유로운 세계인들의 의식에서 국경이나 비행 거리, 비용 같은 제약들이 사라진 것처럼 보이는 시대다. '워치 앤 칠'에 실린 차이 시리즈의 〈포시즌스〉(2010)에는 태국의 치앙마이 풍경이 잠깐 나온다. 작품의 메시지와는 무관하게 내가 그 작품을 보며 무슨 생각을 했을까. 그때 방콕만 들르지 말고 치앙마이도 갔었어야 했다는 생각이었다. 그리고 나서 줄이어 떠오른 생각들, '팬데믹만 아니면 갈 수 있을 텐데…'와 '백신접종 증명서류와 자가격리는 어떻게 해야 하지…'와 '귀국해서도 다시 자가격리를 해야겠지…'라는 한숨 섞인 생각들이 즐거운 상상을 어지럽혔다.

여행이 편해졌다고 해서 국경이나 먼 비행 거리 같은 제약들이 실제로 사라진 것은 아니다. 다만 일반적이고 평범한 상황에서 의식되지 않을 뿐이다. 그리고 팬데믹이 시작됐고, 우리가 의식 아래로 밀어두었던 온갖 제약들이 다시 삶 한가운데로 떠올랐다. 이제 태국처럼 우리 한국인에게 연휴에 잠깐 다녀오곤 하던 아시아의 나라마저, 국경을 넘을 때면 백신접종 증명서와 자가격리 절차를 거쳐야 하는 장소가 됐다.

전시를 보러 가서 한 곳만 보고 오는 경우는 드물다. 미술 전시는 보통 반 시간이면 볼 수 있는 규모이고, 따라서 가까운 거리에서 열리는 전시들을 여럿 묶어서 보게 된다. 이것이 미술 관람이 영화나 공연 관람하고 다른 점이고, 이런 이유로 인사동이나 청담동 같은 소규모 화랑들이 모인 화랑가가 형성되기도 한다. 화랑가를 돌 때면 나는 종종 여행하는 기분이 들곤 한다. 하나의 작품, 하나의 전시가 그 나름대로 하나의 세계를 구현하고 있다고 본다면 여행하는 기분이 딱히 틀린 것은 아니다. 우리는 비행기를 타고 나가서 보통은 한 나라, 한 도시만 보고 오지 않는다. 이

Part. 3

"Living Room Museum":
A Place We Will Be Arriving at Before Long

Baek Minseok (Novelist)

A few days ago, I was listening to the radio when the host read off of a list of historic cities in Spain, explaining that they hoped the pandemic would end quickly so they could travel there. It may have been the sense of deep longing in their voice, but as I was preparing my late breakfast in the kitchen, I also thought about how I'd like to go on the Santiago de Compostela pilgrimage that I've been "planning" for the past several years. But I got the sense too that the host saw Spain—all the way over at the end of Europe—as being too much like Korea. It was as though Spain were part of Korea's territory like Jeonju or Gunsan—a place we could pop off to whenever we wanted.

Spain has an agreement that allows Koreans to enter without a visa, so for ordinary travelers, it really is like Jeonju or Gunsan, a country we can visit without restrictions. There's nothing to stop us from boarding an airplane, arriving at the airport, finding lodgings, and visiting the different tourist sites. We would have to travel in an airplane for a pretty long time, but that kind of inconvenience isn't any real obstacle to a pleasant trip. Even the financial constraints wouldn't seem too bad if we used one of the more inexpensive airlines. This is how we come to emotionally view someplace like Zaragoza or Cordoba as if it were another Korean city.

As restrictions on overseas travel were lifted, Koreans were freed to travel around the world without concerning ourselves with borders. In the minds of cosmopolitans with the freedom to travel, the 21st century is an era without constraints of national borders, flight distances, or costs. The Thai city of Chiang Mai appears briefly in *Four Seasons* (2010), a work by Chai Siris that appears in *Watch and Chill*. Quite apart from the message of the work, what I found myself thinking as I watched it was this: "I really should have gone to Chiang Mai too when I went to Thailand, rather than just stopping in Bangkok." More and more thoughts came to mind, as my pleasant imaginings were unsettled by thoughts of regret. I'd be able to go if it weren't for the pandemic. I wonder how they do the proof of vaccination and quarantine. I suppose I'll have to quarantine again once I get back.

The convenience of travel doesn't mean constraints like borders and long distances have actually gone away. We just don't pay them much mind under ordinary circumstances. But when the pandemic started, all the different constraints that had been pushed down below the surface of our awareness were suddenly back at the center of our lives. Even other Asian countries like Thailand that Koreans would briefly visit during national holidays were now places where we would have to present proof of vaccination and go through quarantine procedures once we crossed the border.

When I go to see exhibitions, it's rare for me to go only to one place. The scale of art exhibitions is typically such that I can see it all in about a half an hour, so I'll also go to

나라 저 나라를 돌아보고, 이 도시 저 도시를 돌아보고 오게 여행 계획을 짠다. 그러면서 우리는 이곳과는 다른 또 하나의 세계를 경험하고 오는 것이다. 미술 전시를 관람하는 일은, 전시장이라는 장소에 구현된 하나의 세계를, 전시의 작가가 평생 일궈온 그만의 또 다른 세계를 접하고 느끼고 경험하는 일이다.

팬데믹은 여행처럼 전시 관람도 불편하게 만들었다. 여행자들이 의식하지 않았던 국경 같은 제약들이 미술 전시를 보러 나선 관람객들에게도 갑자기 나타났다. 바로 전시장의 문턱이다. 관람객은 전시장의 문턱을 넘을 때마다 한 나라의 국경을 넘을 때처럼 체크인과 체온 측정 절차를 거쳐야 한다. 화랑이나 미술관의 문턱은 팬데믹 이전에는 내가 결코 의식하지 못했던 있는 줄도 몰랐던 제약이다. 한 번 화랑가를 찾아 여러 전시를 도는 관람객에게 전시장 문턱을 넘을 때마다 매번 체크인해야 한다는 제약은 사소하지 않다.

그렇지 않아도 일일이 화랑이나 미술관을 찾아다니며 관람하는 일은 쉽지 않다. 미술 관람이 습관이 아닌 사람에겐 일상의 지루한 흐름을 끊는 신나는 여행 같을 수 있겠지만, 나처럼 미술 관람보다 더 애정이 가는 취미가 별로 없어 전시장을 자주 찾는 사람에겐 때로는 시간에 쫓기고 다리가 아픈 일일 수 있다. 얼마 전 리움미술관에선 오후 2시에 입장해서 5시 반에 나왔다. 전체 관람에 3시간 반이 걸렸다. 3시간 반을 전시장 곳곳을 오르내리다 보면 취미가 노역이나 다름없이 느껴지는 순간이 온다. 인사동이나 청담동 화랑가의 전시를 두루 둘러보려면, 화랑들 사이의 이동에도 적잖이 발품을 팔아야 한다.

그렇게 미술 관람은 여러 이유에서 가성비가 떨어지는 취미 활동이 된다. 시간이 있으면 체력이 없거나 체력이 있으면 구미가 당기지 않는다. 나는 전시에 가면 언젠가 쓸 일이 생길지 모른다는 생각에 작품 사진을 찍어 보관하곤 한다. 지금 열어보니 작년 10월에 정화림 작가의 폴더를 만들어놓고는 중단했다가, 올해 10월에 권기자 작가부터 다시 폴더를 만들기 시작했다. 일 년이나 미술 관람을 거의 하지 않았다는 의미다. 했어도 기록으로 남길 만큼 인상적인 전시는 없었을 수도 있다. 작년 이맘때쯤 화랑에 들어갈 때마다 온도를 재고 체크인을 하는 게 귀찮아서 '젠장, 쉬어볼까'하고 생각했던 게 기억난다. 예약제로 운영되는 미술관들이 늘어난 것도 관람을 그만둔 한 이유였다. 전시에 갔다가 예약을 하고 오라는 소리에 발길을 돌린 적이 몇 번 있었다. 이번 리움미술관은 인원 제한까지 있어 예약도 쉽지 않았다. 팬데믹 상황이 길어지면서 볼만한 기획전시들이 줄어든 것도 관람을 그만둔 한 이유고, 내가 아무래도 코로나 블루에 걸린 듯이 취미생활에 흥이 떨어진 것도 한 이유였다.

팬데믹은 이처럼 여행과 전시 관람을, 평소에는 의식하지 못했던 온갖 제약들로 복잡하고 불편하게 만들었다. '제약'의 의미는 "조건을 붙여 내용을 제한함. 또는 그 조건."(표준국어대사전)이다. 제약들이 자꾸 쌓이다 보면, 그리고 예외적 상황이 2년 넘게 장시간 지속되다 보면, 어느새 본래의 "내용"마저 변하게 되는 모양이다. 신작 영화의 개봉이 온라인 개봉으로 바뀌더니 비대면 공연이 늘어나고 방구석 해외여행 프로그램이 서비스되고 있다. 미술계에서는 팬데믹 초기에 한동안 문을 닫았던 국립현대미술관의 주최로 '워치 앤 칠' 같은 "구독형 아트 스트리밍 플랫폼"(전시 설명)이 새롭게 등장하기도 했다. 온라인에 전시 플랫폼이 있다면 팬데믹 같은 예기치 않은 상황에서도 미술관은 제 역할을 해낼 수 있다.

온라인 전시인 '워치 앤 칠'을 보면, 팬데믹 기간에 겪어야 했던 일들이 자연스럽게 떠오른다. 팬데믹은 화랑이나 미술관 같은 장소로서의 전시가 아닌, 온라인 전시 플랫폼 같은 비장소로서의 전시의 활용을 적극적으로 고려해보는 계기가 되지 않았을까. 비장소로서의 전시라면 관람에 방구석 같은 작은 공간만 있으면 된다. 방구석이라면 시간과 인원수 같은 온갖 제약으로부터 자유로워질 수 있다. 그렇지만 온라인 전시가 팬데믹으로 곤란을 겪는 미술계의 임시방편이란 뜻은 아니다.

see various other exhibitions that are taking place in the neighborhood. In this respect, viewing art is different from watching films or theatrical performances; it's also for this reason that we have developed neighborhoods with lots of small galleries, like Insadong or Cheongdam in Seoul. When I visit these gallery neighborhoods, I often get the sense that I'm traveling. It's not exactly wrong to feel that way, if you consider each artwork and each exhibition to constitute its own sort of world. When we get on an airplane to travel somewhere, we don't usually visit only one country or one city. We put together travel plans that allow us to tour different countries and see different cities. In the process, we experience another world that is different from the one here. To view an art exhibition is to see, feel, and experience a world realized in the gallery setting—the different and unique world that the exhibited artist has spent a lifetime charting.

Much like traveling, the pandemic has also made viewing exhibitions inconvenient. Visitors going to see art exhibitions have suddenly found themselves facing the same kind of "borders" and other constraints that travelers used to pay no mind to. It's the border we find at the gallery entrance: whenever visitors pass through the door to enter a gallery, they have to go through the same check-in and temperature check procedures they would if they were crossing a national border. The door to a gallery or art museum is something I never conceived of as a "constraint" before the pandemic—something I never even noticed, really. For the visitor who arrives in an art neighborhood to tour several different galleries, having to check in at every gallery entrance is no small constraint.

It's difficult anyway to go around to different galleries and art museums and view the artwork there. To the person who isn't in the habit of viewing art, it may seem like an exciting departure, a break from the tedious daily rut. But to someone like me—a person who often visits exhibitions, a person who finds no other pastime more pleasant than viewing art—it can end up leaving me with sore legs and the feeling like I'm racing against the clock. Not long ago, I arrived at the Leeum, Samsung Museum of Art at 2 pm and ended up leaving at 5:30 pm. My viewing experience took three-and-a-half hours all told. When you spend three-and-a-half hours traveling up and down through a museum, your pastime may start to feel a lot like drudgery. Seeing all the different exhibitions in a neighborhood like Insadong or Cheongnam means putting in quite a lot of legwork simply traveling from one gallery to the next.

The result of this is that art viewing becomes a less cost-efficient leisure activity in various ways. When I have the time, I don't have the energy; when I have the energy, I can't work up the appetite. I'll sometimes take photographs of the artwork when I visit exhibitions, thinking there might be some call to use them someday. Looking through them now, I see that I took a long break after the folder I made for Jeong Hwarim in October 2020, starting up again in October this year with another folder for Kwon Kija. That means I scarcely viewed any art at all for a whole year. If I did, the exhibition may not have been impressive enough to leave a record of. I can remember how irritating it was checking in and getting my temperature checked each time I entered a gallery around this time last year. "For crying out loud," I thought at the time. "Maybe I should take a break." Another reason I stopped viewing art was the fact that more and more museums and galleries were operating on a reservation-only basis. There were a few times when I went to see an exhibition, only to be turned away at the door and told that I needed to make an appointment. With my Leeum visit, it was tough even making a reservation because they had restrictions on the number of people. Yet another reason I stopped going to see art was a decline in the number of worthwhile special exhibitions as the pandemic dragged on. Meanwhile, my own "corona blues" left me feeling less enthusiastic about any of my leisure activities.

In these ways, the pandemic has made traveling and exhibition viewing complex and inconvenient with various restrictions that we never had to think about before. The dictionary defines a "constraint" as "the restriction of something by adding some condition,

대안도 아니다. 실제로 온라인 전시는 현대미술의 흐름을 보더라도, 팬데믹 시국의 임시방편을 넘어서 현대미술이 언젠가는 가닿게 될 결과에 가깝다. 비슷한 시기에 서울시립미술관에서 열린《하루하루 탈출한다》전은 온라인 전시가 어째서, 머잖아 도달하게 될 보편적인 전시 양식의 하나가 될 것인지 의도치 않게 보여줬다.《하루하루 탈출한다》는 전시된 작품 상당량이 비디오 작품인 까닭에, 온라인 전시가 아니고서는 모든 비디오 작품을 제대로 감상하기 어려웠다. 물론 시간 예술이기도 한 비디오 작품이 늘어가는 흐름에서, 이는 이 전시만의 문제만은 아니게 될 것이다.

보통 전시에서 비디오 작품은 칸막이 쳐진 작고 어두운 공간을 만들어놓고 크고 작은 스크린과 모니터를 통해 감상하게 되어 있다. 관람객이 앉는 자리는 대개 딱딱한 나무로 짠 직사각형의 임시벤치인데, 착석감이 나빠 오래 앉아 감상할 수가 없다. 어떤 경우엔 개방된 공간에 디스플레이를 설치하고 소리가 새어 나가지 않도록 헤드폰을 주기도 하는데 이땐 서서 보기도 한다. 비디오 작품의 상영시간엔 창작자의 상상력에 제한이 없는 것처럼 정해진 한도가 없다. 짧게는 일이십 분에서 길게는 한두 시간이 넘어가기도 한다. 예를 들어 서울시립미술관 홈페이지에는《하루하루 탈출한다》전에 41명의 작가가 참여해 58점의 작품을 출품했다고 나와 있다. 나는 비디오 작품이 너무 많아 예약한 시간(팬데믹으로 관람 시간에 제한이 있었다. 팬데믹은 예약제를 만들고 인원 제한을 만들고 관람 시간에까지 제약을 만들었다.) 내에 다 볼 수 없으니 맛만 보자는 생각으로 작품들 앞에 잠깐씩만 앉았다 일어나곤 했다.

58점 가운데 비디오가 많은 비중을 차지하고 있었고, 상영시간을 어림만 잡아보아도 주어진 시간 안에 다 보기 어렵다는 계산이 나온다. 그리고 보통의 관람객이라면 그렇게 긴 시간을 미술관에서 보내지 않는다. 결국 나는 한 작품도 끝까지 다 보지 못했다. 일반 극영화라면 예고편을 보거나 연출진의 명성을 보고서 끝까지 볼 작품을 선택할 수 있다. 하지만 비디오 작품은 예고편도 없고 작가들 이름은 낯설기만 하다. 따라서 비디오 작품 전시에서, 관람객 대부분은 어느 작품은 맛만 보고 어느 작품은 끝까지 볼 것인지 미리 선택할 수 없다.

그런 비디오 작품들이 이제는 어느 기획 전시를 가나 주류가 되어가고 있다. 내 기억에 그리 오래지 않은 과거에는, 우리나라 미술관에서 비디오 작품은 전시에 감칠맛을 더해주는 색다른 볼거리였다. 평면 회화를 밀어내고 혼합재료 설치 작품들이 전시장의 바닥 면적을 차지하기 시작한 것도 그리 오랜 일은 아니다. 이제는 평면 회화가 걸려있던 벽에 모니터가 걸려있고 비디오 작품이 상영된다.《하루하루 탈출한다》전도 "대중 미디어를 기획의 출발점"으로 삼았다는 전시 설명이 있기는 하지만, 비디오 작품 전시를 콘셉트로 내세운 것은 아니었다. 그러나 비디오라는 매체를 내세우지 않아도 출품작의 많은 비중을 비디오 작품이 차지하고 있었다. 출품 작품 상당수가 비디오 작품이라면《하루하루 탈출한다》전은, 전체 상영 시간을 고려해 온라인 전시, 방구석 미술관 전시와 병행됐어야 하는 것이 아닐까.

요즘 볼 수 있는 비디오 작품들은, 텔레비전이라는 영상 매체 자체를 오브제로 삼았던 초기의 비디오 작품들과는 상당히 다른 모습이다. '워치 앤 칠'에 실린(플랫폼이므로 '싣다', '실리다'라는 표현이 아마 가장 잘 어울릴 것이다.) 작품 중 백남준과 샬럿 무어먼의 1971년 작품과 같은, 비디오의 매체적 특성을 문제시하고 오브제로 삼은 작품은 없다.〈TV, 첼로, 비디오테이프를 위한 협주곡〉(1971)에서 무어먼은 첼로 모양으로 쌓아놓은 텔레비전 수상기를 끌어안고 연주를 하듯 활로 켜는 퍼포먼스를 보여줬다.

백남준이 비디오 아트로 세상의 이목을 끌던 1960-1970년대에, 비디오라는 매체는 아직 예술적 탐구의 대상이었을 것이다. 그리고 21세기가 된 지금, 비디오는 유튜브와 틱톡 같은 개인 제작 영상이 홍수를 이룰 만큼 대중적인 매체가 됐다. 비디오의 매체 특성을 탐구하려는 시도는 보이지 않는다. 인류의 삶에 밀착되고 익숙해진 나머지 그럴 이유가 사라진 것이다. 요즘

or that condition." As the constraints keep piling on, and as this extraordinary situation persists into its third year, even the "something" itself has transformed. First, movie releases began taking place online. Since then, we've seen a proliferation of non-in-person performances and "living room travel" programs. In the art world, we've witnessed the emergence of things like *Watch and Chill*, the "subscription-based art streaming platform" (as the exhibition explanation puts it) organized by the National Museum of Modern and Contemporary Art, Korea (MMCA), which had to close its doors for a time early on in the pandemic. When it has an online exhibition platform, an art museum can play its role even under unexpected circumstances like a pandemic.

As I view the *Watch and Chill* exhibition, I naturally find myself thinking of all the things we've had to experience during the pandemic. The pandemic seems to have prompted an active exploration of using exhibitions not as "places," like galleries and museums, but as "non-places," such as online exhibition platforms. For non-place exhibitions, all you need for viewing is a small space like your own living room. At home, you can avoid all sorts of constraints, including things like time limits and restrictions on the number of visitors. But the significance of an online exhibition is not limited to the sense of an expedient approach by an art world that has been left in difficult circumstances by the pandemic.

It's also not an alternative. Indeed, if you consider the trends in contemporary art, online exhibitions seem more like an inevitable destination than a simple makeshift response to the pandemic. The 2021 exhibition *One Escape at a Time* at the Seoul Museum of Art (SeMA) unwittingly showed how the online exhibition could end up becoming the universal format that we arrive at before long. *One Escape at a Time* consisted largely of video works, which made it difficult to really view all of them through anything but an online exhibition.

Ordinarily, video works at exhibition are viewed on screens and monitors of large and small sizes in tiny, darkened spaces that are set aside and walled off by some kind of partitioning. The viewer usually sits on some hard wooden rectangle of a bench, which is so uncomfortable that they can't watch for very long because it is so difficult to remain seated there. Sometimes the video will be shown on a display in an open setting, with headphones handed out to prevent the sound from bleeding out; in those cases, we remain standing as we watch. When it comes to video running times, there are no prescribed limits, just as there are no constraints on the creator's imagination. They can run for anywhere from 10 to 20 minutes to upwards of an hour or two. According to the SeMA homepage, a total of 41 artists took part in *One Escape at a Time*, with 58 works presented in all. There were so many videos that I couldn't watch all of them during my scheduled visit (the pandemic led to restrictions on viewing times—another new constraint on top of the reservation system and visitor limits also caused by the pandemic), so I would sit down briefly in front of one just to get a taste before standing up and moving along.

Given that most of the 58 works were moving image works, an estimated running time of all the works would take way over the time I was given to see the entire exhibition. Most ordinary visitors won't spend that much time at a museum. I wasn't able to watch a single video through to the end. If these were ordinary movies, we could choose which ones to watch all the way through by viewing the trailer or considering the reputations of the filmmakers. But video artworks don't have trailers, and we don't recognize the artists' names. So when videos are being exhibited, most viewers can't choose ahead of time which works to sample and which to watch all the way through.

Those kinds of video works seem to have become the mainstream now at any special exhibition you might visit. In the not-too-distant past (as I can recall it), the video works at Korean art museums were a novel kind of spectacle that added a certain extra flavor to exhibitions. It wasn't even all that long ago that mixed-media installations began displacing two-dimensional painting and taking up more and more gallery floor space.

세상에서는 완타니 시리파타난눈타쿨의 〈모든 이는…〉(2017)에서 앵무새가 툭툭 내뱉는 말처럼 (카메라만 다룰 줄 안다면) "모든 이는 현대미술가"가 될 수 있다. 비디오 테크놀로지는 더는 기존 예술과 갈등 관계에 놓이지 않는다. 어떻게 하면 비디오를 더 잘 활용할 것인가만이 문제가 된다. '워치 앤 칠'에서도 우리는 갖가지 세분된 비디오 촬영 기법을 만나게 된다. 현대미술 전시에서 흔히 만나게 되는 비디오 작품은 디스플레이를 캔버스처럼 이용한 작품들이다(이는 사진이 평면 회화를 대체할 가능성을 탐구하던 백 년 전의 미술을 떠올리게 한다). 국립현대미술관의 《올해의 작가상 2021》에 나온 네 작가 중 두 작가가 비디오 작품을 선보이고 있는데, 넓은 전시공간을 활용해 대형 스크린과 모니터를 네 개, 다섯 개씩 설치한 대형 작품들이다. 이들이 보여주는 스펙터클한 규모의 예술은 인상적이게도, 비디오 미술이 평면의 세계를 떠나 입체라는 육체성까지 띠게 됐음을 보여준다.

　　　　카위타 바타나즈얀쿠르의 〈어머니와 나(진공청소기 III)〉(2021)는 단순히 영상만을 본다면, 가상 공간 캔버스에 띄워놓은 움직이는 오일 페인팅 같은 느낌을 준다. 휴대전화에 달린 카메라나 디지털카메라에는 사진으로 오일 페인팅의 색감을 낼 수 있는 다양한 필터들이 장착되어 있다. 해상도가 높은 디스플레이는 움직이는 회화작품을 담는 미래의 보편적인 캔버스가 될 가능성이 크다. "콜라주 기법이 유화를 대신했듯이 음극관이 캔버스를 대체할 것"[1]이라는 백남준의 예언은 너무 느린 감은 있으나 어쨌든 실현되고 있다.(예언이 실현되는 과정에서 음극관이 먼저 LED 디스플레이로 대체됐다.) 캠프의 〈만에서 만을 거쳐 만으로〉(2013)는 바타나즈얀쿠르의 작품과는 다른 의미에서 눈에 띈다. 여러 해 동안 바다를 떠도는 선원들이 휴대전화 같은 개인 장비로 촬영한 영상들을 편집한 작품이다. 창작자의 역할은 영상 편집 작업에 머문다. 이 작품은 영상 편집도 창작의 영역이고, 편집만으로도 작가성이 확보될 수 있다는 사실을 일깨운다.

　　　　나는 지난주에 '워치 앤 칠' 플랫폼으로 방구석 여행을 다녀왔다. 아직 공개되지 않은 몇몇 작품이 있지만, 출국일에 쫓겨 다 둘러보지 못하는 아쉬움은 어느 여행에서나 흔하다. 나는 '워치 앤 칠'을 여행자의 마음으로 둘러봤다. 여행은 여행지에 정주하지 않는 사람만이 누릴 수 있는 호사다. 여행지에 대해 책임질 필요도 없고, 그곳의 상황에 대해 근심할 이유도 없다. 여행자는 여행지에 자리를 잡고 살지 않기 때문에, 부담 없는 마음으로 그저 둘러보다 떠나면 그만이다. 나는 '워치 앤 칠' 플랫폼에 실린 작품들에 대해서도, 내가 여행지에서 하던 대로 그곳에 정주하지 않는 사람, 떠나면 곧 잊게 될 여행자로서 보고 말하고 있다.

　　　　전시의 작품을 대하는 관람객의 태도는 여행지에 대한 여행자의 태도와 같다. 관람객도 작품의 소유자가 아니다. 작품을 구매할 수는 있지만 대개는 전시장에 잠깐 머물다 나올 뿐이다. 작품에 애정을 갖고 작가에게 존경심을 품을 수는 있지만, 전시의 상황에 대해 관람객은 책임을 지지 않는다. 어떤 관람객도 작품의 운명을 놓고 자기 소유물에 그런 것처럼 근심하지 않는다.

　　　　'워치 앤 칠' 플랫폼을 처음 열었을 때 나는 거기서 무엇을 봐야 할지 알 수가 없었다. 메인 페이지의 소개 글을 읽긴 했지만 설명과 실제가 같을 리 없다. 여행지에 도착하면 여행자는 처음에는 그곳에서 무엇을 봐야 할지 모른다. 가이드북이 있지만 가이드북이 제공하는 정보는 나만의 특별한 경험과 깨달음을 얻길 바라는 여행자에겐 큰 도움이 되지 않는다. 전시도 마찬가지다. 그냥 작품을 쭉 훑는 것은 누구나 할 수 있지만 그런 건 누구에게도 별 의미가 없는 일이다. '워치 앤 칠'에 실린 비디오 작품들을 순서대로 틀어볼 수는 있겠지만, 나는 '워치 앤 칠'에서 특별히 무엇을 보고 느끼고 생각해야 할까.

[1]　　할 포스터 외, 『1900년 이후의 미술사』, 배수희 외 옮김, 세미콜론, 2012, p.605.

전시를 둘러보면서 자기만의 특별한 경험과 깨달음을 얻는 일이 무엇인지 잘 보여주는 작품이 시린 세노의 〈꽃을 따는

These days, videos appear on monitors that hang on the walls where two-dimensional paintings once hung. The *One Escape at a Time* exhibition includes an explanation that popular media were a "starting point for the planning," although the event was not conceived as a video exhibition per se. Instead, you could see it as a case of an exhibition where they reached out to the artists and received their artwork, and half of it ended up being in the video medium. With so many of the works consisting of videos, the *One Escape at a Time* exhibition ought to have had a concurrent online "living room art museum" exhibition, giving the combined running time of them all.

The kinds of video work you see today are quite different from the early examples of the form, where the television medium itself was regarded as an art object. None of the work loaded onto *Watch and Chill* (since it is a "platform," it seems most appropriate to take of work being "loaded" there) problematizes the characteristics of the video museum or treats it as an art object the way Nam June Paik and Charlotte Moorman did in 1971. The work, titled *Concerto for TV, Cello, and Videos*, had Moorman staging a performance in which she clutched an assemblage of television sets in the shape of a cello and ran a bow over it as if she were playing music.

Back when Paik was drawing the world's attention with his video art in the 1960s and 1970s, the video museum would still have been an object of artistic exploration. In the 21st century, video is a popularized medium, as we can see with the deluge of personally produced videos on platforms like YouTube and TikTok. We don't see any experiments that investigate the properties of video as a museum; it is so closely integrated with human lives, so familiar, that any reason to do so has disappeared. As the parrot declares in Wantanee Siripattananuntakul's *Everyone Is…* (2017), today's world is one where "everyone is an artist" (as long as they know how to work a camera). Video technology is no longer in a relationship of conflict with established art. The only question now is how we can make better use of video. In *Watch and Chill*, we encounter all sorts of specialized video filming techniques. Often, the video work we see at contemporary art exhibitions uses the display as if it were a canvas. (This recalls the art from a century ago, which explored the potential for photography to replace the two-dimensional canvas.) Of the four finalists for MMCA's *Korea Artist Prize* in 2021, two of them have presented their work in the video medium: large works that involved installing four of five enormous screens or monitors in a spacious exhibition setting. The spectacular scale of their artwork shows, strikingly enough, how video art has ventured beyond the two-dimensional realm into that of three-dimensionality.

If we simply look at the video, Kawita Vatanajyankur's *My Mother and I (Vacuum III)* (2021) gives the sense of a moving oil painting that floats on a canvas in virtual space. Our mobile phone cameras and digital cameras come with various filters that can produce the color sense of an oil painting in photographs. It seems very likely that high-resolution displays will become the universal "canvases" of the future, capturing moving works of painting. "As collage technique replaced oil paint, the cathode-ray tube will replace the canvas,"[1] predicted Nam June Paik—a prophecy that seems to be coming true, albeit very slowly. (While it was being realized, the cathode-ray tube was first replaced by the LED display.) *From Gulf to Gulf to Gulf* (2013) by CAMP stands out in a different sense from Vatanajyankur's work. For this work, the images have been compiled from ones taken over the course of several years by sailors traveling over the seas, using their own mobile phones and other personal devices. The role of the creator is confined to editing the images. It is a work that helps us to see how film editing is a creative realm in its own right, and how authorship can be achieved through editing alone.

[1]   Hal Foster et al., *Art Since 1900* (expanded edition), Korean trans. Bae Suhee et al., Semicolon, 2012, p.605.

Last week, I took a trip in my own home through the *Watch and Chill* platform. Some of the works have yet to be shown, but that feeling of

것〉(2021)이다. 이 작품은 작가가 미군 점령기에 벌목촌에서 찍힌 오래된 흑백 사진들을 한 장씩 넘기면서 설명해주는 형식의 작품이다. 식생에 대한 설명, 벌목꾼들에 대한 설명, 지역의 역사에 대해 설명해나가다가 문득 커다란 나무에 올라탄 남성들을 찍은 사진에서 설명을 끊고는 이런 감상을 덧붙인다. "자연을 배경으로 한 사진들은 특징이 있다. 남자들이 자연을 지배하는 것이다. 나무보다 작은 남자들이 나무를 밟고 서 있다." 이 감상은 언뜻 〈꽃을 따는 것〉의 작품 의도와 무관한 돌발적인 발언처럼 들린다. 해설에도 작품은 "식물과 나무의 이야기"이고 옛 사진들을 통해 필리핀의 과거와 "자본주의 발달 이면의 뒤엉킨 뿌리를 사유"하는 작품이라고 나온다. 〈꽃을 따는 것〉이 속한 '워치 앤 칠'의 파트는 반려 관계에 관한 파트, '내 곁에 누군가' 파트다.

　　그럼에도 "자연을 배경으로 한 사진들은 특징이 있다."라는 깨달음은 작가가 옛 벌목촌 사진들에서 과연 무엇을 꿰뚫어 봤는지, 통찰했는지를 인상적으로 들려준다. 필리핀에서 백인 남성들은 자기보다 훨씬 큰 나무를 짓밟고 서 있었던 것이다. 벌목촌 사진들에서 자본주의에 훼손되어 가는 필리핀의 자연을 읽어내는 일은 누구나 할 수 있다. 작가도 처음에는 그 누구나 볼 수 있는 사실에 대해 말하려는 의도였을 것이다. 옛 사진들은 인간이 식물과 나란히 선 사진, 반려 식물에 대한 사진들로도 읽힐 수 있다. 하지만 그런 사진을 한 장 한 장 넘기다 보니, 한 장씩 그 의미를 따지다 보니, 그 모든 옛 사진들을 관통하는 또 하나의 진실이 눈에 띄었고, 말하지 않을 수 없었던 것이다. 당시에 남성들이 자연을 지배했다는 통찰은, 벌목 회사를 세우고 식민지 경영을 하며 노예처럼 필리핀인들을 부렸던 지배자들에 대한 더 깊은 이해를 가능하게 한다. 그들은 자본가, 지주, 주인, 세도가이기 이전에 무엇보다 남성들이었고, 그 같은 깨달음으로부터 우리 같은 관람객도 필리핀의 식민지 시절을 더 잘 이해할 기회를 얻는다. 내가 '워치 앤 칠'에서 원하는 것이, 시린 세노가 옛 사진에서 얻은 것 같은 나만의 깨달음, 통찰이다. 나는 '워치 앤 칠'에서 모두가 다 볼 수 있는 것만을 보고 싶지 않다. 어느 전시에 가든 마찬가지다. 나는 어느 전시에 가서나 누구나 다 생각할 수 있는 것을 생각하다 오고 싶지 않다.

　　'워치 앤 칠'에는 음악이 인상적인 작품이 두 편 있다. 지앙 지의 〈날아, 날아〉(1997)와 구동희의 〈타가수분〉(2016)은 비디오가 시작 매체이면서 청각 매체이기도 하다는 점을 적극적으로 활용한 작품이다. 두 편 모두에서 영상과 음악(음향)은 서로를 반어적으로 보완해주고 있다. 〈날아, 날아〉는 날갯짓하는 손을 따라, 아마도 베이징의 서민층이 거주하는 듯한 비좁은 아파트 안을 비춰준다. 아파트 내부는 비루하기가 이루 말할 수 없다. 거실 천장과 침실에는 배관이 노출되어 있고(세입자를 더 들이기 위해 불법 개축해 공간을 나눈 아파트일 수 있다), 벽에는 곰팡이로 보이는 얼룩들이 줄지어 있고, 언젠가는 더 나은 집으로 옮겨가리라는 희망을 상징하듯 베이징 시내 지도가 걸려있다. 주방은 불결하고 출입문은 녹이 슬었고, 공용인 듯한 화장실에는 쭈그리고 앉아야 하는 화변기가 설치되어 있다. 이 암담한 가난의 공간에서 손 하나가 춤을 추듯 날아다닌다. 그리고 그 배경으로 19세기 프랑스 작곡가 마스네의 오페라 〈타이스〉에 나오는 〈명상곡〉이 흘러나온다. 우아한 손동작과 감미로운 오케스트라의 연주는 가난의 암울함을 반어적으로, 강렬하게 드러내 보여준다.

　　〈타가수분〉도 음향효과와 음악을 효과적으로 사용한다. 작품은 두 공간을 교차해서 보여주는데, 하나는 어느 부잣집의 근사한 욕실처럼 보이는 곳이고 하나는 맥주와 간단한 안주를 파는 주점이다. 영화의 도입부에서 욕실에는 틀어놓은 수돗물 소리가 요란하고, 주점에는 뽁뽁이로 불리는 에어캡을 터뜨리는 소리가 요란하다. 영화의 음향효과는 관람객이 흔히 접할 수 있는 생활 소음들이다. 〈타가수분〉은 일부러 생활 소음의 볼륨을 높여놓아, 관람객의 귀를 따갑게 해 영상보다는 음향에 더 집중하도록 만들었다. 〈타가수분〉에도 음악이 나온다. 림스키-코르사코프의 〈왕벌의 비행〉인데, 아마도 클라이맥스인 부분(시간상으로 이쯤이면 클라이맥스일 텐데 하는 생각이 드는 지점)에 배경으로 쓰인다. 이 경쾌한 관현악곡은 작품 후반부에 수수께끼 같은

disappointment over not getting to see everything before your departure date is a common part of every trip. I approached my *Watch and Chill* tour with the mind of a traveler. Travel is a luxury that can only be enjoyed by people who do not live in the destination. We don't need to take responsibility for the place, nor do we have to worry about the situation there. The traveler has no roots in the destination, which means that they are free to see the sights and then go on their way. I approached the work loaded on the *Watch and Chill* the same way as I had approached my travel destinations: viewing and speaking as a person who did not reside there, as a traveler who would soon forget once I left that place behind.

Indeed, the viewer's attitude toward an exhibited artwork is similar to the attitude of a traveler toward a destination. The viewer is not the artwork's owner. Some of us might purchase works of art, but most of us simply spend some time in the gallery and then go on our way. We might feel a sense of attachment to the artwork and respect for its artist, but as viewers we assume no responsibility for the exhibition's situation. No viewer frets over the artwork's fate as they do over their own possessions.

When the *Watch and Chill* platform first opened, I had no way of knowing what I was supposed to see there. I read the introductions on the main page, but the reality is obviously not the same thing as the explanation. Similarly, the traveler arriving in a destination does not know at first what they ought to see there. There are guidebooks, to be sure, but the information supplied in the books is of little help to the traveler who hopes to achieve their own special experience and unique epiphanies. An exhibition is the same. Anyone can simply scan their eyes over the artwork, but that holds little meaning for anybody. I could conceivably play each of the video works loaded onto *Watch and Chill* in sequence, but what in particular should I be seeing, feeling, and thinking here?

As I viewed the exhibition, the work that best showed what it is to gain some special experience and unique epiphany was Shireen Seno's *To Pick a Flower* (2021). For this work, the artist goes one at a time through old black-and-white photographs taken in a logging community during the American occupation of the Philippines, offering an explanation of each one. As she explains about the vegetation, about the loggers, and about the region's history, she suddenly breaks off at a photograph showing men up in a large tree, where she adds the following observation: "In the photographs I found of people in relation to nature, men were usually photographed as conquistadors, exerting their power over trees, despite being much smaller in scale." Her observation seems at first like a non sequitur with no connection to the artistic intentions of *To Pick a Flower*. The explanation describes the work as "a story about plants and trees," which uses old photographs to "contemplate the tangled roots on the underside of capitalism" and the past of the Philippines. The part of *Watch and Chill* that includes *To Pick a Flower* is titled "By the Other Being," which has to do with companionships.

Yet this epiphany—the "quality" that photographs against a natural backdrop share—is strikingly effective at conveying what the artist saw and perceived in those old logging community photographs. In the Philippines, white men stood atop a "tree" that was far larger than them. In the photographs of the logging village, any viewer can see the nature of the Philippines as the way it has been ravaged by capitalism. Perhaps the artist herself meant to speak about that easily visible point. The old photos may also be seen as images of people standing side-by-side with plants—pictures of "companion plants." But as Seno went through each of those photographs, as she examined the meaning of each one, she perceived another truth running through all of those old images, and she felt compelled to speak it. The insight about the men who dominated nature at the time allows for a deeper understanding of the overlords who created the logging company, who operated the colony and drove the Filipino people like slaves. Ahead of their being capitalists, landowners, masters, and men of power, they were first and foremost white men—and with that realization, viewers like us gain the opportunity to better understand the colonial era in the Philippines. What I want from *Watch and Chill* is the same kind of unique epiphany

장면들이 이어질 때 느닷없이 끼어든다. 흥미롭게도 〈왕벌의 비행〉은 생활 소음에 비교해 더 크지도 더 작지도 않은, 같은 레벨의 볼륨을 갖는다. 생활 소음이 배경음악과 똑같은 비중으로 쓰인다는 사실은 소음의 존재를 더욱 두드러지게 하는 효과를 가져온다.

공간이 교차하면서 음향효과 역시 교차한다. 물소리와 강냉이를 꺼내는 소리, 비누를 깨뜨리는 소리와 새우를 씻는 소리, 기름이 끓는 소리와 자쿠지에서 거품이 흘러나오는 소리 등등이 작품 내내 이어진다. 수수께끼 같은 후반부 장면들의 의미를 도무지 알 수 없는 것처럼, 작품에서 공간의 교차, 음향의 교차가 무엇을 의미하는지는 명확하지 않다. 빈부 격차가 가져온 문화적 괴리일 수도 있고, 사적 공간과 공적 공간의 대비일 수도 있다. 이 대비의 불분명한 의미 역시 작가의 의도인 듯하다. 이분법적 갈등에서 벗어난 대비로, 관람객이 작품을 다양하게 해석할 수 있도록 길을 열어놓은 것이다.

음향효과의 쓰임을 봐도 알 수 있듯 〈타가수분〉은 극영화적인 기법들을 가장 적극적으로 연출에 활용한 작품이다. '워치 앤 칠'의 다른 작품들이 영화적인 과장을 보여주더라도 대개 회화적(오민의 〈에이 비 에이 비디오〉(2016)처럼 몇 개의 정지 화면을 이어붙인 듯한)인 구성으로 되어 있거나, 차재민의 〈안개와 연기〉(2013)처럼 다큐멘터리 같은 사실적인 촬영과 편집으로 제작된 것에 비하면, 확실한 차이를 보여준다. 때문에 〈타가수분〉은 미학적으로 비디오 작품을 미술로 볼 것인가, 단편 극영화로 볼 것인가라는 근원적인 질문을 던지게 한다. 비디오 작품이 만약 미술이라면, 극영화와 미학적으로 구별되는 비디오 미술만의 요소는 무엇인가라는 질문을 다시 던질 수 있다. 나는 미학자가 아니므로 손쉽고 상식적인 답변밖엔 떠오르지 않는다. 20세기 초 뒤샹의 레디메이드 작품들이 그랬듯이, 제도의 맥락에 따라 미술관에 전시되면 미술품이고 영화관에서 상영되면 극영화라는 답변이다. 하지만 이러한 '제도의 맥락'은 시대가 흐르면서 너무 단순하고 편의적으로 미술을 재단하는 구분법이 된 듯하다. 나 같은 비전문가조차, 미술인가 영화인가를 구분하는 일에 훨씬 다양하고 복잡한 요인들이 개입한다는 사실을 알고 있다. 비디오 미술이 영화 기법의 활용에 능숙해질수록, 사람들은 비디오 미술이 극영화와 같아지기를, 극영화와 같은 기술적 완성도를 보여주기를 바랄 것이다. 그러면서 한편으론 모순되게도, 극영화가 보여줄 수 없는 비디오 미술만의 가치와 영역은 무엇일지 묻게 될 것이다.

〈날아, 날아〉와 〈타가수분〉의 엔딩 크레딧에는 작품에 어떤 음악을 썼는지 나오지 않는다. 아니, 엔딩 크레딧 자체가 없다. '워치 앤 칠'에 실린 작품 대부분에 엔딩 크레딧이 없다.(이 사실 또한 비디오 작품이 아직은 평면 회화처럼 개인의 순수한 창작물이라는 사실을 은연중에 드러낸다.) 방구석 미술 관람의 장점은 여기서도 느낄 수 있다. 나는 휴대전화의 음악 검색 프로그램을 열어 스피커에 가져다 댔고, 네이버의 인공지능이 십 초도 지나지 않아 작품에 쓰인 곡의 곡명을 알아냈다. 나는 방구석이 아니면 가질 수 없는 느긋하고 게으른 태도로, 작품을 잠시 멈춰놓고 유튜브와 내가 가진 음반들로 〈명상곡〉과 〈왕벌의 비행〉을 감상했다. 방구석 미술관에선 하나의 작품을 여러 차례 끊어서 볼 수도 있고 여러 번 반복해 볼 수도 있고, 배경음악이 마음에 들면 다른 채널로 얼마든지 잠시 나갔다 들어오는 일이 가능하다.

'워치 앤 칠'은 "가상의 공간을 통해 미디어 환경으로 변화한 집의 다층적 연결성을 사유하"(전시 소개)려는 시도다. 언뜻, 내게 주어진 '여행'이라는 글의 주제와는 맞지 않아 보인다. 여행은 집을 떠나야 성립되는 행위이기 때문이다. 하지만 팬데믹이 갑자기 모든 것을 다른 방식으로 생각하도록 만들었다. 미술관이 문을 닫아도 우리는 방에서 클릭 몇 번으로 '워치 앤 칠'의 비디오 작품들을 즐길 수 있고, 나 역시 양말도 신지 않은 채 '워치 앤 칠' 플랫폼 곳곳을 돌아다니며, 어떻게 여행이 미술 관람 행위와 공통된 함의를 가지는지, 팬데믹이 그 함의를 어떻게 더 명료하게 만들었는지 이야기하고 있다. 내 글은 여행과 관람 행위의 최근 변화에 관한 이야기지만, 사실상 팬데믹에 의해 가장 크게 변한 것은 우리의 '집'이고 초고속 인터넷이 깔린

and insight that Shireen Seno seems to have gleaned from those old photographs. I don't wish to see the things that everyone can see from *Watch and Chill*. It's the same at every exhibition I visit: I don't want to travel there and have the same thoughts as everyone else before heading on my way.

Two of the *Watch and Chill* works were striking for their use of music. *Fly, Fly* (1997) by Jiang Zhi and *Cross×Pollination* (2016) by Koo Donghee both made active use of the fact that video is both a visual and an auditory medium. In both of them, the moving images and music (sounds) complement each other in ironic ways. *Fly, Fly* follows a fluttering hand as it shows the interior of a cramped apartment—the kind that might be home to a member of Beijing's working class. Inside, the apartment is indescribably grotty. Pipes lie exposed in the living room ceiling and bedroom (the apartment may have been illegally renovated to divided in up into more units that could be rented out), the walls are mottled by what appear to be mildew stains, and a map of downtown Beijing hangs there as though symbolizing the home of someday moving to a better place. The kitchen is foul, the front entrance is rusted, and the (seemingly shared) bathroom has a squat toilet in it. Within this space of grim poverty, the hand flutters about as if dancing. In the background, we hear the "Meditation" from Thaïs, an opera by the 19th century French composer Jules Massenet. The elegant hand movements and sweet orchestral performance underscore the direness of the poverty in an ironic and powerful way.

Cross×Pollination also makes effective use of sound effects and music. It alternates between two spaces: one a finely appointed bathroom in what seems to be a wealthy person's home, the other a bar selling beer and light snacks. At the start of the film, the noise of water running from the bathroom's tap is loud, as is the sound of bubble wrap being popped in the bar. The sound effects in the film are the sorts of everyday sounds that viewers might encounter often in their lives. *Cross×Pollination* has the volume of these everyday sounds mixed deliberately loudly, assailing the viewer's ears and making them focus more on the sounds than on the image. *Cross×Pollination* also has music: "Flight of the Bumblebee" by Rimsky-Korsakov, which is used the background music for what may be the "climax" (i.e., the point where one might expect a climax to be based on the running time). This spirited orchestral composition abruptly intrudes upon an enigmatic series of scenes in the later part of the film. Interestingly, "Flight of the Bumblebee" is mixed at the exact same volume level as the everyday sounds—no louder or softer. The fact that the everyday sounds are used at the same proportion to the background music has the effect of making their presence seem more pronounced.

As the spaces alternate, so too do the sound effects. Throughout the work, we hear the sounds of water and of corn being taken out, the sounds of soap snapping and the sounds of shrimp being washed, the sound of sizzling oil and the bubbling of water jets. Just as it is impossible to figure out the meaning of the enigmatic ending sequence, it is not clear what the work intends with its alternation of spaces and sounds. It could be something about the cultural gap brought about by the wealth divide, or the contrast between personal and public spaces. The lack of clear meaning to this contrast also seems to have been the artist's intention. By using contrasts that deviate from dualistic oppositions, she leaves rooms for the viewer to interpret the work in different ways.

As the use of sound effects alone shows, *Cross×Pollination* makes the most proactive use of cinematic techniques in its staging. It clearly contrasts with other *Watch and Chill* works that adopt a generally painterly composition even as they incorporate cinematic exaggeration (such as Oh Min's *ABA Video* (2016), which resembles several still images spliced together), or that were created with documentary-like realism in their filming and editing, like Cha Jeamin's *Fog and Smoke* (2013). In that sense, *Cross×Pollination* aesthetically poses a basic question about the video medium: should a work be viewed as art, or as a short film? If video is an art form, that may raise another question, namely what elements belong exclusively to video art to distinguish it aesthetically from ordinary film. I

'방구석'이다. 어느새 "우리의 집은 거주의 사적 기능을 넘어 공적인 영역으로 진입했고, 팬데믹은 집의 이러한 현실을 더욱 드러나게"(전시 소개) 했다.

감염병으로부터 안전한 공간이라는 집의 가치는, 집을 더욱 사적인 공간, 격리된 공간으로 만들었다. 한편, 집 밖의 공간은 거꾸로 이런저런 제약으로 부자유와 답답함의 공간이 됐다. 우리는 사회적 거리두기의 단계에 따라 달라지는 이동 거리와 모임 인원의 제한, 영업시간의 단축이라는 제약을 받게 되었다. 집 밖은 언제든 감염의 위험이 있는 규제의 공간이다. 해외여행도 마찬가지여서, 우리는 팬데믹이 끝나도 여행의 자유를 전만큼 누릴 수 없을지도 모른다. 국경은 열려도 팬데믹으로 타격을 크게 입은 나라는 치안이 좋아질 때까지 여행할 수 없을지도 모른다.

그래서 집 바깥에 없는 자유를 찾아 스스로 격리된 우리는 무엇을 할 수 있을까. 오민의 〈에이 비 에이 비디오〉는 팬데믹 이전에 제작되었음에도, 지금 우리가 무엇을 할 수 있는지를 재미나게 보여준다. 이 작품에서 주인공은 끊임없이 거실과 주방 집기들의 위치를 옮기고 쌓고 다시 배열한다. 팬데믹이 없었다면 아마도 다르게 이해되었을 이 작품의 주인공은, 내 눈에는 집안의 물건을 이리저리 마음껏 배치하면서 자유에 대한 열망을 무의미하게나마 충족시키고 있는 듯 보인다. 말하자면 팬데믹 시대의 '혼자 놀기'다.

위안 광밍의 〈주거〉(2014) 역시 팬데믹이 아니었다면 다르게 이해되었을 작품이다. 하지만 지금 내 눈에 이 작품은 집 안에 격리되어 머물며 시간을 보내다 실제 세계에 대한 현실 감각을 잃어버린 사람의 몽롱세계로 보인다. 현실 감각을 잃어버리자 눈앞의 현실(거실)은 어항 속에 설치된 이미테이션의 세계, 몽롱세계처럼 보이기 시작한다. 이유는 알 수 없지만 시간이 흐를수록 스트레스와 분노와 긴장이 차오르기 시작하고, 결국 한계에 이르러 그 몽롱세계는 폭발하게 되는 것이다. 설명 하나 없이 몽상적인 이미지들로만 이뤄진 〈주거〉는, 팬데믹으로 집 안에 스스로 갇힌 우리의 내면에 끓어오르는 부정적인 에너지를 극적인 방식으로 드러낸다.

아이러니하게도, 우리는 좁은 집안에서 마스크를 벗고 가족들과 접촉하는 자유를 만끽한다. 집 밖에서는 무슨 일을 당할지 모른다. 그래서 여행의 막바지에 공개된 차지량의 〈뉴 홈〉(2012)과 씨씨 우의 〈유만혼의 미완된 귀환〉(2019)가 들려주는 이야기는 흥미롭다. 〈뉴 홈〉의 등장인물들은 자기 소유의 집이 없는 사람들이다. 월세나 전세를 사는 이들은 밤마다 취미생활을 위한 동호회 모임처럼 모여 비어있는 집들을 탐험한다. 아직 입주가 이뤄지지 않은 빈집(이들이 세를 들어 사는 집보다 크고 안락한)의 문을 열고 들어가 각자 방을 나눠 갖고, 언젠가 자신들 소유의 집이 생기면 할 법한 집안 꾸미기 놀이를 한다. 각자 삶을 이야기하고 각자 꿈을 이야기한다. 이들은 당장 생활할 집은 있지만 언제 쫓겨날지 모른다는 희미한 불안을 안고 사는 이들이고, 오늘 밤 점거한 집 같은 번듯한 집을 영원히 살 수 없으리란 절망의 흐릿한 냄새를 맡고 있는 이들이다. 〈유만혼의 미완된 귀환〉의 주인공은 오래전에 실종된 소년이다. 그는 작품 속에서 "부모와 형제"가 기다리고 있는 집의 바깥을 십수 년째 떠돌고 있다. 집 밖에 있는 그에게 집 바깥은 현실로, 집 안은 장난감 동물들과 함께 놀 수 있는 아련한 꿈속 같은 공간으로 존재한다. 그는 아직도 현실에서 꿈으로 귀환하지 못했다. 〈뉴 홈〉과 〈유만혼의 미완된 귀환〉은 집 없는 이들에게 집이란 무엇일지를 묻는 작품이다. 집이 안전하고 자유로운 공간이라는 팬데믹 시대의 분석은 집이 없는 이들에겐 무의미하다.

'워치 앤 칠' 플랫폼 같은 방구석 미술관은 무궁무진한 가능성을 갖고 있다. 지금은 뛰어넘을 수 없을 듯이 느껴지는 여러 한계는, 촬영과 디스플레이 테크놀로지의 발전으로 점차 극복되리라는 예상을 어렵지 않게 할 수 있다. 비디오 미술에 관한 일반의 인식도 어떻게든 바뀔 것이다. 우리는 머잖아 집에서도 큰 디스플레이로 빌 비올라의 스펙터클한 비디오 작품을 감상하게 될 것이고, 조지 시걸의 등신대 조각들을 가상현실을 통해 집안으로 불러들일 것이고, 고해상도 모니터가 잭슨 폴록의 어지러운 물감 뿌린 자국과 색채의 미세한 변화까지 잡아내 집 거실을

am not an aesthetician, and no answers come to mind beyond the simple and sensible ones. Like Marcel Duchamp's ready-made works of the early 20th century, it is a matter of institutional context: if it's exhibited in an art museum, it's art, and if it's shown in a movie theater, it's a movie. But that institutional context seems to have turned over time into all too simple and convenient a way of distinguishing art. Even a layperson like me knows that there are much more complex and varied factors influencing the distinction between art and film. As video art comes to command cinematic techniques with greater and greater proficiency, people will hope to see it become more like theatrical films and show the same kind of technical polish. At the same time, they will also paradoxically ask what values and domains belong exclusively to video art—things that theatrical films cannot show.

Neither *Fly, Fly* nor *Cross×Pollination* mentions what music was used in their ending credits—because there aren't any ending credits. Indeed, most of the works loaded onto *Watch and Chill* have no ending credits. (This fact also subtly illustrates how video artwork is still purely the creation of an individual, much like two-dimensional painting.) Here, too, we may sense some of the advantages of viewing art within our home. I opened up a music search program on my phone and put it up to the speaker; less than ten seconds later, AI gave me the name of the music played in the work. With the sort of casual, even lazy attitude that I could not adopt if I were not in my own home, I paused the video and listened to recordings of Meditation and Flight of the Bumblebee on YouTube and in my own music collection. In the "living room museum," you can pause a single work multiple times, you can watch it over and over, and if you like the background music, you can pop over to a different channel and listen.

As the exhibition introduction explains, *Watch and Chill* is meant to "consider the multilayered connections of homes that have transformed into media environments" through virtual spaces. At first glance, this might not seem to jibe with the "travel" theme assigned to me for this essay. Travel is an act that requires you to leave your home. But the pandemic has suddenly forced us to think about everything in different ways. Even when museums are closed, we can enjoy *Watch and Chill* videos with a few clicks in the comfort of our room; without even putting my socks on, I can travel all around the platform, talking about how travel shares some of its connotations with the act of art viewing, and how the pandemic has thrown those connotations into even sharper relief. I am writing here about recent changes to the acts of traveling and viewing art, but the places that have changed the most due to the pandemic are really our homes, and our rooms equipped with high-speed internet. "Our homes have gone beyond the mere private function of 'dwelling' and have long entered into the public realm," as the exhibition introduction puts it. "The pandemic has only exposed this reality even more."

The value of the home as a space that is "safe" from contagion has turned it into an even more private and isolated setting. Conversely, spaces outside the home have become places of non-freedom and frustration due to all the different restrictions. We face constraints in the form of changing travel distances, restrictions on private gatherings, and shorter operating hours, depending on the social distancing level. Outside the home is a regulated place where the threat of infection lurks. The same is true for overseas travel, and it may be that we will not be able to enjoy the same sort of travel freedoms as before even after the pandemic has ended. Even as borders open, we may not be able to travel in the hardest-hit countries until their security situation improves.

So what does that leave for us to do, isolated as we are in search of a freedom that does not exist outside the home? Oh Min's *ABA Video* (2016) was actually made before the pandemic, but it provides an entertaining glimpse at what we are capable of doing now. The figure in this work endlessly moves fixtures around her living room and kitchen, stacking them up and rearranging them. It is a work that might have been understood differently if the pandemic had not occurred; as the protagonist keeps arranging the items

명화의 방구석 미술관으로 만들어줄 것이다. 차재민의 〈엘리의 눈〉(2020)에는 '엘리'라는 이름의 인공지능 아바타가 등장해 살아있는 사람들을 상담한다. 이 아바타는 내담자의 신체 반응을 살펴 심리분석에 이용할 만큼 복잡한 사유가 가능한 존재다. 우리는 미술품의 제작, 재현, 전시에 도움이 될 테크놀로지가 얼마나 어디까지 발전하게 될지 예단할 수 없다.

　　　　그렇지는 않을 것이라고? 텔레비전의 등장이 영화관을 사라지게 하지 않은 것처럼, 사람들은 살냄새와 숨소리와 살갗의 감촉이라는 아날로그 감수성을 영원히 잊지 않을 것이라고? 사람들은 여전히 국립현대미술관 과천관 같은 진짜 미술관에 모여 함께 발품을 팔고 북적거리며 작품을 감상하길 바랄 것이라고? 물론 나도 그렇게 생각한다. 세상은 아날로그든 디지털이든 한 방향으로만 흘러가지 않을 것이다. 하지만 아날로그 감수성이 가리키는 방향성은 지금에 절대적으로 고정된 것이 아니다. 아날로그 감수성의 방향 역시 세상이 변화함에 따라 함께 수정을 거듭하게 될 것이다. '워치 앤 칠!' 플랫폼이 오랜 세월이 흐른 다음에는, 그저 방구석에서 접속할 수 있었다는 의미에서 '아날로그적이었다'며 그리움의 대상이 될 수도 있다. 펜데믹이 우리 인류에게 보여준 것은 세상이 어떻게 나아갈지 아무도 예상할 수 없다는 사실의 명백함이다.

백민석　　　　　　　　　ⓘ
소설가

───────────────────

소설을 쓰면서 이따금 여행, 미술 같은
본업을 벗어난 글을 쓰고 있다. 단편집
『혀끝의 남자』, 『수림』, 『버스킹!』, 장편소설
『공포의 세기』, 『교양과 광기의 일기』, 『해피
아포칼립스!』, 『플라스틱 맨』, 에세이 『러시아의
시민들』, 『이해할 수 없는 아름다움』, 『과거는
어째서 자꾸 돌아오는가』이 있다.

in her home, it appears to our eyes like she is satisfying the desire for freedom, albeit in a meaningless sort of way. It is, in a sense, the kind of "playing around by ourselves" that people have taken to during the pandemic era.

Yuan Goang-ming's *Dwelling* (2014) is another work that would have been taken a different way if it hadn't been for the pandemic. But to viewers today, it seems to show the dream world of someone who has been isolated in the home, only to end up losing their sense of the real world. As they lose their sense of reality, the actual living room in front of them starts to look like a dream world—an imitation in a fish tank. For unclear reasons, feelings of stress, anger, and tension begin to build over time, until they reach critical mass and the dream world explodes. Consisting solely of oneiric images without any explanation, *Dwelling* dramatically illustrates the negative energy that seethes inside of us as the pandemic traps us in our homes.

Ironically, it is within the cramped confines of our homes that we are able to take off our masks and enjoy the freedom of communing with our family. We have no way of knowing what might happen to us outside. In that sense, some fascinating stories are shared by two of the works that were unveiled toward the end of my journey: Cha Jiryang's *New Home* (2012) and Cici Wu's *The Unfinished Return of Yu Man Hon* (2019). The people who appear in New Home have no homes of their own. Living in rented apartments and houses, they gather each night to explore empty houses as a kind of leisure activity club. They open the door to an empty home that has yet to be occupied (a home that is also larger and more comfortable than the places they rent) and go inside, dividing up the rooms and play-acting the kind of home decoration they might do if they got a house of their own someday. Each of them talks about their life and their dreams. These are people who have a place to live right now, but live with the vague fear that they might someday be driven out; they are people who sense the faint whiff of despair—the worry that they might never in their lives have the chance to live in a place as nice as the one they're occupying tonight. In *The Unfinished Return of Yu Man Hon*, the main character is a boy who disappeared many years earlier. In the work, he has been wandering for over a decade outside the home where his "parents and siblings" await his return. As he remains outside the house, the exterior is his reality, while the interior exists as a dreamlike place where he can play with stuffed animals. He remains unable to return from the reality into the dream. Both *New Home* and *Unfinished Return* ask what the "home" means to people who do not have one. A pandemic-era analysis of the home as a "safe" and "free" space means nothing to them, as they have none.

"Living room museums" like the *Watch and Chill* platform harbor endless possibilities. We can easily imagine how many of the limitations that seem insurmountable today will be overcome over time through advancements in photography and display technology. Our ordinary perceptions of video art will also change in some way or another. Before long, we will be able to turn our living rooms into museums for the greatest artwork: enjoying the spectacular video work of Bill Viola on large displays, summoning George Segal's life-sized sculptures into our rooms through virtual reality, and capturing even the tiniest changes in color and the dizzying marks of paint in a Jackson Pollock work through high-resolution monitors. In Cha Jeamin's work *Ellie's Eye* (2020), an AI avatar named "Ellie" appears to counsel living people. The avatar is capable of complex enough thinking that it can be used for psychological analysis as it examines the patient's physical responses. We have no way of predicting what kind of developments lie in store for the technology that will assist with creating, reproducing, and exhibiting works of art.

Perhaps you think this is not so. Perhaps you think that people will never forget the analog touch, the smells and breaths and touch of flesh, just as the advent of television never displaced the cinema completely. Perhaps you expect that people will still gather at real museums—like MMCA—to put in the legwork, crowding around to view the artwork on display there. I certainly think so too. The world will not flow in any one direction alone,

be it analog or digital. But the direction that the analog sensibility points is not entirely fixed even now. As the world changes, so the direction of the analog sensibility will be revised. After enough time has passed, even the *Watch and Chill* platform could end up an object of nostalgia, something we remember as having been "analog" simply for the way we could access it in our own living room. What the pandemic has shown humankind is the certainty that no one can predict how the world will progress.

Baek Minseok   (i)

Novelist

Author of numerous short story collections (*Man at the Tip of the Tongue, Surim, Busking!*), novels (*Century of Fear, The Diary of Cultivation and Madness, Happy Apocalypse!*) and essays (*Citizens of Russia, Incomprehensible Beauty, Why Does the Past Keep Coming Back?*).

《우리 집에서, 워치 앤 칠》 연계 심포지엄
MMCA × MCAD × MAIIAM × M+ 인터내셔널

《우리 집에서, 워치 앤 칠》 그 다음은? 팬데믹 이후 미술관의 디지털 프로그램
: 물리적 영역과 디지털 영역을 아우르는 전시 기획 전략

3.17. 14:00 - 17:00 (HKT, GMT+8)

비공개 세션 1
M+, MCAD

14:00 – 14:10 (HKT, GMT+8)

정도련

환영 인사 및 소개
디지털이 미술 활동에 미친 영향은 무엇일까? 물리적 영역과 가상의 영역에서 디지털은 어떻게 큐레토리얼 실천과 관객의 행동을 변화시키나? 물리적 건축물을 넘어선 M+ 브랜드의 강력한 온라인 정체성이 지닌 중요성에 관해 이야기한다.

14:10 – 15:00 (HKT, GMT+8)

카테린 에르노
위니 라이

얼랜다 블레어
케이트 구

윌리엄 스미스
다이앤 왕

디지털 영역과 물리적 영역의 큐레토리얼 실천 및 관객 참여에 대한 M+의 접근법
디지털 행위를 미술관 안으로, 또 전시 실천을 온라인 공간 속으로 옮김으로써 디지털과 물리적 환경 간의 상호연계를 분명히 보여주는 최근 M+의 주요 프로젝트 세 가지를 소개한다. 핵심은 쌍방향성에 있다.

· 캐비닛
'캐비닛'은 40개의 이동식 패널로 구성된 전시 공간으로 M+의 소장품 중 200점 이상을 선보인다. 방문객이 모바일 기기를 이용해 참여하는 해석 게임의 형식으로, 진화하는 전시 디스플레이는 뜻밖의 방식으로 오브제와 개념을 결합시킨다.

· 미디어테크와 M+ 파사드
갤러리 겸 자료실 겸 라운지로 설계된 미디어테크는 M+가 소장한 250점 이상의 영상 작품을 방문객에게 온디맨드 방식으로 제공하며, 초청 프로그램을 비롯해 특별 기획 비디오 전시를 선보인다.
미디어테크의 아늑한 공간에서 가장 공개적인 M+ 파사드의 스크린까지, 다양한 방식과 규모로 관객의 참여를 이끌고 자율성을 어떻게 선사할 것인가?

· M+ 웹사이트
M+의 웹사이트는 풍성한 내용의 콘텐츠 플랫폼으로, 소장품 연구, 큐레토리얼 프로젝트, 교육 및 해설 등의 내용을 전 세계 관객에게 제공한다. 언어와 특정 소셜미디어 플랫폼을 활용하여 우리는 어떻게 지역의 관객들에게 도달하는가?

15:05 – 15:50 (HKT, GMT+8)

디지털 영역의 큐레토리얼 실천과 관객 참여에 대한 MCAD의 접근법
대학 소속 미술관이자 국제적으로 활발한 교류 활동을 하고 있는 기관으로서 MCAD의 방향성에 대해 소개한다.

호셀리나 크루즈, 라라 아쿠인

이안 카를로 하우시안, 매리 안 페르니아

제임스 루이지 타나

· MCAD와 초창기 프로그램
· 범위의 확장—새로운 미디어 플랫폼을 통한 관객의 참여와 디지털 네이티브인 대학생들과 협업
· 공간의 확장—미술관의 물리적 공간 너머의 활동

15:50 – 17:00 (HKT, GMT+8)

소그룹 분과 토론

3.18. 10:00 - 13:00 (HKT, GMT+8)

비공개 세션 2
MAIIAM, MMCA

10:00 – 10:10 (HKT, GMT+8)

환영 인사 및 소개, 세션1 요약

10:10 – 11:00 (HKT, GMT+8)

키티마 차리프라싯

그리드티야 가위웡

조이 버트

디지털 영역의 큐레토리얼 실천 및 관객 참여에 대한 MAIIAM의 접근법
지방도시의 사립미술관으로서 MAIIAM의 사명과 위치: 큐레토리얼을 통한 관객 접근

· 에라타: 관계의 수집과 체화된 역사
일련의 공공 프로그램들 - 지역의 관객 vs 국제적인 관객

· 폴리네이션
지역에서 지역으로, 기관이 주도한 개인간 관계 맺기의 필요성

11:05 – 11:50 (HKT, GMT+8)

현대미술1과, 기획총괄과 공동 발표
이지회

MMCA 4개 분관 전시 부서 공동 발표
박주원, 박혜성, 이수연, 이지회,
이현주, 현오아

미술정책연구과, 홍보고객과 공동 발표
김남인, 윤승연

디지털 영역의 큐레토리얼 실천 및 관객 참여에 대한 MMCA의 접근법
최근 MMCA가 수행한 다양한 디지털 활동을 살펴보며 미술관의 각기 다른 전문가들이 어떻게 디지털 환경에 대응하고 있는지 이야기한다.

· MMCA와 웹사이트
MMCA 조직 및 4개 분관
최근 개편된 웹사이트

· 적극적인 디지털 큐레토리얼 프로젝트 사례
'워치 앤 칠', '프로젝트 #', '모바일 아고라' 외 메타버스 및 VR·AR 관련 프로젝트

· 미술관 정책
미술관의 연결성을 주제로 한 온라인 공공 프로그램 및 디지털 영역에서의 다양한 홍보 및 관객과의 상호작용

11:50 – 12:50 (HKT, GMT+8)

소그룹 분과 토론

12:50 – 13:00 (HKT, GMT+8)

맺음말 및 향후 프로젝트 전망

3.17. 19:00-20:30 (HKT, GMT+8)

디지털 영역에서도 진정한 영상 문화를 창출할 수 있을까? 우리의 공동체를 찾고 집단 관람 경험의 공간을 어떻게 되찾을까? 온·오프라인 혼합 형식의 작품을 만들고 발표하기 위해 작가들이 채택한 전략은 무엇일까?

가상 상영을 통한 새로운 영상 문화 만들기: '워치 앤 칠' 사례 연구
온라인 공개 토크

19:00 – 19:10 (HKT, GMT+8)

이지회, 실케 슈미클

환영 인사 및 소개

19:10 – 19:20 (HKT, GMT+8)

김희천
시린 세노
씨씨 우
카와타 바타나즈얀쿠르

영상 작업들에 대한 설명과 '워치 앤 칠' 사례 연구

19:20 – 20:00 (HKT, GMT+8)

'워치 앤 칠' 및 기타 온·오프라인 혼합 전시/상영에 관한 작가적 경험 공유
'워치 앤 칠'이 마련한 새로운 맥락으로 인해 창작 과정에 변화가 생기거나 작품의 유연한 발표 방식에 관해 어떻게 생각하는지?

20:00 – 20:20 (HKT, GMT+8)

관객과 함께하는 라운드테이블

20:20 – 20:30 (HKT, GMT+8)

맺음말

3.18. 19:00 – 21:00 (HKT, GMT+8)

미술관이 온라인 스트리밍 플랫폼과 겨룰 수 있을까?
미술관 소장품의 온·오프라인 혼합 전시는 왜 중요한가

미술관과 디지털 문화: 생산적 긴장의 장
온라인 공개 토크

M+ 무빙 이미지 팀

19:00 – 19:10 (HKT, GMT+8)

환영 인사 및 '워치 앤 칠' 프로그램과 협력 미술관 소개

· '워치 앤 칠'에 참여한 4개 미술관의 프로젝트 발표
공동 기획, 주제, 작품 선정, 미술가 협업 내용 공유
온라인 플랫폼 및 오프라인 전시 제작 및 설계

이지회
호셀리나 크루즈
키티마 차리프라싯
실케 슈미클

· 참여 큐레이터와 청중이 함께하는 토론: 관객 개발 및 참여에 대하여
집단/개인의 관람 경험, 파악 가능한 관객과 파악 불가능한 관객, 지역 관객과 국제 관객
새로운 유형의 관객 참여가 가져올 과제와 기회

Watch and Chill Symposium
MMCA x MCAD x MAIIAM x M+ International

What's next? Museum's digital offerings beyond the pandemic
: What are some of the strategies to maintain curatorial offerings in
both, physical and digital realms?

3.17. 14:00-17:00 (HKT, GMT+8)

Closed door session 1
M+, MCAD

14:00 – 14:10 (HKT, GMT+8)

Chong Doryun

Welcome greeting, introduction
What impact does the digital have on our sector and activities? How
does it change curatorial practice and audience behaviours in the
physical and virtual realms? Sharing on the establishment of M+
without a physical building and the importance of the brand's strong
online presence and identity.

14:10 – 15:00 (HKT, GMT+8)

**M+'s approach to curatorial practice and audience engagement in
the digital and physical realms**
Presentation of three recent M+ key initiatives that articulate the
interconnection between the digital and physical by bringing digital
behaviour into the museum and exhibition practice into the online
space. Interactivity is key.

Catherine Erneux
Winnie Lai

· The Cabinet
The Cabinet is an exhibition space consisting of 40 movable panels
showcasing over two hundred works from the M+ Collections. The
evolving display brings together objects and ideas in unexpected ways
in the form of an interpretative game where visitors use their own
mobile devices.

Ulanda Blair
Kate Gu

· Mediatheque and M+ Facade
Designed as a gallery, library, and lounge, the Mediatheque makes
over 250 M+ Moving Image collection works available to visitors on
demand, and presents guest programmes and specially curated video
exhibitions.
How do we engage audiences and give them agency in various ways
and scales, from the intimate space of the Mediatheque to the most
public screen of the M+ Facade?

William Smith
Diane Wang

· M+ Website
The M+ Website is the museum's rich content platform which makes
collection research, curatorial projects, learning and interpretation
available to audiences worldwide. How do we target regional audiences
through the use of language and specific social media platforms?

15:05 – 15:50 (HKT, GMT+8)

MCAD's approach to curatorial practice and audience engagement in the digital realm
The positioning and prospects of MCAD as a museum within a university, while it being known as an internationally active art institution.

· MCAD and its initial programs.

· Broadening the scope—audience engagement across new media platforms and working with the college's students who are digital natives.

· External spaces and engagement outside of the museum's physical space.

Joselina Cruz
Lara Acuin

Ian Carlo Jaucian
Mary Ann Pernia

James Luigi Tana

15:50 – 17:00 (HKT, GMT+8)

Breakout session in smaller groups

3.18. 10:00 – 13:00 (HKT, GMT+8)

Closed door session 2
MAIIAM, MMCA

10:00 – 10:10 (HKT, GMT+8)

Welcome greeting, quick refresher on key findings of session 1

10:10 – 11:00 (HKT, GMT+8)

Kittima Chareeprasit

Gridthiya Gaweewong

Zoe Butt

MAIIAM's approach to curatorial practice and audience engagement in the digital realm
MAIIAM's mission and positioning as a private museum in a marginal city: how we approach audiences through curatorial practices.

· Errata: Collecting Entanglements and embodied histories
Series of public programs—Local and regional vs. international audiences.

· Pollination
Local to local, the need to lead institutions with a focus on in-person engagement.

11:05 – 11:50 (HKT, GMT+8)

Co-presented with Planning and Management Department
  Lee Jihoi

Co-presented with Curatorial Departments of MMCA's 4 branches
  Hyun Oh-ah, Park Hyesung, Park Joowon, Lee Hyunjoo, Lee Jihoi, and Lee Sooyoun

Co-presented with Museum Policy and Research Department and Communications and Audience Department
  Kim Namin and Tiffany Yun

MMCA's approach to curatorial practice and audience engagement in the digital realm
An overview of various digital activities that MMCA have conducted in recent days.

· MMCA and its website
MMCA's organization and 4 branches.
Recently renewed website.

· Digitally motivated curatorial projects
Watch and Chill, *Project #*, *Mobile Agora*, and other projects that engages with Metaverse, VR and AR.

· Museum policies
Online symposia on connectivity and various public relations for MMCA's digital presence.

11:50 – 12:50 (HKT, GMT+8)

Breakout session in smaller groups

12:50 – 13:00 (HKT, GMT+8)

Concluding remarks, outlook of future projects

3.17. 19:00-20:30 (HKT, GMT+8)

Can we create an authentic film culture in the digital realm?
How do we find our community and reclaim space for collective
viewing experience? What strategies do artists employ to create and
present artworks in a hybrid of on- and offline formats?

Public online talk
Fostering a new Film Culture through Virtual Presentations:
Watch and Chill, a Case Study

Lee Jihoi
Silke Schmickl

19:00 – 19:10 (HKT, GMT+8)

Welcome greeting, introduction

19:10 – 19:20 (HKT, GMT+8)

Case study of *Watch and Chill*, with film stills and info about the works

19:20 – 20:00 (HKT, GMT+8)

Kim Heecheon
Shireen Seno
Kawita Vatanajyankur
Cici Wu

Sharing of individual experiences around *Watch and Chill* and other
hybrid exhibitions/screenings.
Individual impressions, challenges, and excitement. Does the new
context change the process of creation or enables new thinking around
adaptable presentations?

20:00 – 20:20 (HKT, GMT+8)

Round table discussion amongst artists with the audience

20:20 – 20:30 (HKT, GMT+8)

Concluding remarks

3.18. 19:00-21:00 (HKT, GMT+8)

Can museums challenge online streaming platforms?
Why do hybrid on-and offline exhibitions of museum collections
matter.

Public online talk
Museums and Digital Culture: A Field of Productive Tension

19:00 – 19:10 (HKT, GMT+8)

M+ Moving Image Team

Welcome greeting, introduction of *Watch and Chill* and institutional
partners

223

19:10 – 20:15 (HKT, GMT+8)

· Project presentation by the 4 institutions
Sharing of joint curatorial approach, theme, film selection, collaboration with artists.
The production and design of the online platform and various physical exhibitions.

Lee Jihoi
Joseline Cruz
Kittima Chareeprasit
Silke Schmickl

20:15 – 21:00 (HKT, GMT+8)

· Discussion between curators and the audience: Audience development and engagement
Collective vs. individual viewing experience, known and unknown, local and international audiences.
Challenges and opportunities of the new type of audience engagement.

국립현대미술관

이지회

국립현대미술관의 학예연구사(2017-현재). 온라인 스트리밍 플랫폼 '워치 앤 칠'과 연계 국제 순회전을 기획했으며, 3년(2021-2023)에 걸쳐 아시아, 유럽, 미주권 등 지역으로 협력망을 확장 중이다. 광주 국립아시아문화전당의 《새로운 유라시아 프로젝트》(2015-2017) 큐레이터, 2014년에 베니스 건축 비엔날레에서 황금사자상을 수여받은 한국관의 부큐레이터로 활동했다.

건축농장 (최장원)

최장원은 2013년 '건축농장'을 설립하였다. 그의 작품 〈신선놀음〉은 국립현대미술관과 뉴욕현대미술관, 현대카드가 공동 주최한 '젊은 건축가 프로그램'의 첫 번째 당선작(프로젝트팀 문지방)으로 선정되었고, 2015년 문화체육관광부가 주관하는 '오늘의 젊은 예술가상' 건축부문을 수상하였다. 이후 다양한 분야를 넘나들며 질감과 형태, 오브제와 공간 사이의 균형적 관계를 고찰하는 작업을 꾸준히 진행하고 있다.

김희천

김희천은 서울에서 활동하는 미술가다. 아트선재센터(2019), 두산갤러리(2017) 등에서 개인전을 개최하였고, 부산비엔날레(2020) 광주비엔날레(2018), 이스탄불비엔날레(2017), 미디어시티서울(2016)과 리움미술관(2021), 쿤스트할베가(2021), 아시아문화전당(2020), 국립현대미술관(2019), ZKM(2019), 마닐라 현대미술디자인미술관(2019) 등의 단체전에 참여했다.

구동회

서울을 기반으로 활동하는 구동회는 설치, 조각, 영상,사진 이미지 등 다양한 매체를 활용하여 작업한다. 작가는 일상에서 발견되는 독특한 양상을 공간 설치와 영상으로 변형하여 현실에 드러나는 현상과 비가시적 세계의 3차원적 구조 이면의 진실을 보여준다.

오민

오민은 시간을 둘러싼 물질과 추상적 사유의 경계 및 상호 작용을 연구한다. 주로 미술, 음악, 무용의 교차점, 그리고 시간 기반 설치와 라이브 퍼포먼스가 만나는 접점에서 신체가 시간을 감각하고 운용하고 소비하고 또 발생시키는 방식을 주시한다. 서울대학교와 예일대학교에서 피아노 연주와 그래픽 디자인을 공부했으며, 국립현대미술관, 토탈미술관, 대전시립미술관, 수원시립미술관, 독일 모르스브로이 미술관(레버쿠젠)과 에어퍼트 미술관, 플랫폼엘 컨템포러리 아트센터, 포항시립미술관, 아트선재센터, 아뜰리에 에르메스, 서울시립 북서울미술관, 네덜란드

드메이넨 미술관(시타르트), 대구시립미술관, 아르코미술관 등에서 작품을 전시했다. 펴낸 책으로는 『토마』,『부재자 참석자 초청자』, 『스코어 스코어』 등이 있다.

차재민

차재민은 서울에서 거주 및 활동하고 있으며 영상, 퍼포먼스, 설치 작업을 한다. 그는 합성 이미지보다는 촬영한 영상을 사용하며 시각예술과 다큐멘터리의 가능성과 무력함에 대해 질문한다. 또한 현장 조사와 인터뷰를 통해 개인들의 현실에 접근하고, 그 개인들의 삶 안에 사회가 어떻게 스며들어 있는지를 주목한다.

차지량

차지량은 미디어를 활용한 참여 프로젝트를 진행하며 시스템과 개인에 관한 현장을 개설하는 작업을 이어왔다. 2008년 〈이동을 위한 회화〉를 시작으로 젊은 세대들과 온라인 커뮤니티를 만들어 일시적으로 공간을 점유하는 프로젝트 〈미드나잇 파라다이스〉(2010), 〈일시적 기업〉(2011), 〈뉴 홈〉(2012)을 발표했다. 이후 미래의 균형이 어긋난 상황을 공유하는 '한국 난민' 시리즈(2014-2024), 해외 이주를 경험한 사람들과 'BATS' 프로젝트(2016-)를 진행하며 다양한 장소에서 관객과 만나왔다.

마닐라 현대미술디자인미술관

호셀리나 크루즈

마닐라 성베닐드 라살대학의 현대미술디자인미술관에서 관장 겸 큐레이터를 맡고 있다. 마닐라 로페스기념관과 싱가포르미술관에서 큐레이터로 근무했으며, 제2회 싱가포르비엔날레(2008) 큐레이터, 제13회 자카르타비엔날레(2009) 네트워킹 큐레이터, 제57회 베니스비엔날레 필리핀관 큐레이터를 맡은 바 있다. 미술 및 문화에 관한 에세이, 리뷰, 비평, 해설 저술 작업도 이어가고 있다.

코코이 럼바오

전통적인 영상 제작 방식에 도전하는 비디오 아트 및 설치 작품을 만든다. '로스트 프레임스'의 설립 멤버이며, 도록 및 전시 노트 등의 글도 저술한다. 현재는 필리핀대학교 미술대학에서 미술사를 가르친다.

마크 살바투스

도시 풍경 속 역동적인 자연과 우연한 만남들에 초점을 맞춘다. 2016년 히라노 마유미와 함께 다양한 프로그램을 통해 현대 미술을 생산하고 제시하는 다양한 방식을 탐구하는 미술 및 연구 프로젝트인 '로드 나 디토 프로젝트'를 설립하였다.

시린 세노

기억, 역사, 이미지 만들기를 집이라는 개념과 결부하여 작품을 만든다. 존 토레스와 함께

영화와 미술의 교차 지점에 집중하는 스튜디오 겸 플랫폼인 '로스 오토로스'를 운영한다. 영화 및 미술 집단 '티토&티타'의 일원이기도 하다.

치앙마이 마이얌현대미술관

키티마 차리프라싯

태국 치앙마이의 마이얌현대미술관 큐레이터. 2016년 실험적 워크숍 겸 아트 퍼블리싱 스튜디오인 '웨이팅 유 큐레이터 랩'을 공동 설립했다. 태국과 남동아시아의 비판적 역사와 사회·정치적 이슈를 다루는 현대 미술과 문화에 특히 관심을 둔다. 다양한 배경의 학자, 미술가, 기관, 예술 공간과 함께 여러 플랫폼과 프로젝트에 걸쳐 활동한다.

카위타 바타나즈얀쿠르

2015년 재규어아시아퍼시픽테크아트상 최종 후보에 올랐고, 사치갤러리에서 열린 《태국의 눈》전에 참가했다. 2017년에는 제57회 베니스비엔날레와 나란히 베니스에서 열린 《해류 속의 섬들》을 비롯해, 멜버른예술센터에서 열린 아시아공연예술트리엔날레, 대만 아시아미술비엔날레 《미래 교섭》에 참여한 바 있다. 2018년에는 방콕 비엔날레의 일환으로 작품을 선보였고, 2019년에는 뉴욕 올브라이트녹스미술관에서 개인전을 가졌다.

완타니 시리파타나눈타쿨

완타니 시리파타나눈타쿨은 사회, 정치, 경제, 문화적 이슈에 대한 비판적 시각을 취하는 작품들을 보여준다. 각각의 프로젝트는 종종 조각, 사운드, 비디오, 인터랙티브 설치 등 여러 매체로 구성되는데, 매체들은 특정 주제와 메시지를 중심으로 묶여 있다. 2007년 태국 미술가들을 대표하는 작가로 선정되어 제53회 베니스비엔날레에 참가하였으며, 2016년 방콕의 컬렉터들이 꼽은 13인의 신진 미술가 중 한 사람이기도 하다.

차이 시리스

방콕 로열 그라운드의 노숙자들과 함께 작업하며 미술 실천을 시작한 그는 점쟁이, 건설 노동자, 주부 등 여러 직업의 사람들과 협업을 이어가고 있다. 영상과 사진이 주를 이루는 그의 작업은 개인과 사회의 역사 재구성, 국경 분쟁, 젠더, 삶과 죽음 등의 문제를 다룬다. 아피찻퐁 위라세타쿨 감독과 함께 독립영화사 '킥 더 머신 필름스'에서도 일하고 있으며, 치앙마이에서 생활하며 작업 중이다. 현재 태국-버마 국경 지역에 사는 여러 소수민족 집단을 다루는 영화 프로젝트를 진행하고 있다.

타다 행삽쿨

성적 주제를 대립과 권력의 수행으로 표현하는 누드 사진을 매체로 활용한다. 15살 때부터 지금까지, 친구들과 가까운 지인들의 관계를 포착하는 방식으로 사진 기술을 발전시켜왔다. 그의 작품은 태국 사회의 경계를 구획하는 전통,

정교적 신념, 도덕적 가치를 실험하고 질문하며
경계를 밀어붙이는 시도 속에 자리한 사고의
과정을 다룬다. ‹통과 노트›(2011) 연작에서
보듯, 그는 생면부지의 벌거벗은 두 사람의 만남을
주선해, 아무 규칙 없이 서로 교류하게 한다. ‹같은
하늘 아래›(2016)에서는 베트남전 당시의 정치적
장소에 깃든 역사를 특히 과거가 남긴 물리적
흔적과 물건들에 초점을 맞추어 연구와 현장
조사를 진행하며 본인의 접근법을 발전시켰다.

사룻 수파수티벡

방콕 실파콘대학에서 2015년 복합매체예술
학사 학위를 받았다. 과거 기록된 적 없는
장소들에 관한 구술사와 개인의 서술담에
관심을 두고 있다. 종종 지리적 장소에서 찾은
잔여 물질을 설치 작품 속 영상, 형상, 사운드로
변모시킨다.

M+

실케 슈미클

홍콩 M+의 무빙이미지 부문 수석
큐레이터이다. 이전에는 싱가포르 국립미술관과
싱가포르 현대미술연구소의 큐레이터로 일했고,
파리 소재 독일미술사센터 연구원, 파리/싱가포르
기반의 큐레토리얼 플랫폼이자 미술작가들의
영상 작품 퍼블리싱 하우스인 로웨이브의 설립
디렉터로도 근무했다. 중동, 아프리카, 아시아의
신진 미술계에 집중한 다수의 미술 및 영화
프로젝트를 시작하고 이끌었으며, 여러 미술관
및 비엔날레와 국제적으로 협력하며 전시들을
기획했다.

왕 공신

본래 베이징에서 사회주의 리얼리즘 스타일의
유화 화가로서 교육을 받았지만 선구적인 미디어
아티스트가 되었다. 1987년 장학생으로 미국
유학을 한 이후로 비디오, 전자예술, 3D 설치로
예술 언어를 확장했다. 1993년 이래로, 타당한
일상 경험의 인식을 놀라움과 긴장으로 전복하는
일련의 개념적 미디어 작품들을 발전시켜왔다.

위안 광밍

대만 비디오 아트의 선구자이다. 기술, 인간
정신, 의식의 경계를 탐구하며, 당대적 존재의
상태를 질문한다. 활동하는 동안 여러 매체, 형식,
재료에 걸쳐 작업해왔으며, 다수의 국제 전시,
비엔날레, 페스티벌에 참가했다.

차오 페이

2001년 광저우미술학교를 졸업했다. 현대
중국 사회의 빠르고 혼란스러운 도시화 과정이
담긴 비디오, 멀티미디어 설치, 인터넷 작업으로
알려져 있다. 다수의 국제 비엔날레에 참가하였고,
2010 퓨처제너레이션아트프라이즈와 2010
휴고보스프라이즈 최종후보에 올랐다. 2006년
중국현대미술상에서 최우수젊은작가상을 수상한
바 있다.

씨씨 우

설치작품 및 대기를 이용한 작업을 위주로 한다.
시네마를 해체해 조명 조각의 빛 입자로 만드는
시도에서부터 장편 영화를 끊임없이 참조하고
번안하는 작업에 이르기까지, 다양한 수단으로
무빙 이미지 개념을 재고한다.

지앙 지

1995년 중국미술학원을 졸업하고, 선전
지역의 잡지사에서 베이징 주재 리포터로 일했다.
비디오, 드로잉, 사진, 설치, 텍스트를 포함해
다양한 매체로 작업을 진행해왔다. 허구와
현실의 경계를 흐리는 실험적 기법을 활용해
일상의 경험과 시각 언어 사이의 복잡한 관계를
드러내는데, 특히 자아의 개인적 표현과 사회의
공공성에 관한 질문에 주목한다.

캠프

2007년 샤이나 아난드, 산자이 방가르, 아슉
수쿠마란이 뭄바이에서 결성한 인도의 미술
집단/스튜디오이다. 영화, 설치, 사진, 인쇄물,
퍼포먼스, 디지털 플랫폼 등 광범위한 매체와
형식을 가지고 작업하며, 기술적·예술적 실험의
접점을 탐색해왔다. 학제를 교차하는 이들의
실천은 종종 특정 집단 및 공동체와 오랜 시간에
걸쳐 관계 맺고 협력하며, 세계적 현상의 여파를
검토하고 기성의 권위 체제를 심문한다.

MMCA

Lee Jihoi

Curator of the National Museum of Modern and Contemporary Art (MMCA), Korea (2017-current). She initiated *Watch and Chill* online streaming platform, a project accompanied by offline traveling showcases in Asia and other regions of the world (2021-3). Previously, she curated a number of exhibitions at the Asia Cultural Center, Gwangju (2015-7) and was Deputy Curator for the Korean Pavilion at the 2014 Venince Architecture Biennale, which won the Golden Lion.

Farming Architecture (Choi Jangwon)

Choi Jangwon founded the "Farming Architecture" in 2013. His work *Shinseon play* was selected as the first winner (project team Moon Ji Bang) of the Young Architects Program organized by the MMCA, the MoMA and Hyundai Card, and he received the Today's Young Artist Award from the Ministry of Culture, Sports and Tourism of Korea in 2015. Since then, he has been focused on balancing between materiality and mass, object and space, as he exploring and experimenting in various genres.

Kim Heecheon

Kim Heecheon is an artist who lives and works in Seoul. He has held solo exhibitions at Art Sonje Center (2019) and Doosan Gallery (2017) and has participated in several biennales including the Busan Biennale (2020), Gwangju Biennale (2018), Istanbul Biennale (2017) and Seoul Mediacity Biennale (2016) and group exhibitions at Kunsthalle Bega (2021), Leeum (2021), ACC (2020). MMCA (2019), ZKM (2019) and MCAD (2019).

Koo Donghee

Koo Donghee works with various media, including installation, sculpture, video, and photographic images. Donghee Koo captures unique aspects discovered in daily life, transforming them into spatial installations and moving images to show the truth beneath real-world phenomena and the three-dimensional structures of the invisible world.

Oh Min

Oh investigates the boundaries and interactions of perception, substance, and thought that surround time. Trained with musical performance as a native tongue, she explores how the body senses, operates, consumes, and even generates time where visual art, music, and dance intersect and also where film and live performance meet. Oh received bachelor's degrees in piano performance and graphic design at Seoul National University and received her MFA at Yale University, New Haven. Her work has been presented at MMCA, Total Museum, Daejeon Museum of Art, Suwon Museum of Art, Morsbroich Museum, Pohang Museum of Steel Art, Art Sonje Center, Atelier Hermès, Buk-Seoul Museum of Art, Museum De Domijnen, Daegu Art Museum, Arko Art Center, Kukje Gallery, Nam June Paik Art Center, and Kunsthalle Erfurt. She published *Thomas, Absentee Attendee Invitee, Score by Score* among others.

Cha Jeamin

Cha Jeamin works variously between film, performance, and installation. She lives and works in Seoul. Cha's works are not constituted of synthesized images, but lens-based, and ask about the possibilities and helplessness of visual arts and documentaries. She approaches the reality of individuals through processes of interviews and field studies, notes how society permeates their lives.

Cha Ji Ryang

Cha Ji Ryang has led numerous media-based participative projects and worked on initiating theme-based sites that focus on systems and individuals. In 2008, with *The Expressions to Move* as a start, he created an online community with the emerging young generations to work on projects on temporary occupation of spaces such as *Midnight Parade* (2010), *Temporary Enterprise* (2011), and *New Home* (2012). He continued to meet with the public in various places while leading projects like *K-Refugees* series sharing the future that is out of balance and *BATS* project with people having experienced emigration.

MCAD

Joselina Cruz

Joselina Cruz is the Director and Curator of the Museum of Contemporary Art and Design (MCAD), De La Salle-College of Saint Benilde, Manila. Cruz worked as a curator for the Lopez Memorial Museum in Manila and the Singapore Art Museum. She was a curator for the 2nd Singapore Biennale (2008), a networking curator for the 13th Jakarta Biennale (2009), and curator of the Philippine Pavilion at the 57th Venice Biennale (2017). She continues to write essays, reviews, criticism and commentary on art and culture.

Cocoy Lumbao

Cocoy Lumbao creates video art and installations known to challenge conventional methods of producing moving images. He is a founding member of Lost Frames, has also written catalogues and exhibition notes, and currently teaches art history at the University of the Philippines' College of Fine Arts.

Mark Salvatus

Mark Salvatus focuses on the dynamic nature and chance encounters within the urban landscape. Together with Mayumi Hirano, he co-founded "Load na Dito Projects" in 2016, an artistic and research initiative that explores various modes of producing and presenting contemporary art through a wide range of programs.

Shireen Seno

Shireen Seno's work addresses memory, history, and image-making, often in relation to the idea of home. With John Torres, she runs "Los Otros," a studio and platform dedicated to the intersections of film and art. She is part of "Tito & Tita," a film and art collective.

MAIIAM

Kittima Chareeprasit

Kittima Chareeprasit received her MA in Curating and Collections from Chelsea College of Arts. She is a curator from MAIIAM Contemporary Art Museum in Chiang Mai, Thailand. In 2016, she co-founded the experimental workshop and art publisher studio "Waiting You Curator Lab." Her interest lies in contemporary art and culture, which revolves around critical history, social and political issues, specifically of Thailand and Southeast Asia. She works across various platforms and projects with academics, artists, institutions and art spaces from diverse backgrounds.

Kawita Vatanajyankur

Kawita Vatanajyankur has achieved significant recognition since graduating from RMIT University (BA, Fine Art) in 2011. In 2015 she was a Finalist in the Jaguar Asia Pacific Tech Art Prize and curated into the prestigious *Thailand Eye* exhibition at Saatchi Gallery, London. In 2017, her work has been curated into *Islands in the Stream* exhibition in Venice, Italy alongside the 57th Venice Biennale, Asia Triennale of Performing Arts at the Melbourne Arts Centre, as well as *Negotiating the Future*, Asian Art Biennial Taiwan. In 2018, she showed her works as part of the Bangkok Art Biennale, followed by a solo exhibition at Albright Knox Art Gallery in New York in 2019.

Wantanee Siripattananuntakul

Wantanee Siripattananuntakul's artworks take a critical view on social, political, economic and cultural issues. Each project often consists of different media such as sculptures, sound, videos and interactive installations, grouped around specific themes and messages. Although there may not always be material simi-larities between different projects, they are linked by recurring themes and genuine concerns on the subject matter. In 2007, she was chosen to be the representative of Thai artists to join the 53rd Venice Biennale and she are one of 13 Thai emerging artists who were chosen by Bangkok collectors in 2016.

Chai Siris

Chai Siris started his art practice when he worked with homeless people at Bangkok's Royal Ground. He continues to collaborate with people from various professions such as fortune tellers, construction workers, and housewives. His work, often video and photograph, deals with reconstruction of personal and social history, border conflicts between countries, gender, life and dead. He also works with Apichatpong Weerasethakul in an independent film company, "Kick the Machine" Films and currently lives and works in Chiang Mai, Thailand. He is currently working on a film project deals with ethnic groups along the Thai-Burmese border.

Tada Hengsapkul

Tada Hengsapkul is well known for his use of nude photography as a medium to express the sexual themes of confrontation and the performance of power. Tada began developing his photography skills by capturing relationship narratives of his friends and close acquaintances from the age of 15 until present. His works push boundaries, experiment and question with the tradition, religious beliefs and moral values that continually demarcate the boundaries of Thai society. As in the *Tong & Note* series (2011), the artist arranged a rendez-vous between two complete strangers, both naked, and prompted them to interact with each other under no rules whatsoever; or for *Under The Same Sky* (2016), Tada developed his approach through research and on-site investigation about the history of the political sites during the Vietnam war, focusing particularly on the physical traces and objects left behind from the past.

Saroot Supasuthivech

Saroot Supasuthivech graduated with a Bachelor's degree in mix-media arts from the Faculty of Painting, Sculpture and Graphic Arts, Silpakorn University, Bangkok, in 2015. His interests lie in oral histories and personal narratives of different places that have never been recorded before. He often transforms remaining substances found in geographical locations into moving images, figures, and sounds in his installations.

M+

Silke Schmickl

Silke Schmickl is the Lead Curator, Moving Image at M+ in Hong Kong. She was previously curator at the National Gallery Singapore, the Institute of Contemporary Arts Singapore, a researcher at the German Art History Center in Paris and the co-founding director of Lowave, a Paris/Singapore based curatorial platform and publishing house for artists' moving images. She has initiated and directed numerous art and film projects dedicated to emerging art scenes in the Middle East, Africa and Asia and has curated exhibitions in partnership with museums and biennials internationally.

Wang Gongxin

Wang Gongxin is a pioneering media artist. Initially trained as an oil painter in the socialist realist style in Beijing, he expanded his artistic langue after a scholarship in the US in 1987 with video, electronic art, and 3D installations. Since 1993, Wang has developed a series of conceptual media artworks that subvert the logical perception of everyday experiences with surprise and tension.

Yuan Goang-ming

Yuan Goang-ming is a pioneer of video art in Taiwan. His practice explores the boundaries between technology, the human mind, and consciousness, questioning the state of contemporary existence. Throughout his career, Yuan has been working across different mediums, forms, and materials and has participated in a number of international exhibitions, biennials, and festivals.

Cao Fei

Cao Fei graduated from the Guangzhou Academy of Fine Arts in 2001. She is known for her video, multimedia installation, and internet work that reflect the rapid and chaotic urbanisation occurring in the Chinese society today. Cao has participated in numerous international biennales and was a finalist of the Future Generation Art Prize 2010 and the Hugo Boss Prize 2010. In 2006, she received Best Young Artist Award by Chinese Contemporary Art Award (CCAA).

Cici Wu

Cici Wu focuses on creating installations and atmospheric works. She revisits the very notion of moving image by different means—from her attempts to deconstruct cinema into illumination particles that form light sculptures to her constant referencing and adaptation of feature films.

Jiang Zhi

Jiang Zhi worked as a Beijing-based reporter for a Shenzhen magazine after graduating from the China Academy of Art in 1995. He has worked with a diverse range of media, including video, drawing, photography, installation, and text. Using experimental techniques to blur the boundaries between fiction and reality, he reveals a complex relationship between everyday experience and visual language, paying particular attention to questions concerning the intimate expressions of the self and the public nature of society.

CAMP

CAMP is an Indian collective/studio founded around 2007 in Mumbai by Shaina Anand, Sanjay Bhangar, and Ashok Sukumaran. They have worked with a wide range of mediums and forms, such as film, installation, photography, printed matter, performance, and digital platforms, exploring the juncture of technological and artistic experimentation. Their cross-disciplinary practice often engages and collaborates with specific groups and communities over a long period of time, examining the impacts of various global phenomena and interrogating the established systems of authority.

《우리 집에서, 워치 앤 칠》
https://watchandchill.kr
2021.8.24.–2022.2.28.

국립현대미술관 서울, 6전시실
2021.8.24.–10.24.

마닐라 현대미술디자인미술관,
도밍가 주차장, 자동차 극장
2021.10.29.–12.9.

치앙마이 마이암현대미술관,
원형 감상 공간
2021.12.10.–2022.1.3.

홍콩 서구룡문화지구 M+,
미디어테크
2022.1.7.–2.28.

MMCA×MCAD×MAIIAM×M+
인터내셔널
2022.3.17.–3.18.

주최
국립현대미술관

협력
마닐라 현대미술디자인미술관
치앙마이 마이암현대미술관
홍콩 서구룡문화지구 M+

기획
이지회
호셀리나 크루즈
가티마 차리야프라셋
실케 슈미들
김은주
〈나만 아는 이야기〉 기획
진행
이수연, 이안 카를로 하우시안,
티트라차난 퐁파니크,
카트린 라우, 코엘 추
그래픽 디자인·플랫폼 개발
위크스
자막
푸르모디티
번역
김정화, 이재희, 콜린 A. 모엣

국립현대미술관

관장
윤범모
학예연구실장
김준기
현대미술1과장
류지연, 박미화
학예연구관
박수진, 이주영
공간디자인
건축농장(최장원)
전시운영
정제환
전시지원
윤해리
홍보·마케팅
이성희, 윤승연, 박우리, 채지연,
김홍조, 김민구, 이민지, 기성미,
신나래, 장라윤, 김보윤
고객지원
김은재
사진
이은주, 추현철, 주다란
영상 프로덕션
몽규

(재)국립현대미술관문화재단
협찬
DK 동국제강

마닐라 현대미술디자인미술관

관장
호셀리나 크루즈
기술 총괄
제임스 루이지 타나
전시 설치
알드윈 타부에나
교육 및 연계 행사
메리 엔 페레니아
홍보·마케팅
패트리시샤 파레데스
그래픽 디자인
마틴 미란다
기술 보조
사진
웰델 아베에라
트레일러 제작
엘 제로 라바오
자막, 캡션
조이스 아리엘 얌보스,
알렉스 줄리안 라텀럼
공공 프로그램 조사
조슈아 바레라,
소피아 아이비 신조,
리앤 루앙골라스,
제니나 케이틀린 로페즈,
다니엘 루이스 메로카도,
자니카 피오나 블랑크타스,
프란체스카 아리아나 톨라비에

치앙마이 마이암현대미술관

관장
에릭 분낭 부스
공간 디자인
폼볼스튜디오
공간 디자인 팀
칸 칸행, 타나찻 숙사와디,
프라데이쿨로이 마하통차이
설치·운영
시와 시리
전시 설치
여반폼 CO., LTD.
고객지원
아낫 투탐지, 나탄야 몽사왓,
패타마 판통, 사이핀 수파
사진
카린 몽쿨판, 폼볼스튜디오
그래픽 디자인
세타파 프롬몸맏드
트레일러 제작
손파낫 팟포

홍콩 서구룡문화지구 M+

관장
수한야 라펠
부관장·수석큐레이터
정도련
기술 총괄
데니스 핑
콘텐츠 테크니션
트레이션 아우
프로젝션
KH 라우
관내 총괄
체이스 리
제작 보조
에드먼드 라이
디지털, 에디토리얼 콘텐츠
엘리슨 펑, 글로리아 퍼네스,
SJ 지앙, 나타니엘 라우,
프란시스코 로, 윌리엄 스미스
홍보·마케팅
카일 찬, 에니 찬, 메기 쳉, 얄피 청,
센디 리
사진
독형

감사의 말씀

디자인아트룸, 박경린, 샤넬 콩,
스튜디오 하포-보듬, 양혜규,
잉크 오코하마, 전경린, 전효경, 홍초선,
TKG+ 갤러리 외 《우리 집에서,
워치 엔 칠》의 개최를 위해 도움 주신
모든 분들께 깊은 감사의 말씀을 드립니다.

이미지 크레딧

표지
© 김경태

차재민, 〈엘리의 눈〉, 2020.
© 차재민, MMCA 제공
7쪽

시릿 수파수티벳, 〈보안인의 CCTV〉, 2019, 설치 전경.
© MMCA, 사진: 홍철기
8쪽

위안 광밍, 〈주가〉, 2014.
© 위안 광밍, TKG+ 갤러리 소장, M+ 제공
9, 16쪽

오민, 〈에이 비 에이 비디오〉, 2016.
© 오민, MMCA 소장
10, 225쪽

차오 페이, 〈아지랑이와 안개〉, 2013.
© 차오 페이, M+ 소장, 비타민 크리에이티브 스페이스, 스푸르스 마거스 제공
10, 18쪽

차이 시리즈, 〈포시즌스〉, 2010.
© 차이 시리즈, MAIIAM 제공
11, 18쪽

지양 지, 〈날이, 날아〉, 1997.
© 지양 지, M+ 지그 컬렉션 제공, 기증
12, 19쪽

국립현대미술관 전시 전경.
© MMCA, 사진: 홍철기
12, 14, 19, 21, 23, 185, 187-190, 226쪽

캠포, 〈만에서 만을 거쳐 만으로〉, 2013.
© 캠포, M+ 소장
13, 20쪽

시린 세토, 〈꽃을 따는 것〉, 2021.
© 시린 세토, MCAD 제공
13, 19쪽

왕 공신, 〈브루클린의 하늘—베이징에서 구명파기〉, 1995.
© 왕 공신, M+ 소장
14, 21쪽

씨씨 우, 〈유만훈의 미완된 귀환〉, 2019.
© 씨씨 우, M+ 소장, 2021년 M+ 뉴아트핀드위원회, 홍콩 엠티 갤러리 제공
15, 22, 186쪽

김희천, 〈썰매〉, 2016, 설치 전경.
© MMCA, 사진: 홍철기
23쪽

김희천, 〈나홀로 '댐볼'보기〉, 2020.
© 김희천
24쪽

차오 페이, 〈아지랑이와 안개〉, 2013, 설치 전경.
© MMCA, 사진: 홍철기
185쪽

마닐라 현대미술디자인미술관 자동차 극장 전경.
© MCAD, 사진: 웰비 아비에라
191-192쪽

치앙마이 마이암현대미술관 원형 감상 구역 전경.
© MAIIAM, 사진: 카린 몽콜판, 폼불스튜디오
193-194쪽

M+ 미디어테크 전경.
© M+, 사진: 록 쳉
195-196쪽

출판

발행인
윤범모

편집인
김준기

제작총괄
류지연, 박수진

책임편집
이지회

기획편집
권태현

편집보조
임미주

글
백민석, 실케 슈미클, 유현주, 윤향로, 이기리, 이지회, 조은비, 기타마 차리프라닷, 훗셀리나 크루즈

디자인
워크스

표지 사진
김경태

인쇄제본
청산인쇄

ISBN
978-89-6303-312-9

정가
25,000원

발행처
국립현대미술관
03062 서울시 종로구 삼청로 30
02-3701-9500
www.mmca.go.kr
발행일 2022.3.31.
© 2022 국립현대미술관

Watch and Chill: Streaming Art to Your Homes

https://watchandchill.kr/en
8.24.2021.–2.28.2022.

Exhibition at MMCA Seoul, Gallery 6
8.24.2021.–10.24.

Drive-in Theatre at MCAD, Manila,
Dominga Car Park
10.29.2021.–12.9.

Circular Viewing Zone at MAIIAM,
Chiang Mai
12.10.2021.–1.3.2022.

Mediatheque at M+, West Kowloon
Cultural District, Hong Kong
1.7.2022.–2.28.

MMCA × MCAD × MAIIAM × M+
International
3.17.2022.–3.18.

Organized by
The National Museum of Modern
and Contemporary Art, Korea

In Partnership with
Museum of Contemporary Art &
Design, Manila
MAIIAM Contemporary Art
Museum, Chiang Mai
M+, West Kowloon Cultural
District, Hong Kong

Curated by
Lee Jihoi
Joselina Cruz
Kittima Chareeprasit
Silke Schmickl

The Tales I Tell Curated by
Kim Eunju

Coordination
Lee Suyeon, Ian Carlo Jaucian,
Taratchanan Pongpanich,
Catherine Lau, Koel Chu

Graphic Design and Platform
Development
WORKS

Subtitles
Furmo DT

Translation
Colin A. Mouat, Yi Jaehee,
Sophie Kim

MMCA

Director
Youn Bummo

Chief Curator
Gim Jungi

Head of Exhibition Department 1
Liu Jienne, Park Mihwa

Senior Curator
Park Soojin, Lee Chuyoung

Space Design
Farming Architecture
(Choi Jangwon)

Technical Coordination
Jeong Jaehwan

Exhibition Construction
Yun Haeri

Public Communication and
Marketing
Lee Sunghee, Yun Tiffany,
Park Yulee, Chae Jiyeon,
Kim Hongjo, Kim Minjoo,
Lee Minjee, Ki Sungmi,
Shin Narae, Jang Layoon,
Kim Boyoon

Customer Service
Lee Eunsu, Chu Hunchul,
Ju Daran

Photography
Hong Cheolki

Trailer and Film Production
Mon Q

National Museum of Modern
and Contemporary Art
Foundation, Korea

Supported by

MCAD

Director
Joselina Cruz

Technical Supervision
James Luigi Tana

Exhibition Construction
Aldwin Tabuena

Learning and Special Projects
Mary Ann Pernia

Marketing
Patricia Paredes

Graphic Design
Francis Tadeo

Tech Support
Martin Miranda

Photography
Wendell Abiera

Trailer Production
Earl Jerome Labao,
Maria Jessica Chavez,
Matthew Jose Reyes

Subtitling and Captions
Joyce Ariel Ambas,
Alecx Julianne Literal

Public Programs Research
Joshua Barrera,
Sophia Ivy Cinco,
Leanne Lumanglas,
Janina Caitlin Lopez,
Daniel Luis Mercado,
Janica Fiona Balagtas and
Francesca Arianna Flavier

MAIIAM

Director
Eric Bunnag Booth

Space Design
Pomballstudio

Space Design Team
Karn Khamhaeng,
Tanachat Sooksawasd,
Praeploy Mahathongchai

Technical Coordination
Siwa Siri

Exhibition Construction
URBANFORM CO., LTD.

Customer Service
Anat Tubtimsri,
Nuttanya Muangsawat,
Pattama Pantong,
Saipin Supa

Photography
Karin Mongkonphan,
Pomballstudio

Graphic Design
Setapa Prommolmard

Trailer Production
Sornpanath Patpho

M+

Director
Suhanya Raffel

Deputy Director, Curatorial
and Chief Curator
Chong Doryun

Technical Supervisor
Dennis Fung

Content Technician
Tracy Wu

Projectionist
KH Lau

House Supervisor
Chase Li

Production Assistant
Edmond Lai

Digital and Editorial Content
Alison Fung, Gloria Furness,
SJ Jiang, Natalie Lau,
Francisco Lo, William Smith

Marketing and Communication
Kyle Chan, Yanny Chan,
Meggy Cheng, Alfie Chung,
Sandy Lee

Photography
Lok Cheng

Special Thanks to

Design Maroon, Hong Cho-sun,
Jeon Hyokyong, Jeon Kyoungrin,
Chanel Kong, Park Kyoungrin,
Studio Half-bottle, TKG+ Gallery,
Haegue Yang and Ikko Yokoyama

First Edition March 31st, 2022
© 2022 National Museum of Modern and Contemporary Art, Korea

This book is published on the occasion of *Watch and Chill: Streaming Art to Your Homes*, an online exhibition at https://watchadnchill.kr/en, a subscription-based streaming platform and accompanied by offline traveling presentations at the National Museum of Modern and Contemporary Art (Seoul), Museum of Contemporary Art and Design (Manila), MAIIAM Contemporary Art Museum (Chiang Mai) and M+, West Kowloon Cultural District (Hong Kong) from August 28th, 2021 to February 28th, 2022.

Publication

Publisher
Youn Bummo

Production Director
Gim Jungi

Managed by
Liu Jienne, Park Soojin

Chief Editor
Lee Jihoi

Managing Editor
Kwon Taehyun

Editorial Coordination
Lim Mjiu

Contributors
Jo Eunbi, Joselina Cruz, Kittima Chareeprasit, Lee Gi-ri, Lee Jihoi, Silke Schmickl, Yoo Hyunjoo, Yoon Hyangro

Design
WORKS

Cover Photography
Kim Kyoungtae

Printing and Binding
Chungsan

ISBN
978-89-6303-312-9

Price
25,000 KRW

Published by
National Museum of Modern and Contemporary Art, Korea
30 Samcheong-ro, Jongno-gu, Seoul 03062, Korea
+82-2-3701-9500
www.mmca.go.kr/en

Image Credit

Cover
© Kim Kyoungtae

Cha Jeamin, *Ellie's Eye*, 2020.
© Cha Jeamin, Provided by MMCA
p. 7

Installation view of Saroot Supasuthivec, *CCTV of Security Guard*, 2019.
© MMCA, Photo: Hong Cheolki
p. 8

Yuan Goang-ming, *Dwelling*, 2014.
© Yuan Goang-ming, Courtesy of TKG+ Gallery, Provided by M+
pp. 9, 16

Oh Min, *ABA Video*, 2016.
© Oh Min, MMCA collection
pp. 10, 225

Cao Fei, *Haze and Fog*, 2013.
© Cao Fei, M+ collection, Courtesy of Vitamin Creative Space, Sprüth Magers
pp. 10, 18, 185

Chai Siris, *Four Seasons*, 2010.
© Chai Siris, Provided by MAIIAM
pp. 11, 18

Jiang Zhi, *Fly, Fly*, 1997.
© Jiang Zhi, Provided by M+ Sigg Collection, By donation
pp. 12, 19

MMCA exhibition view.
© MMCA, Photo: Hong Cheolki
pp. 12, 14, 19, 21, 185, 187-190, 226

CAMP, *From Gulf to Gulf to Gulf*, 2013.
© CAMP, M+ collection
pp. 13, 20

Shireen Seno, *To Pick a Flower*, 2021.
© Shireen Seno, Provided by MCAD
pp. 13, 19

Wang Gongxin, *The Sky of Brooklyn—digging a hole in Beijing*, 1995.
© Wang Gongxin, M+ collection
pp. 14, 21

Cici Wu, *The Unfinished Return of Yu Man Hon*, 2019.
© Cici Wu, M+ collection, Council for New Art Fund in 2021, Courtesy of Empty Gallery, Hong Kong
pp. 15, 22, 186

Installation view of Kim Heecheon, *Sleigh Ride Chill*, 2016.
© MMCA, Photo: Hong Cheolki
p. 23

Kim Heecheon, *Watching 'Mumbling in Hell, Tumbling Down the Well' Alone*, 2020.
© Kim Heecheon
p. 24

View of Drive-in Theatre at MCAD.
© MCAD, Photo: Wendell Abiera
pp. 191-192

View of Circular Viewing Zone at MAIIAM.
© MAIIAM, Photo: Karin Mongkonphan, Pomballstudio
pp. 193-194

View of M+ Mediatheque.
© M+, Photo: Lok Cheng
pp. 195-196

Watch & Chill